MASTERING

BACKGROUND TO BUSINESS

MACMILLAN MASTER SERIES

Astronomy
Australian History
Background to Business
Banking
Basic English Law
Basic Management
Biology
British Politics
Business Communication
Business Law
Business Microcomputing
Catering Science
Chemistry
COBOL Programming
Commerce
Computer Programming
Computers
Data Processing
Economic and Social History
Economics
Electrical Engineering
Electronics
English Grammar
English Language
English Literature
Financial Accounting
French
French 2
German
German 2
Hairdressing
Italian
Italian 2
Japanese
Keyboarding
Marketing
Mathematics
Modern British History
Modern European History
Modern World History
Nutrition
Office Practice
Pascal Programming
Physics
Practical Writing
Principles of Accounts
Restaurant Service
Social Welfare
Sociology
Spanish
Spanish 2
Spreadsheets
Statistics
Statistics with your Microcomputer
Study Skills
Typewriting Skills
Word Processing

MASTERING BACKGROUND TO BUSINESS

TERRY PRICE

M
MACMILLAN

First published by Pan Books Ltd as *Background to Business* in the Breakthrough series in 1983.

Fully updated and revised edition first published 1989 by
MACMILLAN EDUCATION LTD
Houndmills, Basingstoke, Hampshire RG21 2XS
and London
Companies and representatives
throughout the world

Typeset by TecSet Ltd., Wallington, Surrey.

Printed in China

British Library, Cataloguing in Publication Data
Price, Terry, *1938–*
Mastering Background to Business
1. Business practices
I. Title
650
ISBN 0–333–48801–6
ISBN 0–333–48802–4 Pbk
ISBN 0–333–48803–2 Pbk export

CONTENTS

Acknowledgements viii

Introduction ix

1 Goods and services

1.1 Goods and services 4
1.2 Changes in consumer expenditure 7
1.3 Primary, secondary and tertiary production 10
1.4 The working population 12

2 Business organisation

2.1 Sole trader 19
2.2 Partnerships 23
2.3 Limited companies 26
2.4 A public company 29
2.5 Public enterprises 32
2.6 Other types of business organisation 36

3 Internal organisation of companies

3.1 The Board of Directors 41
3.2 The Company Secretary 42
3.3 The Managing Director 42
3.4 Internal communications 44

4 Marketing and advertising

4.1 Market research and product planning 48
4.2 Promotion of the product 53
4.3 After-sales service 60
4.4 Marketing 61

CONTENTS

5	**Distribution – retailing, wholesaling and other markets**	5.1	Retailing	65
		5.2	Wholesaling	80
		5.3	Other markets	84
6	**Finance**	6.1	Balance sheets, and profit and loss accounts	88
		6.2	Expansion of the business	93
		6.3	Company finance	96
		6.4	How a company obtains additional finance	98
7	**The Stock Exchange**	7.1	How shares change hands on the Stock Exchange	103
		7.2	The Big Bang and Stock Exchange changes	103
		7.3	The importance of the Stock Exchange	106
8	**Insurance and business insolvency**	8.1	Insurance	107
		8.2	Business insolvency	119
9	**Banking services and business**	9.1	Functions of the bank	124
		9.2	Types of account	125
		9.3	Cheques	127
		9.4	Methods of payment using the bank	132
		9.5	Bank credit	134
10	**Personal finance**	10.1	Borrowing	138
		10.2	Lending	146
		10.3	Investment management	150
11	**Transport and communications**	11.1	Transport	153
		11.2	Communications and new technology	158
12	**International trade**	12.1	Balance of Payments	166
		12.2	Protection and free trade	169

	12.3	Exporting	170
	12.4	Importing	174
	12.5	Trading blocs	175
13 Trading documents	13.1	The Letter of Enquiry	178
	13.2	The Quotation	179
	13.3	The Order	180
	13.4	The Acknowledgement	181
	13.5	The Advice Note	182
	13.6	The Delivery Note	182
	13.7	The Invoice	183
	13.8	Value Added Tax	184
	13.9	Credit Notes and Debit Notes	185
	13.10	Statement of Account	185
14 Consumer protection	14.1	Rights under the Sale of Goods Act 1979	188
	14.2	Trade Descriptions Act 1968 and 1972	189
	14.3	Other Acts of Parliament which protect the customer	191
	14.4	Other protection	192
	14.5	Consumer credit	192
	14.6	Other types of credit	194
15 Business and the government	15.1	Monopolies and restrictive practices	199
	15.2	Government aid to industry	200
	15.3	Planning permission	201
	15.4	Employment and the government	202
	15.5	Health and safety	204
16 Taxation	16.1	Direct tax	206
	16.2	Indirect taxes	210
	16.3	Other forms of government revenue	212
	16.4	Summary	216
Answers to Exercises			218
Index			242

ACKNOWLEDGEMENTS

To:
John Meed and Tim Burton of the National Extension College for their many helpful comments.

Keith Martin and Anne Bown for their help with the chapter on Distribution.

John Paget and Susan Bennett, librarians at Canterbury College of Technology, for their valuable assistance in obtaining up to date information on the business environment.

David Hogg, Senior Technician at Canterbury College for all his assistance.

Ian Cooke, Chief Accountant, Canterbury City Council, for his help with aspects of local taxation.

The Halifax Building Society, Barclays Bank and the Midland Bank for their assistance with building society and banking matters.

Pat Roberts who assisted with some of the typing and editing.

Finally to my wife Sheila whose help and encouragement made it possible for me to complete this book.

The author and the publishers acknowledge and thank the following companies and organisations for allowing the use of illustrative material: Access (Midland Bank), Barclay Card, The Burton Group, Canterbury City Council, General Motors Acceptance Corporation, Lufthansa, Marks & Spencers Charge Card, Midland Bank, NEC and Storecard Ltd.

INTRODUCTION

How to use this book. Throughout the book you will find questions which you are encouraged to answer before reading on. There are two types of question sections: exercises and activities.

Exercises Usually short questions requiring quick answers. They either help to prepare you for the text which follows, or they provide a means for you to test yourself whether you have understood a particular principle or technique. Answers can be found at the back of the book. It is obviously best for you to try to answer the question before reading on, but, whether you think you have got it right or wrong, read the answer before moving on to the next topic. If you have somehow made a mistake the answer will usually tell you where you might have gone wrong. Exercises placed at the end of a chapter or at the end of a section are intended to review your understanding of several principles or techniques. You can, of course, 'cheat' and read the whole book from beginning too end without attempting to answer the questions at all. But if you do, there is only one person you are cheating. Guess who?

Activities Again, designed to test your understanding of the text, but they usually ask you to use some information which you will not find in the text. To answer these questions you have to use your own experience or discover some fresh facts for yourself. Sometimes an activity is simply an opportunity for you to stop and think about an important point raised in the text.

This book describes the situation as it exists in 1988. Remember that the business world is a changing environment and throughout the book readers are encouraged and given ideas on how to keep up to date.

To Sheila

CHAPTER 1

GOODS AND SERVICES

John Percival is a maintenance fitter at a limestone works in Derbyshire. He is married to Jean and they have two boys, Simon aged nine and Mark aged four. John earns £200 per week but after various stoppages for tax, national insurance, pension contribution, union fees, etc. his take-home pay is £140 per week. Jean has a part-time job for which she receives net (after stoppages) £45.50 per week. The child benefit for the two boys comes to £14.50 per week so that the combined family income is £200.

Like most families, the Percivals face economic decisions. They have unlimited wants but limited resources. If John, Jean and the two children could buy anything they wanted in a week, the weekly expenditure would well exceed £200. Commerce centres around the problem of unlimited demands and limited resources. The Percivals try to obtain the best out of their resources (£200). They are a fairly typical family and their weekly expenditure is shown as follows:

Food	£50
Housing, expenses, mortgage, rates, insurance	£50
Bills – electricity, telephone, gas	£25
Entertainment including saving for holidays	£20
Jean's weekly visit to the hairdressers	£5
Clothes	£10
Car expenses, petrol, oil and maintenance	£20
Hire purchase and credit	£10
Savings	£10
	£200

This expenditure pattern can be shown quite well by the use of what is called a pie chart (Figure 1.1).

Figure 1.1 *Pie chart showing the weekly expenditure of the Percival family*

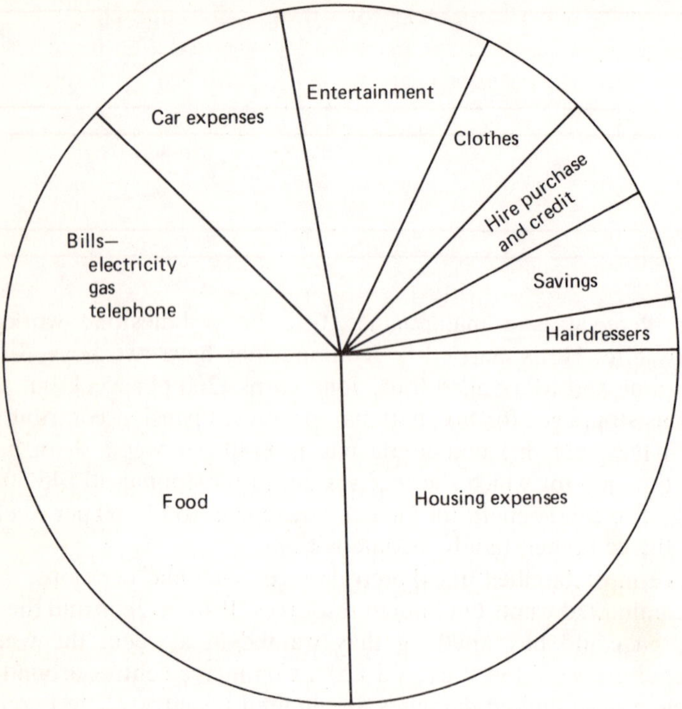

This is a good visual way of showing the allocation of certain things and is popular in business. The circle represents the total income, i.e. £200. As you will remember from school geometry, a circle has 360 degrees and each segment is calculated by multiplying 360 by the fraction of expenditure on that particular item, e.g. the Percivals spend £50 on food out of a total of £200; therefore the segment is

$$\frac{50}{200} \times 360 = 90°$$

We will use the example of the Percival pattern of expenditure to explain the differences between consumable and durable goods, between private sector goods and services, and the changes in patterns of consumer expenditure over the last twenty years.

Exercise 1
Mr Syd Oliver is a pensioner receiving £90 per week. He spends £45 on food, £15 on rent and housing expenses, £15 on electricity and gas and £15 for various entertainments, e.g. a few packets of cigarettes, beer and the occasional outing. Draw a pie chart to represent Mr Oliver's expenditure pattern using four segments.

Activity
Either using your own income or your family's draw up a list of the items on which the weekly income is spent.

Let us return to the Percivals. John gives his wife £65 each week of which she uses £50 for food, £10 for clothing and £5 for hairdressing. The £50 which is spent upon food is being spent on what is called 'consumables'; i.e. those goods are used up (consumed) and have to be replaced regularly. Clothing, especially for a growing family, would also be regarded as consumable goods. There are some goods, however, which last longer and are sometimes called 'durable' goods; i.e. they last for a longer period. You will note that John spends £10 of his income on hire purchase and credit. This is because over the past two years John has bought a new washing machine, a fridge and a secondhand car. Because he could not afford to buy these goods outright John took out an instalment agreement whereby he paid monthly. Items such as cars, washing machines, fridges, electric and gas stoves, and freezers are often known as 'durables'. However, they do not need to be bought on instalments, and many people buy them outright, i.e. they pay cash.

Exercise 2
Study the following list and say whether you think the goods in question are 'consumable' goods or 'durables'.

1. lamb chops
2. dishwasher
3. vacuum cleaner
4. breakfast cereal
5. petrol
6. dining-room suite
7. washing powder
8. electric kettle

When we look more closely at the way in which consumer expenditure has changed in the last few years we will see that there has been a growth in amounts of money spent on durable goods. This growth is both in 'absolute' and 'relative' terms. By absolute we mean the actual amount of money spent on the goods in question has risen as prices have risen while if we looked at the proportion of income spent on 'durables' we would find that there had been relative increases, i.e. increases in *relation* to other expenditure. In other words, a higher percentage of people's income is spent on durable goods.

1.1 GOODS AND SERVICES

If we look at the Percival list again we will notice yet another distinction. Some of the expenditure is on food and clothing. Food and clothing are examples of goods but there are also examples of expenditure on services. Quite a large amount of money, £25 per month, goes on services such as electricity, gas and telephone. Gas and electricity are basic necessities and of course more and more families are beginning to regard the telephone as essential. You will note that £20 per week is spent on entertainment and this for the Percivals includes an occasional visit to a restaurant in the town. John is interested in football and he usually goes to see Manchester City play when they are at home. This costs £4 admission plus the train fare from Buxton to Manchester, £3 return. Here we have examples of other services. A restaurant provides a service to its customers, Manchester City Football Club provides entertainment to its paying spectators and British Rail provides a service by transporting passengers. The Percivals always go to Torbay for their holidays and stay at a holiday camp; again, the holiday firm is providing a service. Jean's visit to the hairdressers is yet another example of a service.

The distinction between goods and services is an important one in commerce and business, and in the last twenty years or so there has been a vast increase in the number of firms providing services rather than goods. It has been a feature of expenditure in the last twenty years or so that a bigger and bigger proportion of people's income is being spent upon services.

£50 per week is spent on housing expenses. Many people buy houses by means of a mortgage which means that a building society or bank has provided most of the money for the house and John will have to pay interest on the loan each month. In addition you will have noticed that he has to pay rates. These are sums payable to the local authority; in John's case, because he lives in Buxton, to the High Peak Borough Council. The money is to pay for the services which are provided by both the district (High Peak) and the county

(Derbyshire) and cover such things as schools, fire service, ambulance, street lighting, refuse clearing. Thus, the rates are yet another example of spending money on services. (The rating system is due to be replaced in 1990 by a community charge called a 'poll tax'. We will return to the subject of rates in Chapter 16.)

John, like most sensible people, has taken the precaution of making sure that his house is insured against fire, etc. and insurance companies provide the service of undertaking the risk on his behalf. We notice that John had paid part of his salary in tax and national insurance and a good deal of this money paid to the government is to help finance many of the services provided by the government, e.g. medical services, education, law and order, defence.

Exercise 3

From the following list of expenditure distinguish goods from services:

1. holidays
2. books
3. technical college courses
4. motor-car repairs
5. motor-car accessories
6. fresh vegetables

Public sector and private sector goods and services

A distinction is sometimes made between goods and services produced and provided by the public sector and goods and services produced and provided by the private sector. Let us think again for a moment about the Percivals' weekly expenditure.

Some of the services which John and Jean have purchased are provided by public corporation, e.g. electricity is sold to the Percivals by the North West Electricity Board (Norweb). This is a state-owned corporation which therefore is owned by the public.

If John or his family travel by train then this will again be an example of a public sector service; British Rail, a publicly owned board, is responsible for the network of railways in this country. When John goes to see his favourite football team play he travels by rail, therefore using a public service. Jean travels by bus into town; she may use a public service since some of the bus routes throughout the country are operated by the National Bus Company which is publicly owned. Some services enjoyed by the Percivals are 'free', e.g. street cleaning, refuse collection, police, education. These are however paid for through taxation and rates. The services paid for by the rates and taxes are of course provided by the government and are therefore yet more examples of public sector services. There are, however, a range of services which are provided by the private sector. When the Percivals go on holiday to Torbay they use a local coach firm which is privately owned; the holiday firm is a private firm. Jean's hairdressers are a small private business, and when John gets his car serviced he goes to a privately owned garage. We learned that John insures his house and contents and this he does through one of the large insurance companies, which has shareholders and is in the private sector.

When people buy goods, they usually purchase from the private sector. Jean buys most of her food from one of the local supermarkets (Fine Fare) which is part of a large privately owned and organised chain of shops. Clothing is purchased from privately owned shops, such as Burtons, Fosters, Marks & Spencer and, in the main, is manufactured by companies in the private sector. Some imported clothing has been manufactured abroad, sometimes in government-owned factories.

John runs a 1.3L Metro, an Austin–Rover car. Austin–Rover, part of the Rover group formerly government owned but recently purchased (1988) by British Aerospace. Although the Percivals do not heat their home with solid fuel, many families do and coal is produced by British Coal, which is a public corporation owned by the State. When John buys petrol for his car, he sometimes buys from Shell which is a privately owned company but he also buys from BP, a comany which was owned partly by the government. A 32 per cent stake in BP was sold by the government in 1987. In fact it is not always easy to know when goods and services are purchased whether they are publicly or privately produced or provided, and as we have seen the situation is changing.

The last twenty years saw a considerable increase in the range of goods and services provided from the public sector. However, many people felt that the trend had gone too far, something the present Conservative Government (1988) has reversed with the sale of British Telecom, Austin–Rover, TSB, British Gas and British Airways. At present the government is considering privatising part of the electricity industry.

Activity
Think about your own expenditure over the last few weeks and divide it into expenditure on goods and services. At the same time try to distinguish whether they were provided publicly or privately.

Exercise 4

1 Name a service which you can obtain from both the public and the private sector.

2 From the following list of goods and services produce two lists, one for public sector provided goods and services and one for private sector goods and services:

milk	washing machines	Peugot/Talbot cars
beer	televisions	snack bars
coal	Russian-produced Lada cars	furniture
gas		postal services
law and order		

1.2 CHANGES IN CONSUMER EXPENDITURE

Every year, through its Statistical Office, the British Government produces a range of statistics. Figures are produced on consumer expenditure and in this section we will be looking at the changes which have taken place over the last 10–15 years.

In 1970 consumer expenditure in the UK was around £31 000 million. In 1980 this had grown to £132 000 million. In 1982 it was £167 000 million, and by 1986 it was just over £234 000 million. These increases do not necessarily mean that people are so much better off; they can largely be explained by the increases in prices during that period. In recent years, the word 'inflation' – that is a rise in prices – has become almost a household term. In 1975–6 the annual increase in prices rose by 24 per cent; prices were increasing, that is, at the rate of 24p in the £. The average rate of increase in the years 1970–80 was 15 per cent, but since then rate of increase has been much lower.

Each year the British Government's statistical office publishes the annual rate of increase in what is called the Retail Price Index (RPI). This is not a straightforward average of all price changes, rather goods are weighted according to the percentage of money spent on them. For example, around 15 per cent of consumer expenditure goes on food and this will be reflected in the figures.

The graph shown here (Figure 1.2) shows the rate of inflation between 1965 and 1988 and you can see the rate was modest in the early years, rising sharply through the 1970s but was again much more modest in the 1980s. The average rate of inflation for 1987–88 was 3.4 per cent.

Figure 1.2 *Percentage changes in inflation in the UK 1960–88 (RPI – Retail Price Index*

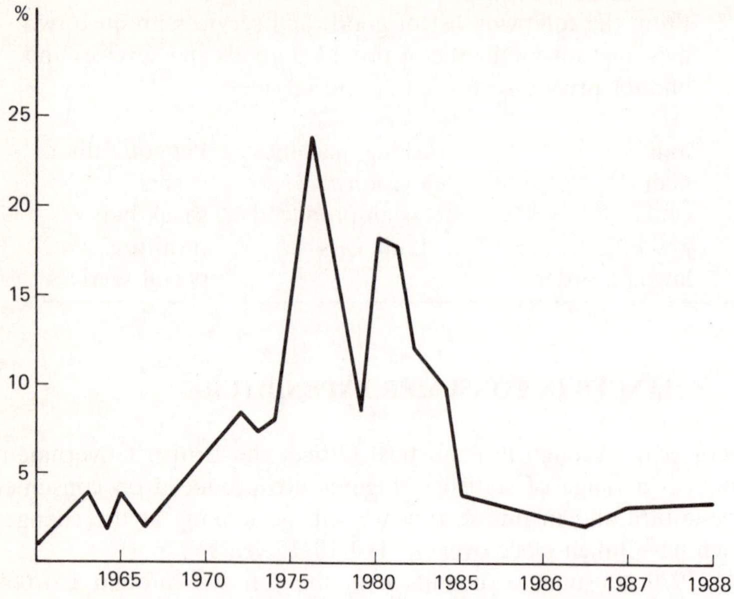

Several reasons have been advanced for the large increases in the 1970s:

1. The large increase in oil prices caused by the decision of OPEC (Oil and Petroleum Exporting Countries) to increase their prices drastically in 1973/4.
2. High wage demands.
3. Easy credit facilities (people could obtain loans to finance expenditure).
4. The low rate of exchange for £ sterling pushed up import prices.

> **Exercise 5**
> If the £ sterling has a low rate of exchange with such currencies as dollars, marks, francs and Yen, why will import prices be high?

Patterns of Expenditure

Not only were there changes in the level of prices during this period, there was also a change in pattern of expenditure.

In 1970, 20p in every £ spent was spent on food. In 1986 this figure had dropped to 14p. During the same period, there was a large increase in expenditure on such goods as televisions, refrigerators, washing machines and videos and at the same time a large increase in spending on transport especially motor cars. In 1986, 20p in the £ was spent on transport and communications – the increase in communications expenditure is very much related to the use of telephones.

During the period 1970–86 there has been a large increase in the amount spent on housing expenses such as rates, mortgages, insurance, heating and lighting. In 1970 the figure was 12p in the £; by 1986 this had risen to 20p in the £.

Patterns of expenditure in 1986 looked like this:

Expenditure in the £ in certain categories:

Housing expenses	20p
Food	14p
Transport and communication	20p
Leisure activities, including holidays	12p
Expenditure on durables, e.g. TV, videos, washing machines, computers	17p
Drink and tobacco	10p
Clothing and footwear	7p
	100p = £1

(*Source:* Central Statistical Office, *Source Trends 18,* 1988, HMSO.)

There are several reasons for the changes which have taken place in expenditure patterns.

1. As increasingly both a husband and wife are at work, there is an increase in demand for labour saving devices such as washing machines and vacuum cleaners.
2. Home-based entertainment has increased in importance as more sophisticated equipment has become available and central heating makes houses more comfortable. Thus the demand for videos and TVs has increased.
3. Holidays have increased in importance, especially travel overseas.
4. Higher petrol costs and higher maintenance costs for cars have increased the proportion of money spent on transportation.

Exercise 6
Answer the following questions, which relate to changing patterns of consumer expenditure.

1 The annual average rate of inflation during the period 1970–80 was: 25%; 20%; 15%; or 10%.
2 Indicate two causes of inflation during the 1970s.
3 The period 1970–86 has seen a rise in the proportion of income spent on food. True or false.
4 Why has there been such a large increase in the demand for labour saving devices such as washing machines and vacuum cleaners?

Activity
Inflation is a topic which needs to be constantly updated. The Government produces an excellent publication called *Social Trends.* Go to your college, school or local library and obtain this book to update the figures given in this section.

1.3 PRIMARY, SECONDARY AND TERTIARY PRODUCTION

We have been considering the various ways in which consumers spend their incomes and we discovered that their spending was on both goods and services. One way of classifying production is to divide it into primary, secondary and tertiary, i.e. first, second and third stages of production.

We will use one example to explain the differences between the three stages: a tin of carrots bought in a local supermarket.

Primary Production

The ingredients are carrots, salt and sugar; they are packed in a tin with a label around it. The ingredients and the packing all began as gifts of nature; the carrots and sugar were cultivated, the salt and the tin and iron mined and the paper from which the labelling was made came from trees. These products – carrots, sugar, salt, tin and paper – came from what are sometimes called the extractive industries, e.g. agriculture, fishing, mining and forestry. All products come originally from such industries and the process is known as primary production, i.e. production concerned with obtaining the direct products of nature.

Secondary Production

These natural products, i.e. carrots, salt, sugar, tin and paper pulp, have to be converted into products which can be used by consumers and there are various secondary stages involved in the manufacture of tins of carrots, e.g. making and printing the labels, producing the tins from steel and tin, combining the carrots, sugar and salt in a way to make them edible. This secondary stage is sometimes known as the manufacturing stage. The manufacturing or secondary stage is concerned with converting natural products.

Tertiary Production

These carrots came to us as a result of a number of activities, e.g. transport, retailing, advertising. These stages do not involve extraction or manufacturing but are services which allow the goods to come to consumers. It is probable that the carrots were ordered using postal or telecommunication services, paid for using banking services, arrived by road or rail transport and then were displayed on the shelves of a supermarket. This third but essential stage is known as the tertiary stage.

Exercise 7
Examine the following list of industries and say whether they are in the primary, secondary or tertiary stage.

1. an oil refinery
2. a coal mine
3. a bakery
4. an insurance company
5. a clothing manufacturer
6. a hospital
7. a sheep farm
8. North Sea oil rigs
9. telecommunications
10. a glass factory

We pointed out that the amount of money spent on services had been increasing in the last decade and this has meant that the tertiary sector has grown. The tertiary sector not only includes those things directly related to goods, i.e. banking, transport, but other services which are not directly related but without which production would not be possible, e.g. medical services, fire services, services providing law and order, education services.

1.4 THE WORKING POPULATION

In the last section we considered the various types of production and divided these up into primary, secondary and tertiary. The various goods and services required by the population would not be provided without the intervention of the workforce. In 1987 there were 23 385 760 persons in the UK who were available for work and of this figure 2 665 500 were registered as unemployed which represents an unemployment rate of 10.5 per cent. This meant that over one in every ten persons available for work was unemployed. A number of reasons have been put forward for this high rate of unemployment.

1. A rapid advance in technology and machinery in many industries which has been labour saving. Automation and computerisation have certainly been one of the causes of the high rate of unemployment.
2. Wage rates have risen sharply in the last ten years or so and this has meant that many firms have found themselves unable to employ the number of workers they did in the past. Trade unions have negotiated large wage increases.

   There has been a particular problem for young people because as trade unions have negotiated large increases for them this has had the effect of pricing them out of the market, and there has been a big rise in youth unemployment.

   The UK has faced enormous international competition in many of its traditional industries such as clothing and textiles, motor vehicles, electrical goods and shipbuilding. A number of countries, particularly in the Far East, have taken advantage of their lower wage levels to out-compete the products of the UK.
3. Perhaps the most important explanation of unemployment is that the British economy like that of many other countries has been in *recession*; this means that demand for goods and services has been low and therefore because a firm cannot sell its products it is forced to reduce its labour force or in some cases 'close its doors'. The number of companies forced into liquidation, i.e. that have 'gone bust', in recent years is considerable and clearly that has had enormous effects upon employment.

Activity
When you are next shopping in a large city, think about the large range of goods available in shops which are from overseas.

Distribution of the Labour Force

You will remember that we divided production up into three stages – primary, secondary and tertiary. It is possible to divide employment up in the same way and the following was the distribution in 1988, showing the percentage of the labour force in each sector:

1. *Primary sector*: extractive industries including agriculture, forestry, fishing, mining and quarrying – 4 per cent.
2. *Secondary sector*: manufacturing including construction – 33 per cent.
3. *Tertiary sector*: service industries including transport, insurance, banking, retailing, hotels, catering, electricity, gas and water – 56 per cent; *also* local and national government – 7 per cent : 63 per cent in all.

This distribution can easily be shown by means of what is called a bar chart (Figure 1.3).

The bar chart represents the total labour force and the divisions represent the proportions in that particular sector. If percentages are used then it is easy to construct by using a bar which is 10 cm or 10 inches in length. 6.3 per cent is represented by 6.5 cm or inches.

The significant feature of the distribution of the labour force is the large percentage involved in the service industries. This percentage has grown quickly in the last ten years which is a reflection of the fact that services have represented a larger proportion of consumers' spending. We must, not forget, however, that services are involved in bringing manufactured goods to the shops and ultimately to our homes.

Exercise 8
1. List three possible reasons for the high level of unemployment in the UK.
2. Construct a bar chart representing the service industries in the UK in 1987 using the following percentages: catering and distribution 27 per cent, financial services 9 per cent,

transport and communications 11 per cent, government, local and national, 12 per cent, professional, e.g. medical, dental, 27 per cent, other services including electricity, gas and water 14 per cent.

Figure 1.3 *Bar chart showing distribution of labour force in the UK in 1988 (percentages)*

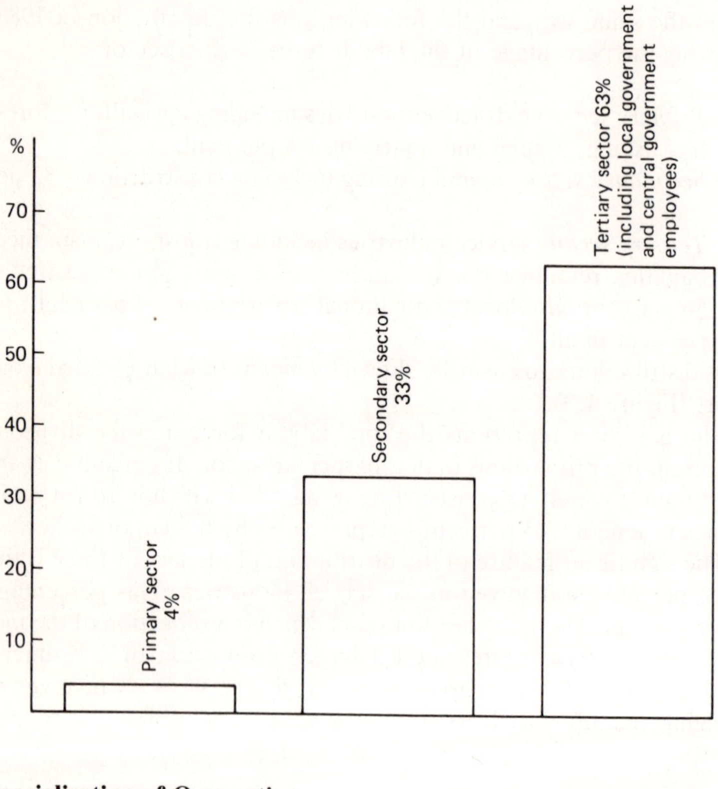

Specialisation of Occupations

You will remember that we have already dealt with the various stages involved in the production of a relatively simple product such as a tin of carrots. A full range of activities was involved in bringing this product to the consumer. Let us think of another example to illustrate the vast range of occupations involved in the manufacture and distribution of goods.

Figure 1.4 *Bar chart showing service industries in the UK in 1987*

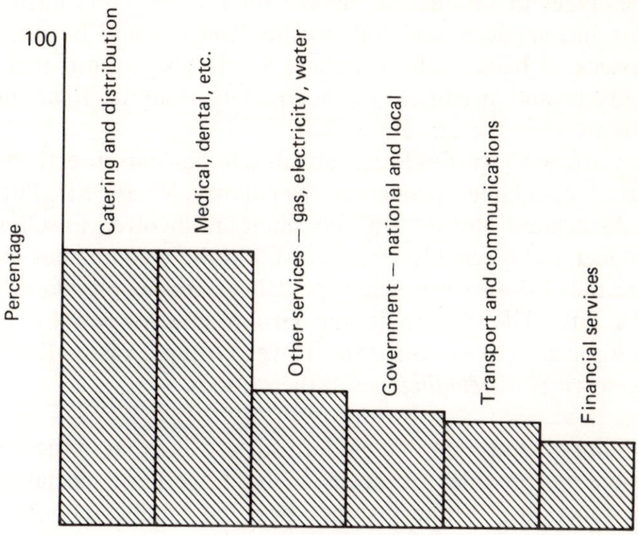

Leslie and Dorothy Pitt have saved hard to buy a motor car and they decide to purchase a British one, the Austin–Rover Metro 1.3. They go along to the local dealer, Associated Motors Ltd. The salesman shows them the range of colours and arranges a test drive. Leslie and Dorothy are particularly interested in the 1.3L, which they purchase for £6200.

The Metro was produced in Austin–Rover's Oxford works but used a vast range of parts from other companies all over the country. To quote just two examples, it is probable that the lighting equipment came from Lucas of Birmingham while the brake linings would have probably been manufactured by Ferodo in Derbyshire. Not only has there been a large number of factory workers, mechanics, foremen, supervisors, etc. involved in the production but also others not involved in the actual production:

1. Before launching the Metro, Austin–Rover wanted to be sure that the product was what the consumer wanted and would be priced correctly; this involves *market research.* Having decided upon the product then Austin–Rover attempted to stimulate demand by *advertising.*

2. At various stages of production of the car, parts have to be brought from other areas of the country and therefore *transport* is involved.
3. The stages of production involve finance. Workers have to be paid and services paid for. Austin–Rover would be using the services of banks. The company would also ensure that their products and premises are adequately insured. *Banking* and *insurance* are therefore involved.
4. As you know, Austin–Rover do not sell their cars directly but use various companies throughout the country. Mr and Mrs Pitt went to Associated Motors Ltd. Salesmen are involved in selling the product and mechanics are involved in these companies making sure that the cars are ready for delivery to people like Mr and Mrs Pitt. The Austin–Rover Group now owned by British Aerospace is to be called the Rover Group. Austin–Rover use the services of *retailing* to sell their goods.

It is quite obvious that in a modern society like that in the UK it is impossible to provide for needs without workers specialising in various functions. We hear sometimes that families choose to be self-sufficient, i.e. they move to remote areas and try to provide all their own needs. In some parts of the world there are people who *subsist*, i.e. they provide for all their needs. Even among these people, however, trading takes place and specialisation develops.

1. Each person does what he has most aptitude for. Some people are good organisers, some are inventive, some have physical strength, some are good at mathematics and so on. Specialisation allows them to concentrate on what they are good at.
2. Because workers specialise they can become expert in their chosen field.
3. Specialisation results in our being able to enjoy the vast range of goods and services available. This would be impossible if everyone tried to produce all he needed himself.

However, there are disadvantages in specialisation as far as workers are concerned:

1. If a person is specialised in a narrow field of activity and the demand related to that activity declines he can be in a difficult position. For example, the advent of electronic watches has proved to be a problem to a watch repairer who has concentrated upon the 'Swiss' movement watches.

2. Specialisation in a narrow range of skills can become very monotonous. A machine worker involved in a repetitive task for eight hours per day does not have the most attractive of occupations.

Exercise 9

These review questions are based upon the whole of the chapter. Try to do these questions without reference to the text. If on checking the answers you find that you have misunderstood a particular aspect read over that appropriate section again.

1. By reference to this list of items explain in a paragraph the difference between consumable goods and durable goods: a suite of furniture, a packet of biscuits, a tin of shoe polish, a shampoo, a television video recorder.

2. Which of the following statements are true?

- **(a)** Electricity is always produced in the private sector.
- **(b)** A motor-car service is an example of a durable product.
- **(c)** British Rail is a privately owned company.
- **(d)** Coal is produced mainly by a publicly owned corporation.
- **(e)** An accountant is an example of a primary occupation.

3. Between 1970 and 1980 certain trends in consumer expenditure were apparent. Study the following statements which refer to 1970–80 and say for each whether it is true or false.

- **(a)** Expenditure in the £ on food fell between 1970 and 1980.
- **(b)** Expenditure in the £ on services also fell between 1970 and 1980.
- **(c)** Inflation during the period 1970–80 averaged 5 per cent.
- **(d)** Housing costs rose sharply between 1970 and 1980 and relative expenditure on this item rose.

4. In the production of a motor-cycle identify one occupation in the three categories: primary, secondary and tertiary.

5. In the UK economy as a whole list the three sectors in order according to the number of employees employed in them.

6. List two advantages and two disadvantages of specialisation.

7. Draw a pie chart representing patterns of expenditure in the period 1986–88, based on the following:

	Per cent
Housing	20
Transport	20
Food	15
Leisure activities	12
Durables	16
Drink and tobacco	10
Clothing and footwear	7

CHAPTER 2

BUSINESS ORGANISATION

2.1 THE SOLE TRADER

Keith Riley is from a fairly wealthy family. He was not, however, interested in going into the family business but took up a career in retailing instead. His first job was as an assistant in a shoe shop which was part of a large chain. Keith went to college one day per week and gained the BTEC (Business and Technician Education Council) national certificate in retailing. He was very keen on retailing and his father gave him, as a twenty-first birthday present £60 000 so that he could start up in business on his own account. Keith bought a shoe shop which was situated near the town centre. He employed two assistants and decided to trade as Surefit (Shoes). Keith obviously had good skills in business and the first three years were very successful indeed. Careful advertising, good customer services and a specialisation in children's shoes brought good business. He made £30 000 profit in his third year.

Keith has been quite successful in his first venture in business and in the first part of this chapter we will be following Keith's career to help us understand the various types of business organisation existing.

Keith is the only owner of Surefit (Shoes). This is an example of a *sole trader* form of organisation. Although Keith employees two ladies as shop assistants they are employees and are paid a weekly wage; they do not have any part in the ownership of the business.

If Surefit (Shoes) does well Keith will get the benefit but if it does badly he will bear the loss. Thus a definition of a sole trader is 'an individual who owns and controls a business, receives all its profits and bears all its losses'.

1. A sole trader is the only owner of the business. Some sole traders

get loans to assist them but the lender is not in any way an owner, he is a creditor (i.e. the trader owes him money).

2. A sole trader controls the business – he has sole responsibility for all decisions. When Keith is away, perhaps buying shoes, he may put the shop under the control of one of his employees. She, however, would only be managing the shop for Keith; he would be responsible.
3. Keith will not need to share any profits he makes because he is the 'sole owner'. If, however, he had lost money, e.g. if losses were £10 000, Keith would have had to bear these losses himself.

These then are the features of a sole trader organisation:

1. sole ownership
2. sole responsibility for profits and losses

There are thousands of businesses in the United Kingdom which are of the sole trader type and this particular form is predominant in other countries. In the last twenty years there has been an increase in the number of large businesses but the sole trader still plays an important part in commercial activity. The continuing existence of the sole trader is due to the fact that this type of organisation has a number of advantages, as we shall see when we look at Keith's business in more detail.

Advantages of the Sole Trader Organisation

1. The business is a very personal one – Keith as owner will see the representatives of firms selling him goods. He will have closer personal contact with his two employees and therefore be able to get the best out of them.
2. The success of the business will be of direct benefit to Keith and so he knows that his efforts will bring rewards to him, not anyone else. Sole traders are often willing to work long hours to benefit the business.
3. Keith does not have to consult others when he wants to make changes. He can decide and act quickly.
4. The sole trader does not have to go through any lengthy formalities to set up his business. Keith bought the shop and began trading the next day. The requirement to register a business name has now been abolished (in 1981) and the only requirement is that Keith on his invoices and bills must indicate 'K. Riley trading as Surefit (Shoes)'. The business must display

its name and the name of the owner. This requirement is necessary only if the business is using a name other than the name of the owner. If Keith's business was known as K. Riley then even the requirement to display would not be necessary.

> **Activity**
> Often you will see shops displaying details of the names of the owner and the business name. Because the legal requirement to register the name has only recently been abolished you may still find the certificates necessary under the 1916 Registration of Business Names Act. In the next few days try to find examples of sole traders trading under names other than their own and perhaps also the display of this information.

5. A sole trader does not need to publish any information about his business to the public. Any member of the public has the right to see details of companies but no right to have details of a sole trader's business. Of course, Keith would have to supply details of his business to the Inland Revenue. This is for tax purposes but these details are not available to the public.

We can see then that the sole trader organisation has a number of quite important advantages. There are, however, a number of disadvantages in this type of business and again we will use the example of Surefit (Shoes) to explain these.

Disadvantages of Sole Trader Organisations

1. Keith has to work long hours to run his business; usually he arrives at the shop at about 8.15 am and does not normally leave until he has cashed up, often about 6.30. Although he sometimes discusses his problems with his wife, Wendy, he has all the worry of the business on his shoulders. In the three years he has operated his business he has never felt he could afford to be away on holiday and although he has fortunately been in good health the effect of absence through illness does worry him considerably. It can be fairly said that a sole trader has a number of personal burdens.
2. Keith's business has prospered, but not all businesses are in this happy position. Let us assume for a moment that instead of £30 000 profit Keith's takings were not even sufficient to pay his bills or his manufacturers for new shoe deliveries. The business

could go bankrupt and Keith could stand to lose not only his £60 000 initial investment in the business, but also his creditors (i.e. those to whom he owes money) could claim his personal possessions to settle the debts, i.e. his house or his car.

A sole trader such as Keith has *unlimited liability*; this means he is liable for the debts of the business over and above money he has put in. In law the business and the owner are treated as though they were one and the owner's personal property could be seized to pay off business debts. As we will see later, companies are not in this position and this is why they often have 'limited' in their title. Unlimited liability is a very serious disadvantage.

3. Keith's business is flourishing and he realises that he could do even better if he could open several other branches. Unfortunately, sole traders do not usually have sufficient reserves to do this and it is often a disadvantage that expansion is limited by insufficiency of capital.
4. Keith, of course, has to do all the work of managing the business himself and some aspects such as the accounts, stocktaking and sales returns he does not like and is not very good at. He could employ someone to do these things, but it is sometimes an advantage to have a business colleague who has that sort of expertise. You cannot expect one person to be good at everything and the sole trader organisation often lacks some essential skills.

Exercise 1

1. What are the three features of a sole trader organisation?
2. The number of sole trader organisations has grown rapidly in the last twenty years. True/false?
3. A sole trader operating a business using a name other than his own must register his name. True/false?
4. Information about sole traders' business activity is freely available to the public. True/false?
5. Michael Harper uses £50 000 of his savings to open a music shop. Michael operates as a sole trader and, having little experience, over-orders stock. He finds he cannot pay his debts and he goes bankrupt. Advise Michael as to whether he could lose more than £50 000.

2.2 PARTNERSHIPS

Keith has established his business and each year his profits increase. Keith is very ambitious and he feels he would like to expand his business by buying two other shoe shops which are for sale in a town nearby. Keith has some money available for the two purchases but not enough so he decides to form a partnership. He contacts a friend who has good retailing experience and the friend decides to come in with Keith and invests £60 000. Keith's wife Wendy also agrees to use her savings of £20 000 to join the partnership. The £60 000, plus the £20 000, together with his own money, allows Keith and his new partners to buy the two shops.

Keith, his friend Kevin Bradd and Wendy decide to draw up a partnership deed and go to see their solicitor. A partnership deed is not a necessary requirement but it is for obvious reasons, as we will see, advisable.

The partnership deed between Keith, Kevin and Wendy is drawn up and specifies the following points:

1. The partnership capital (i.e. the money in the business) is as follows: Keith £80 000, Kevin £60 000 and Wendy £20 000.
2. The profits to be shared in the proportion 8:6:2, i.e. the profits will be divided into sixteen parts. Keith will get 8/16 ($\frac{1}{2}$), Kevin 6/16 ($\frac{3}{8}$) and Wendy 2/16 ($\frac{1}{8}$). You will have noticed that the agreement lays down that the profits will be shared in exactly the same proportion as the ownership: 80 000, 60 000, 20 000. It is also agreed that the precise amount of profits to be shared will be determined by a meeting of Keith and Kevin. (Many businesses, of course, do not distribute all their profits but use a proportion to put back in the business, e.g. to make improvements. This process is known as 'ploughing back.')
3. The partnership deed specifies that Keith and Kevin will share in the management of the business. The overall policy relating to sales, advertising, sales promotions and ordering will be made by the two partners, but Keith will look after two new shops while Kevin will manage the first one. Kevin will also be responsible for buying stock, keeping accounts and analysing sales. The deed specifies that Wendy will be a 'sleeping partner', i.e. she will have no management duties. All policy decisions will be made by the two partners, Keith and Kevin.
4. The partnership deed also lays down that Keith and Kevin will be paid each an annual salary of £7 000; these salaries will be deducted before the profits are calculated.

A partnership has been formed with three partners, Kevin, Keith and Wendy. A partnership is regarded as being an *association of individuals engaged in business,* and it has the following features.

1. Each partner has unlimited liability – Keith, Kevin and Wendy could lose more than their investment in the business, i.e. 80 000, 60 000 and £20 000.
2. If Surefit (Shoes) did not for any reason pay some of its debts then the creditor could not sue the partnership but would sue the partners by name.
3. If one of the partners makes a contract then he binds the other partner. If Keith decided to improve one of the shops and ordered equipment from a firm of shopfitters then Kevin and Wendy would be liable just as if they had made the agreement themselves.
4. Like a sole trader the partnership does not need to provide any information to the public.
5. The partnership is owned and controlled by the partners.

Although Keith, Kevin and Wendy have obtained a partnership deed it is possible to form a partnership without a deed, but the rules to be followed will be as laid down in the Partnership Act 1890.

Keith and Kevin work very well together, the three shops flourish and the concentration upon good customer service with the specialisation in children's shoes brings the business good returns. Keith and Kevin decide to 'plough back' £12 000 of the net profit to make improvements in the shops. This leaves £64 000 to distribute to the partners.

Exercise 2

1. Explain in a sentence what you understand by 'plough back'.

2. Assuming that £64 000 is distributed using the Surefit (Shoes) partnership deed, calculate the profit to be received by each of the three partners.

Advantages of a Partnership

By looking at the partnership known as Surefit (Shoes) let us examine some of the advantages of partnerships as a form of business organisation.

1. Obviously a partnership allows more capital to be put into the business. Keith wishes to expand but he did not have enough capital (money) to buy the two additional shops; by taking two partners he was able to obtain an extra £80 000. Thus one advantage of a partnership is that it helps to provide additional capital.
2. You will remember that Keith did not like aspects of running a business, e.g. accounts, stocktaking and making sales returns. In the partnership agreement Kevin agreed to take on these tasks. Thus another advantage of a partnership is that it can allow a sharing of the work so that partners can take on what they are particularly good at.
3. Now that Keith has got a partner he can do things which he could not easily do before. For example he can now take a holiday confident that the business is in good hands. Since Kevin is also a partner it is in his interest to do the job well. Also if Kevin or Keith is ill they can cover for each other. Thus a third advantage is that having a partner can take the strain out of running a business.

Disadvantages of Partnerships

There are also some disadvantages of partnerships.

1. Keith is no longer able to do what he pleases; he must consult with Kevin. It is possible that they will not agree and conflict may arise. It is also possible that decisions will be slow because of the need for consultation.
2. Keith, Kevin or Wendy can at any time take their money out of the business and this would present the remaining partners with considerable problems. If Keith decided to leave, to pay him out might mean selling at least one if not two of the shops.
3. As pointed out earlier, both the 'active' partners, Keith and Kevin, can make contracts, e.g. order goods or equipment, Kevin could make a contract which put the business into difficulties and Keith of course, would be equally liable.

Exercise 3
We have then seen that a partnership is another form of business organisation. Answer the following questions, which are based on partnerships.

1. It is a legal necessity for partners to draw up a partnership deed. True/false?
2. A 'sleeping partner' can take full part in management decisions. True/false?
3. Give a definition of a partnership.
4. Give four examples of what might be included in a partnership deed.
5. Give three possible advantages of a partnership as compared to a sole trader.

2.3 LIMITED COMPANIES

The three shops run by Surefit (Shoes) are, as we have seen, doing well and in fact the firm is acquiring a reputation for an excellent sales record. Keith and Kevin realise that their method of running the shops is highly successful and they are anxious to expand their operations throughout the North-West of England. There are a number of shoe shops for sale all over the North-West but there really is not enough money to purchase them. Keith and Kevin decide that their best hope of success is to form a company and following consultation with Wendy, Keith and Kevin set about changing the partnership into a company.

Although a company may be set up by Act of Parliament or by Royal Charter, by far the most common method is to set up the company by registration. The law lays down (Companies Act, 1981) that there must be at least two shareholders.

Setting up a Company

Kevin and Keith are able to interest two other people in their new venture who are willing to invest about £60 000 each. But before a company can be set up the following must be lodged with the Registrar of Companies:

1. The Memorandum of Association
This document is sometimes known as the company's charter and it sets down the main details of the company as they apply to the public. An example is given below.

MEMORANDUM OF ASSOCIATION

1. The name of the Company is Surefit (Shoes) Ltd.

2. The registered office of the Company will be situated in England.
3. The objects for which the Company is established is to retail shoes and associated footwear and to do such other things as may be incidental or conducive to the attainment of such objects.
4. The liability of the members is limited.
5. The share capital of the Company is £330 000 divided into three hundred and thirty thousand £1 shares.

We, the persons whose names and addresses are subscribed, are desirous of being formed into a company in pursuance of the Memorandum of Association and we respectively agree to take the number of shares in the capital of the Company set opposite our respective names:

Names, addresses and description of subscribers		*Number of shares taken by each subscriber*
Keith Riley 14 White Knowle Drive Blandford	Shop manager	100 000
Kevin Bradd 32 High Street Old Compton	Shop manager	80 000
Wendy Riley 14 White Knowle Drive Blandford	Housewife	30 000
	Total shares	210 000

Dated the 4 August, 1988
Witness to the above signatures:
Philip Cheetham
14 Hove Road
Brightford

The memorandum of association contains a statement that the company is limited, i.e. the shareholders can lose only what they have put in. The name of the company will be allowed by the registrar only if it does not conflict with another company. The purpose for which the company is formed must be stated, i.e. the objects and the amount of money to be raised. You will have noted that although the company wishes to raise £330 000 it has only at this stage subscribed £210 000.

2. *Articles of Association*
The second document which must be sent to the registrar is the articles of association. This lays down the internal rules of the company such as voting rights, meetings, etc.

3. *A Statement of the Share Capital of the Company*
This is a statement of what the company will raise. Surefit (Shoes) Ltd would state £330 000. Since tax is payable on the amount companies do not usually indicate an amount over and above what they really wish to raise.

4. *Registration of directors*
Keith and Kevin are to be the two directors of the company and Wendy agrees to be company secretary. The fourth requirement is that a document must be sent to the registrar giving full details of the directors and the secretary together with the signatures indicating that the three people, in this case Keith, Kevin and Wendy, are willing to act.

5. *Registration of Address*
Lastly there must be a statement giving the address of the registered office of the new company: 36 London Road, Blandford. If the registrar is satisfied with the documents he will issue a certificate of incorporation and Surefit (Shoes) Ltd can begin trading as a private company.

A private company has a number of important features:

1. The company is a 'legal entity', that means it can sue, be sued in the courts and face prosecution. All agreements made by the company will be in the company's name. In other words the company is a body quite separate from its individual shareholders.
2. The shareholders have limited liability, which mean Keith, Kevin and Wendy can lose only the amount of their shareholding.
3. A company goes on existing even if its shareholders leave because before they leave they have to sell their shares to other people who will become shareholders.

4. Because Surefit (Shoes) Ltd is a private company it cannot advertise its shares to the public. Moreover if anyone in a private company wishes to sell his shares the other members can restrict his right to sell them as he pleases.
5. The company's affairs are available to any member of the public.

Surefit (Shoes) Ltd is now a company and Keith and Kevin obtain £120 000 from two other people by selling 120 000 £1 shares. This enables the company to expand and buy additional premises. This then is an advantage of a company type of organisation; it allows far more capital investment. The other advantages are that the company does not disappear if shareholders leave and it gives the shareholders limited liability.

However, there are certain disadvantages. Keith and Kevin are not completely in control since they are now answerable to the other three shareholders. Decisions may take longer to be made and to be put into effect. The company must make its affairs known and any member of the public can examine Surefit (Shoes) Ltd's affairs by application to the registrar.

Exercise 4

1. Name three ways in which a company may be set up.
2. What five documents must be given to the Registrar of Companies before he will issue a certificate of incorporation?
3. What is the objects clause?
4. If Surefit (Shoes) Ltd had broken the law then Keith, Kevin and Wendy could face prosecution. True/false?
5. If Keith wished to leave Surefit (Shoes) Ltd, the company would automatically come to an end. True/false?
6. What restriction is placed upon a private company in respect of its shares?

2.4 A PUBLIC COMPANY

Surefit (Shoes) Ltd has certainly come a long way since Keith bought his first shop and operated as a sole trader. It is now clear that the shoe shops controlled by the new company are very successful and the two directors Keith and Kevin realise that there is considerable potential in even further expansion. They know that shops are available in the North-West of England, in the Midlands and in

Yorkshire and they feel that in order to expand they need to go 'public'. To go 'public' means that the private company will become a public company. Following a meeting with the other shareholders the two directors are given permission to apply to the Registrar of Companies to make Surefit a public company.

As we have already learned, a public company means that the shares can be advertised and bought publicly. Let us then use our company Surefit (Shoes) Ltd to see how a public company is created.

1. Keith and Kevin calculate that they wish to raise £1 000 000 by selling £1 million £1 shares.
2. Members of the public who might be interested in the shares would want to be sure that they could resell them if ever they wanted the money. Therefore, it is important that the shares are 'listed' at the Stock Exchange. Before listing any shares, the Stock Exchange carries out a full investigation of the company.
3. Once the Stock Exchange has agreed to list the shares Keith and Kevin issue a 'prospectus' which is a document setting out the main details of the company and inviting the public to subscribe to the £1 share issue. The prospectus is advertised in the newspapers.
4. If the directors (Keith and Kevin) receive applications from the public for 1 million shares or more then they advise the Registrar of Companies.
5. The registrar then issues a certificate of trading, and Surefit (Shoes) Ltd has become a public company.

Since 1981 it has become necessary for public companies to indicate in their title that they are public and Surefit (Shoes) Ltd would become Surefit (Shoes) plc. Plc means 'public limited company'.

Activity

In the new few weeks or so try to find examples of public limited companies. Since 1981 public companies have had to indicate that they are public either in full or by abbreviation.

Although in our example Surefit (Shoes) plc did the work of applying to the Stock Exchange and issuing a prospectus it could have gone to a merchant bank which would have taken on the job for it. The merchant bank buys all the shares and then offers them for sale. The 'offer for sale' document is really the same as a prospectus. As you have probably guessed the merchant bank gets its commission by buying the shares at a cheaper rate than it sells them to the public.

Control of a Company

Surefit (Shoes) plc as it is now called has four director, Keith, Kevin and two new directors, Mrs Jeanette Beckwith and Mr Mark Stacey. These four directors have between them at least 51 per cent of the shares.

A shareholders' meeting is held once a year and each share carries one vote. It can be seen that the four directors cannot be voted out of office by the other shareholders.

Surefit (Shoes) plc like all other public limited companies is:

1. owned by the shareholders;
2. managed by the directors;
3. controlled by those holding a majority of the voting shares.

A public company has all the advantages and disadvantages of a private company but it is also able to raise much more capital because it can invite the public to subscribe.

Exercise 5

1. It is always possible since 1981 to distinguish a public company from a private company. True/false?
2. There are two possible ways in which the public company can invite the public to buy shares. Can you name them?
3. Although it is not a legal necessity why do you think it is important for a public company to get Stock Exchange listing?
4. Before a public company can begin trading what does it need from the Registrar of Companies?

Company Takeovers

Surefit (Shoes) plc is now a successful company with a number of shoe shops around the country. Its shares are quoted on the Stock Exchange at 260p per share. A number of very large shoe retailing companies begin to show an interest in Surefit.

The effect of this is that Surefit shares begin to increase in price.

Two companies make bids for the shares and the price rises to 750p per share.

It is up to Surefit shareholders to decide whether or not to accept the bid and they are guided by the directors. Surefit directors recommend the acceptance of a bid from Easiphit PLC and a price per share of 770p is accepted.

Surefit is now wholly controlled by Easiphit but still continues to trade as Surefit (Shoes).

You probably remember a similar situation in 1988 when two companies from Switzerland, Suchard and Nestlé were trying to gain control of the British company Rowntree. Rowntree's shares increased sharply in price during this time, as the following extract from June 1988 shows:*

1988		
High	*Low*	
$10\frac{5}{8}$	411	Rowntree

The Independent, The Times and *The Daily Telegraph* newspapers regularly publish details of share prices. For each company quoted they show the present price and the high and the low point in a year. Prices are quoted usually in pence e.g. 411 pence but if the price is £10 or above then this is shown as in our example.

In June 1988 Rowntree shares stood at over £10, but during that year had been 411p, i.e. a gain of nearly £6.

Activity

In takeover bids as they are sometimes called, the decisions of institutional investors are often important.

See if you can find out what the term 'institutional investor' means.

Your school, college or public library will be able to help.

(As we all now know, Nestlé were successful and now own Rowntree.) We will be coming back to the subject of shares and share prices in the chapter 'The Stock Exchange'.

2.5 PUBLIC ENTERPRISES

In the first chapter we learned that some of the goods and services purchased by individuals come from what we called the public sector.

Activity
Think for a moment of all the goods and services you have bought or used in the last week or so. You will notice that quite a number are available from the public sector.

A number of the most common services are provided by public corporations, electricity is provided by the Central Electricity Generating Board (CEGB) but distributed by area boards, e.g. North-West Electricity Board (Norweb); rail services are provided by British Rail; some bus services are provided by the National Bus Company; broadcasting is provided by the British Broadcasting Corporation; postal services are provided by the Post Office Corporation. A number of companies have been created from the public sector since 1981. They have been 'privatised'. The list below gives the name of the company, when it was formed, the share price when the shares were first issued and the present [June 1988] price.

Company	*Issue price (p)*	*Present price (p)*
AB Ports (1983)	56	565
Amersham (1982)	142	449
BAA (1987)	245	285
British Aerospace (1981)	150	385
British Airways (1987)	125	144
British Gas (1986)	135	168
British Telecom (1984)	130	237
Britoil (1982)	215	510
Cable and Wireless (1981)	56	344
Enterprise Oil (1984)	185	397
Jaguar (1984)	165	249
Rolls-Royce (1987)	170	123
TSB (1986)	100	97
VSEL Consortium (1986)	100	468

The Government has recently announced plans to 'privatise' Girobank and also parts of the Electricity Industry. Try to make sure that you keep up to date with these developments.

In order to understand the workings of these public corporations let us examine one in detail. As you will remember a number of public corporations have been privatised, that is sold by the government for example, British Gas, British Telecom, British Airways and the Rover Group.

British Rail

British Rail, which is responsible for the railway network in the United Kingdom, is controlled by the British Railways Board.

1. The membership of the board is chosen by the government and the board has a chairman, at present (1988) Sir Robert Reid.
2. Finance is available from the Treasury and is borrowed at a fixed rate of interest.
3. The board must provide annual accounts to Parliament and although the day-to-day running of British Rail is in the hands of the board it is answerable to a Minister, i.e. the secretary of state responsible for transport.

The government has much more say in the running of a public corporation than in an ordinary company and if it (the government) is not happy with the way in which a board is handling its affairs it can refuse to make money available for investment. You may remember that the 1982 disputes with the railway drivers' union (ASLEF) over flexible rostering threatened the provision of government money for a modernisation programme, particularly electrification.

British rail services were privately owned until 1947. Various companies operated the network, e.g. GWR (Great Western Railway), LMS (London Midlands and Scottish), SR (Southern Railways), LNER (London North Eastern Railway). These companies were making huge losses and there was often a duplication of services. Railways were brought into public ownership:

1. to prevent a collapse of the system because of the losses. The government can agree to run a service at a loss and provide the revenue. A privately owned company answerable to its shareholders cannot go on operating at a loss;
2. because as the system is controlled by one body some of the wasteful competition could be got rid of (notice how many stations there are in large cities now and compare this with thirty years ago).
3. Some routes are still operated at a loss. The government regards this as essential because it provides a link between outlying areas and larger cities. Operation of what are called 'uneconomic' routes is more likely under the government than under the private system.
4. The government can, if it wishes, make sums available for modernisation. It is less likely that the enormous sums of money

needed would come from the selling of shares in a private company.

The Reason for Public Ownership

You are probably aware that a lot of controversy surrounds the subject of public ownership. There are some people who believe that public ownership has not really proved successful and it should be gradually handed back to the private sector. Others believe that more and more private firms should be brought under public ownership, and the question is a political one. Generally the Conservative Party is more inclined to favour private enterprise whereas the Labour Party favours public ownership. Without going into the various political arguments it is possible to list some of the advantages and disadvantages of public ownership.

Advantages

1. Some services are so important that it is essential they are operated for the good of the community and industry generally. For example it might be regarded as unsatisfactory if the Post Office became private and, because it did not pay to serve rural areas, postal deliveries and other services were discontinued.
2. In the interests of security certain services must be provided by the state. It would be wrong for there to be private police forces or private armies in this country.
3. Some services cannot be operated at a profit but still ought to be provided. Health services are an example of services which could not be easily operated at a profit but must be available to all who require them.
4. As pointed out earlier, services are brought under public control sometimes because only the government will provide the resources to make them efficient and sometimes because the service under private control was making such heavy losses that its survival was threatened.

Disadvantages

1. When services come under state/public control competition is not allowed to exist. If the area electricity boards put up prices consumers cannot get electricity elsewhere. This is said to be a danger of large public corporations. They become 'monopolies' – i.e. the only producer of a good or service.
2. Since the public corporation gets its money from the Treasury it is said that it need not worry too much about 'profit' because the

Treasury will always 'bale out' the corporation. This is said to result in a lack of efficiency.

3. Some people argue that a large public corporation, because of its size, is too 'bureaucratic', i.e. decisions are slow, there is too much 'red tape'. Workers, because they are working for a public corporation, do not always regard efficiency as important. 'The government will pay' is sometimes an unfortunate attitude.

Exercise 6

1. Given an example of a public corporation which is responsible for: (a) the provision of electricity; (b) the distribution of electricity.

2. Who provides the finance for public corporations?

3. In what three ways does the government control the activities of a public corporation?

4. British Rail is a 'monopoly' – explain in a sentence what you understand by this.

5. The British Broadcasting Corporation obtains finance by selling shares to the public. True/false?

2.6 OTHER TYPES OF BUSINESS ORGANISATION

Before we leave the subject of business organisations it will be useful to examine briefly two other forms of business organisation; in both cases they are non-profit making. The following example will help to illustrate these two.

Mr and Mrs Giles have just got married and they decide to buy a small house for £45 000. The house is situated in 24 Crossways Avenue, Highfield, Oldham. Before their marriage both Mr and Mrs Giles saved with the Abbey National Building Society and they applied to this building society for a mortgage of £35 000. This application is granted and the house is purchased. The interest on the mortgage is 10 per cent which means that the couple have to pay £299.66 per month interest to Abbey National. Mrs Giles works in Oldham and because it is convenient she does all her shopping in the Cooperative Society.

Building societies and the Cooperative Society are the two examples of non-profit-distributing organisations.

Building Societies

Building societies offer facilities to savers who receive interest; the money from savers is used to provide mortgages to house buyers who pay interest. The loans to house buyers are quite safe because they are *secured* by property. The building society holds the deeds of the house, that is the ownership details and, should the borrower fail to repay the building society on a regular basis (usually monthly), the society can sell the house to recover the money it has borrowed.

Building societies are not companies, they are subject to special laws and regulations and must register with the Chief Registrar of Building Societies. Building Societies are owned by the members who are savers and borrowers. The members elect the Board of Directors. It is, however, possible that within the near future building societies will become much more like ordinary companies selling shares to the public.

Nowadays building societies offer a wide range of services and, as you will see in the High Streets of most towns, many have cash dispenser machines. A change in the law, effective from January 1987, has provided opportunities for building societies to widen even further their range of services and unsecured loans are available from some of them such as loans for cars, durables and even holidays. A number of societies have bought estate agencies.

Activity
Try to find examples of Estate Agents owned by (a) building societies; (b) insurance companies.

Building societies are important organisations for they allow people to borrow money quite cheaply to purchase homes. In 1988 the percentage of households living in their own homes had risen to 63 per cent.

Activity
Building societies produce excellent material which provides up-to-date information. The Building Societies Association has produced a very informative booklet 'Key Facts on Building Societies, Savings and Housing'. Try to obtain a copy from your local building society, as well as the range of leaflets available both on saving with a building society and borrowing from it.

Cooperative Societies

These are organisations which are owned, as the title suggests, 'cooperatively', that is by all the customers. Many exist in the retail trade. The principle is that the shoppers are the shareholders. No shopper can have more than a £1 share and this entitles him or her to one vote. Profits are distributed in proportion to the value of purchases made by shoppers and are nowadays in the form of 'dividend stamps'.

Cooperative Societies have their origin in Rochdale, Lancashire. The first society was set up by groups of workers who did not like being exploited by shopkeepers or worse still by employers' shops.

Retail cooperatives are quite numerous, particularly in the north of England and in the face of competition they have improved their image and competitiveness.

Activity
If you have a cooperative society near you, see if you can find out more about how it is organised.

Exercise 7
This review exercise is based upon Chapter 2. Try to answer the questions without reference to the chapter. If on checking your answers you find you have not understood some aspect then read that particular section again.

1. Explain the term 'unlimited liability' as it applies to a sole trader.
2. Explain the term 'sleeping partner'.
3. A partnership deed lays down that profits be shared in the following proportions: John $\frac{3}{8}$, Frank $\frac{2}{8}$, Joan $\frac{1}{8}$, William $\frac{2}{8}$. Calculate the amount of profit available to each shareholder if the partnership receives £20 000 profit but decides to plough back 20 per cent.
4. What five clauses are included in a memorandum of association?
5. A public company can start trading immediately it receives its certificate of incorporation. True/false?
6. Name one difference between a public and a private company.
7. What does the abbreviation 'plc' stand for?
8. (a) Who owns a public company? (b) Who owns a private company?

9. Who elects the directors in a building society?
10. Why is a building society loan much safer for the lender than many other types of loan?
11. What proportion of households in the UK own their own homes?
12. Who owns a Cooperative Retail Society?

CHAPTER 3

INTERNAL ORGANISATION OF COMPANIES

In Chapter 2 we considered how businesses were organised and looked at the various forms of businesses from sole traders to big public companies and corporations. In this chapter we consider the internal organisation of a fairly typical company.

Good Foods plc is a large supplier of a range of food products. The company has concentrated on the manufacture of foodstuffs, reducing as far as possible the use of artificial additives and other ingredients associated with unhealthy living. As a result, the company has gained enormously and is now beginning to exploit some overseas potential.

As in all companies, shareholders own the company but control is in the hands of a board of directors. Day-to-day organisation is the responsibility of the managing director and his/her team; the managing director of the company is Mrs Patricia Roberts. The organisation of the company is set out in Figure 3.1

This is a fairly typical company organisation though clearly there will be differences depending on the sort of business which is operating.

Activity
See if you can obtain an organisation chart from a company that you have contact with.

Let us look at this particular chart in more detail.

Figure 3.1

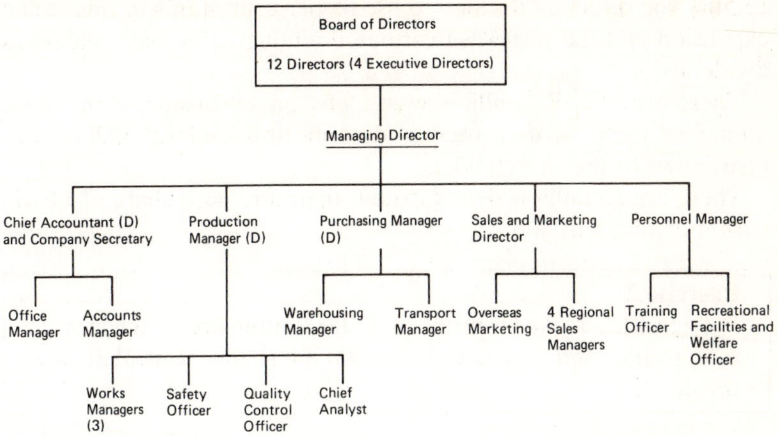

3.1 THE BOARD OF DIRECTORS

The Board makes the policy for the company. It is elected annually by the shareholders, though often there is not an annual change but the same board continues. As you know from Chapter 2, how the board is set up will depend upon the company's articles of association.

In our case there are twelve directors. There is a chairman and four executive directors. 'Executive' directors means they actually work in the company.

Exercise 1
From the chart see if you can identify the four executive directors.

Good Food plc's board meets every two months and the Managing Director, Pat Roberts, will provide a report and will ask the Chief Accountant to provide various statistical material, especially relating to the financial health of the company.

The non-executive board members are directors who do not work at the company but bring different experience to the company. The Articles of Association often lay down that each director must have a minimum shareholding. In this case the minimum shareholding is 3000 £1 shares.

The Board of Directors will determine what happens to the company's profits. In 1988/9 Good Food made a profit after tax of £3.5m. The directors decided to use 65 per cent of this to finance an expansion and the rest was distributed amongst the shareholders as dividends.

Therefore, £2.275 million was spent on expansion – the term 'ploughed back' is often used to describe this – £1.225 million was distributed to the shareholders.

There are £3 million shares issued, therefore each share of £1 will earn a dividend of 40p.

Exercise 2

Portrex PLC makes a profit of £70 000 after tax. It decides to retain 50% and has issued 280 000 £1 shares. Calculate the dividend.

3.2 THE COMPANY SECRETARY

As you can see the Company Secretary is also the Chief Accountant. His name is Donald Mcleod, he is a management accountant and he is responsible for ensuring that the legal requirements are met regarding meetings, procedure and so on. He has to make sure that accounts are lodged in Company House as required. He also acts as administrator to the board and will send out the agenda for board meetings.

3.3 THE MANAGING DIRECTOR

The Managing Director, Pat Roberts, is the head of the company and is responsible to the board for the smooth running of the company and its continued prosperity. She is also a member of the board. She leads the management team which consists of:

1. *The Chief Accountant* – who is also company secretary. The chief accountant is responsible for the administration and the Office Manager reports directly to him. He also has an Accounts Manager who is responsible for salaries and keeping records of costs and revenue. It is the Chief Accountant who keeps the MD, as she is sometimes called, fully aware of the financial position of the company.

2. *The Production Manager* – he is also a director and has full responsibility for production of the variety of products that Good Food plc produce. As you can see from Figure 3.1 the Works Manager, the Safety Officer, the Quality Control Officer and Analyst report to him. The Safety Officer ensures that the company complies with its requirements under the Health and Safety at Work Act. The Works Manager is responsible for the operation of the plant and production process and has a number of Plant Managers under him.

   Business must constantly strive for good quality products and Good Food plc rely upon their Quality Control Department and their analyst to ensure quality and to improve product design.
3. *Purchasing Manager* – he is responsible for the purchase of all raw materials for the company. He is also responsible for warehousing, storage and transport. For these two latter functions he is assisted by two managers. The Transport Manager who is responsible to his boss for the company's fleet of lorries, company cars and for the transport of goods not carried by the company's own vehicles.
4. *Sales and Marketing Director* – Good Foods is no exception to the rule that if the firm's products do not sell then it will not be successful. The Sales and Marketing Director is responsible for a large sales force and as you can see he has four managers in different parts of the country with whom he regularly holds sales meetings. He is also developing the overseas potential and he has recently taken on a new Overseas Sales Manager, Jennie Haslop, who has a degree in foreign languages and marketing.

   You will remember that our Sales Director is also responsible for marketing and he needs to ensure that:

   (a) the firm's products are adequately promoted;
   (b) the advertising campaigns are cost-effective;
   (c) the product range is what the customer wants.

   To help him, he has established a small marketing unit.
5. *Personnel Officer* – Although mentioned last this is a very important post and Sue McCarthy, the present holder, is responsible for staff welfare and training. A well-satisfied, highly trained staff will always be beneficial to a company and it would be difficult to exaggerate the key role of the Personnel Manager. She is assisted by Training Officer who maintains excellent contact with the local technical college and the Training Commission. Sue also has a Welfare Officer who looks after the

company's recreational facilities, the canteen, and deals with personal matters brought to his attention. The Welfare Officer has been very instrumental in establishing for the company a reputation for being a caring concern and the employees certainly welcome this.

Exercise 3

1. State three functions of a company secretary.
2. State three duties of a marketing manager in a company.
3. Give two reasons why a personnel manager is so important in a company.
4. What is a non-executive director?

Activity

Politicians are often on the boards of companies. See if you can find three examples of politicians who have taken non-executive directorships in companies.

3.4 INTERNAL COMMUNICATIONS

Good Food plc is a large company with over 1000 employees. The company prides itself on good employer/employee relationships and this is shown in the number of employees who stay with the company for long periods.

There is, however, always a problem of communications. The *line* of communication often works like this:

From
Managing Director
to
Production Manager
to
Works Manager
to
Plant Supervisors
to
Section Leaders
to
Shop floor employees

Recent research has shown that up to 30 per cent of communication is lost at each level.

Good Food plc has tried to deal with the problem –

1. by involving employees at various management decision levels. Shop stewards (representing the union) attend management meetings and changes which involve the workforce are discussed and agreed. This means they can be introduced more smoothly.
2. By asking the Union/s to nominate one of its members for the board.

Good Food plc has put into operation several other schemes to improve communications and morale.

1. A profit sharing scheme whereby workers obtain a percentage of the profits or can use their profit bonus to acquire shares in the company. The latter method, it is hoped, will encourage employees to take an even greater interest in the affairs of the company.
2. There is a good deal of mundane processing work and the company has come up with a scheme whereby employees are able to rotate around the various jobs. One scheme enables employees to spend a day a month with the transport departments to gain some idea of who the customers are.
3. The social and recreational club is run by a committee of employees and its success is a good reason for high morale.
4. The company pays two bonuses in addition to the profit share. Each employee gets a Christmas bonus plus Christmas fayre and also a holiday bonus, which can be used for a cut price Spanish holiday negotiated by the company.

Good Food plc staff policies are very successful and as a result the company has been able to introduce new technology such as computerised processing and office systems with very little opposition. In this introduction the company

1. held discussions with employees likely to be affected;
2. gave a guarantee of no redundancies;
3. offered better salaries to employees involved in new techniques;
4. offered good training facilities into the new techniques.

Exercise 4

1. What level of loss has been estimated by researchers at each level of communication?
2. State three ways in which Good Food plc introduced new technology successfully.

Exercise 5

Answer the following review questions without reference to the chapter. Check your answers and, if you have not understood any part of the chapter, read it through again.

1. Who owns a company?
2. Who controls a company?
3. What is an executive director?
4. In a company what is the name given to the chief executive director.
5. Name four managers in the production division of Good Food plc.
6. What is the advantage of union members being on the board and at management meetings?

CHAPTER 4

MARKETING AND ADVERTISING

In the last chapter we considered the various types of business organisations. Most business organisations exist to make money. A business uses its resources, i.e. labour, money and materials, to produce a product or a service that the consumer wants. The successful business is usually the one that produces or provides what is required at a price that can be afforded using the minimum costs. It needs market research to find out what product or service is likely to be required, and to bring the product or service to the attention of the consumer often requires advertising. In this chapter we will deal with the ways in which businesses try to find out what consumers want and also look in detail at advertising. The following example will be used to explain the role of marketing, market research and advertising.

John Harris has completed a degree at a polytechnic in languages and business studies. He studied German and French and has become fluent in both the languages especially in relation to business. At the polytechnic he met his wife Francesca who was studying for the same degree with French and Spanish as her languages. Francesca and her parents are Italian, and she can also speak Italian fluently. When John and his wife leave the polytechnic they decide to start up a partnership which is concerned with translation and interpreting. Because of the number of languages available to John and his wife the business does quite well but John is anxious to develop further and he discusses with his wife the possibility of selling holidays whereby costs are kept down to a minimum by families from various countries using each other's homes.

John goes to see his father, who is a wealthy businessman, to discuss his plans and John, Francesca and John's father decide to form a private company known as Home Exchange Ltd. John's father puts a sum of money into the business so that John and Francesca can research into what really is required by consumers.

John and Francesca need to make sure that they provide a service which will:

1. be satisfactory to the user; and
2. bring an adequate return of investment to the company.

They need to do this by means of what is sometimes called a matching process.

Figure 4.1 illustrates this process. John and Francesca need to assess the market, then to ensure that they have the resources to meet the needs and then to plan a service (or product) which is useful and desired by the consumer but will bring adequate returns to the new company.

4.1 MARKET RESEARCH AND PRODUCT PLANNING

The first stage in any marketing process is, of course, to make sure that you know your market. John and Francesca have done a course

Figure 4.1 *The matching process*

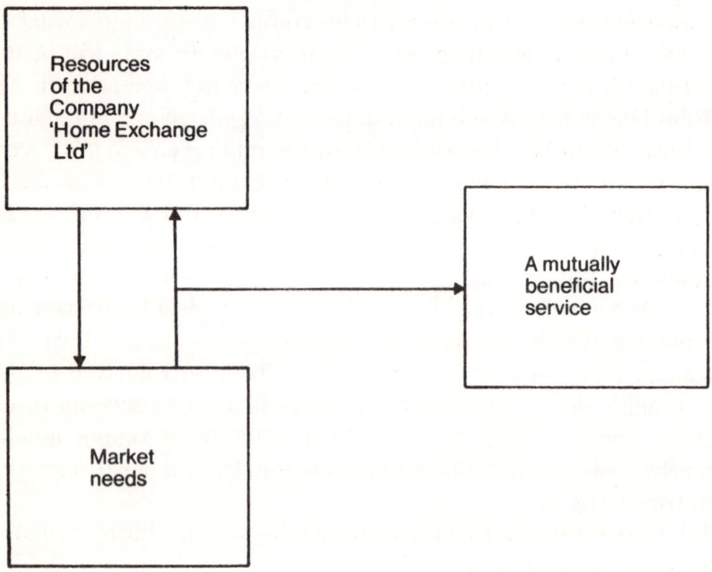

in marketing as part of their degree and they are quite familiar with the stages involved in marketing.

John and Francesca could, of course, have used one of the specialist market research agencies to carry out their research into the market, but they decide to conduct the research themselves. John and Francesca are anxious to discover answers to the following questions:

1. What is the size or potential size of the market for the service which they are planning?
2. Who are the potential users of the service?
3. What type of service do they require?

Desk Research

John and Francesca first of all conduct some 'desk research'; this means that they collect as much statistical and other information as possible relating to the five countries in which they have an interest. They look at information from the various tourist boards and make a thorough study of the tourist industry. Following this quite extensive desk research, John and Francesca come to the conclusion that in France, Britain, Spain, Italy and West Germany, the amount of money spent on holidays as a proportion of total income is increasing. They feel that their most likely market lies among the middle class and skilled working class, i.e. people in such posts as shop manager, clerical officer, works manager, skilled mechanic, electrician, teacher. The sort of holiday which they are planning, they feel, would be attractive to married men and women in the 30–45 age group who have children.

This desk research has revealed for Home Exchange Ltd:

1. The potential market;
2. The potential size of the market.

Various surveys reveal that about 67 per cent of the total population fall into the classifications, i.e. middle and skilled working class. This clearly is a huge market even if only the 30–45 age group is taken into account.

Exercise 1

1. In selecting a product or service a business must ensure two things. What are these?

2. Explain in a paragraph what you understand by the 'matching process' as used in marketing?
3. State three of the purposes of market research.
4. In a sentence explain 'desk research' as it applies to market research.

Market Surveys

Having conducted their desk research, John and Francesca decide what they need is now to sample the population. This means they will take a 'representative' group of the particular classes and age range that they have identified. Representative means the sample should be as nearly as possible identical with the whole. This, of course, is not easy to determine and many a product or service has been launched optimistically based upon a sample which has not turned out to be very representative.

John and Francesca decide to spend between them two weeks in each of the European countries France, Spain, Italy and West Germany and a further four weeks in England. They select a number of cities and towns in each of the countries and attempt to interview a number of families from the two classes suggested above and drawn from the age range 30 to 45. They ask a number of questions, such as:

1. Do you take a holiday each year?
2. What sort of holiday do you take?
3. Have you ever visited England or Europe?
4. If the answer was 'yes' to question (3) more detailed questions are posed:
   (a) Was the holiday a package holiday?
   (b) Why did you take the holiday?
   (c) Were you satisfied with the holiday?
   (d) Are you planning to go again?
5. If the answer was 'no' to question (3) other questions to these are asked:
   (a) Why have you never holidayed in Europe or England?
   (b) Was language a problem?
   (c) Was cost a factor?
6. Questions are then asked as to whether the families would be interested in holidaying where:
   (a) Families swap homes?
   (b) The cost is kept merely to the cost of transport?

(c) The travel company make all the arrangements relating to travel?
(d) The travel company make all the arrangements relating to the house exchange?
(e) Basic language assistance was provided?
(f) All bookings by boat, train or coach are made and car travellers are provided with up-to-date route maps?

John and Francesca's good knowledge of languages enables them to conduct a very good survey and questionnaires are prepared in all five languages, French, English, Spanish, German and Italian.

When John and Francesca and John's father meet to look at the results of the survey, they are very enthusiastic. There is an optimistic feeling that a service could be provided at a cost which would be most attractive to customers, but at the same time would result in a good return to Home Exchange Ltd.

Having then established the existence of a potentially large market it is now necessary to move to the next stage, sometimes known as product design. In this case we are, of course, concerned with a service, so 'the job' of Home Exchange Ltd is to design the service and determine its price. We will call this stage 'product design' even though it is a service which is involved.

Product Design

John and Francesca believe that they need to provide a 'package' which is designed in such a way as to take out most of the problems related to holidaying abroad. The package which they design includes the following:

1. The address and location of the flat or house with any essential information relating to electricity, water, etc., and the whereabouts of the keys on arrival.
2. Tickets for the channel crossing.
3. Route maps to the destination; or
4. coach or rail tickets with reserved seats, and times of departure and arrivals.
5. A series of cards containing key sentences in English and one of the foreign languages which can be used for shopping.
6. Insurance both for the family holidaying and for the property for the period of time they are there.
7. Where necessary overnight stays, booked in modestly priced hotels.

8. As an extra with the holiday pack, cassettes are included providing a basic introduction into the language, culture and history of the country which is being visited.

Pricing Policy

John, Francesca, and John's father spend a good deal of time on this problem because they realise that they must choose an attractive price from two points of view:

1. To be attractive to potential customers.
2. To provide an adequate return to the company.

Following careful research into various costs of Channel crossings, overnight hotel stops, insurance, and taking into account the various administrative costs involved, e.g. matching the families, translating various information relating to properties, correspondence, etc., the company decides that it can advertise holidays at what is thought to be a very attractive price. Several examples are provided of prices as at 1988.

1. An English family of five living in Bristol could have a fortnight in Bordeaux (France) taking their cars for £350 including one overnight stay at a small hotel south of Paris.
2. An English family of four living in Cambridge could have a three-week holiday in Munich (West Germany) using the train for £545 including one overnight stay at a hotel in Cologne.
3. An English family of three living in Oxford could spend two weeks at a coastal resort near Genoa (Italy), travelling by car with two overnight stops in Paris and Nice using their own car for £360.

These attractive prices John and Francesca feel will give them an adequate return on their investment in the company.

John and Francesca have now concluded two major aspects of their marketing, i.e. they have chosen the product and they have determined the price. It will now be necessary for them to determine how they are going to sell their product, sometimes summed up by the two words 'place' and 'promotion', in other words where they are going to promote it. The basis of a marketing operation is sometimes neatly described through the four *p*s.

1. *product;*
2. *price;*
3. *place;*
4. *promotion.*

Exercise 2

1. Explain in a sentence the meaning of the expression 'representative sample'.
2. In deciding upon the price of a product, what two factors will a business take into account?
3. Marketing is sometimes summed up by the four *p*s. What are the four *p*s.

4.2 PROMOTION OF THE PRODUCT

John and Francesca decide that the product (service) will be distributed from an office which they establish in Dover. Setting up offices is expensive and so they decide on just one place and hope they will not have to rent additional premises in Europe.

They know, however, that they must spend a good deal of money in advertising the product. John and Francesca's business knowledge stands them in good stead; they are quite aware of the main purpose of advertising, which is:

1. *to inform* – i.e. in this case merely to tell people about this new type of inexpensive holiday.
2. *to persuade* – i.e. to persuade people that this is what they ought to spend their money on, and that home exchange represents much greater value for money than another type of holiday. Persuasion could also involve persuading people that they ought to have a holiday, i.e. persuading them to spend their money on a holiday rather than on other things.
3. *to remind* – many adverts merely serve to remind consumers that a product still exists. Some adverts just give the name of a product or company and provide little more information.

Activity

1. Look at these advertisements from NEC/Lufthansa. What would you consider to be their main purpose.

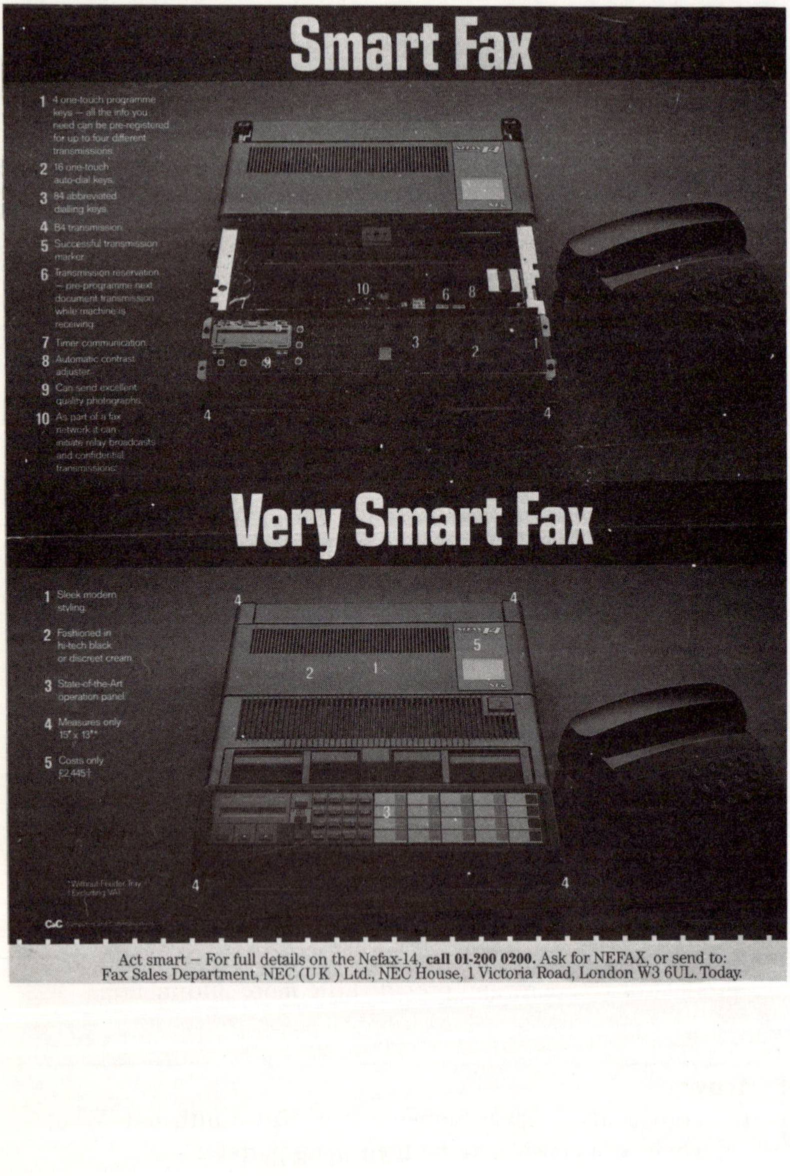

Smart Fax
1 4 one-touch programme keys – all the info you need can be pre-registered for up to four different transmissions.
2 16 one-touch auto-dial keys.
3 84 abbreviated dialling keys.
4 B4 transmission.
5 Successful transmission marker.
6 Transmission reservation – pre-programme next document transmission while machine is receiving.
7 Timer communication.
8 Automatic contrast adjuster.
9 Can send excellent quality photographs.
10 As part of a fax network it can initiate relay broadcasts and confidential transmissions.
Very Smart Fax
1 Sleek modern styling.
2 Fashioned in hi-tech black or discreet cream.
3 State-of-the-Art operation panel.
4 Measures only 15" x 13"*
5 Costs only £2,445†
Act smart – For full details on the Nefax-14, **call 01-200 0200.** Ask for NEFAX, or send to:
Fax Sales Department, NEC (UK) Ltd., NEC House, 1 Victoria Road, London W3 6UL. Today.

2. In the next few weeks pay special attention to the various types of advertising that you see and think about the function of it. Is it mainly to inform, persuade or remind?

John and Francesca plan an advertising campaign to promote their product which has really the twin purpose of informing and persuading. John has a couple of friends who work for advertising agencies and they give him some useful advice on the form of his advertising. Many businesses, of course, do their advertising through advertising agencies. These are firms that, for a price, will take over the advertising of a company; they will produce the advert and place it in what they regard as the appropriate medium, newspapers, magazines, etc. You have probably heard of Saatchi and Saatchi – a very famous advertising agency company. John is rather fortunate in having these two friends because they are able to give him free advice.

John and Francesca decide in their advertising to concentrate upon the theme. 'Why not use your home to provide you with a cheap holiday?' The adverts stress the wastefulness of leaving the family home empty for the weeks the family are on holiday.

The main advert used in England features two houses, one in England and one in France, with an English family arriving at the French house and the French family arriving at the English house. The French house is situated by the sea. Underneath is a caption which reads, 'Home Exchange Ltd can arrange a holiday in the South of France for a fortnight for a famly of five from £350.' Readers are invited to write to Home Exchange Ltd for further details.

Advertising Media

Advertisers have a choice of media, i.e. where they can place their advertisements. The medium chosen will depend upon the target population being aimed for and, of course, the cost.

Newspapers

There are various types of newspaper, some with national circulation and some with only local circulation. Some newspapers are read by particular sections of the community and an advertiser needs to keep this in mind when placing his advert. The cost of advertising depends upon the paper circulation, the size of the advert and also where it is placed. A large front-page advertisement in a newspaper with a large circulation could be very expensive. Home Exchange Ltd chose several newspapers in the five countries involved and placed their advertisement in these.

Magazines
Obviously certain magazines have a particular type of readership. Home Exchange Ltd know the sort of people they are trying to attract and they choose several magazines in the various countries which they feel will attract such people.

Radio and TV
Advertising here is very expensive but one of the great advantages of it is that everyone listening or viewing at that time will hear or see it. When someone reads a newspaper or magazine he may not even notice the advertisng.

John and Francesca recognise the great impact that radio and TV advertising has, but do not feel that the high cost is justified at this stage of the company's life and, therefore, the company does not use this medium.

Outdoor advertising
Advertising is also done by using hoardings, vans, buses, trains, etc. This form of advertising, which mostly uses simple and short messages, has the advantage of being seen by large numbers of people, but Home Exchange Ltd decide not to use this particular form.

Advantages and Disadvantages of Advertising

Advertising has considerable advantages.

1. It informs the public about new products. No one would know about cheap holidays with Home Exchange if there was no advertising.
2. It promotes competition among firms, which hopefully will keep prices down.
3. Because it often results in increased sales, this often means lower costs to the producer and this again has the effect of keeping prices down.

But there are disadvantages.

1. Advertising does cost money and it is argued that this extra cost is passed over to the customer. Take, for example, advertise-

ments for breakfast cereals; if people buy more Shredded Wheat because Ian Botham allegedly eats three a day, this may result in less cornflakes being eaten. The producers of cornflakes may launch a massive advertising campaign to restore sales. What possible advantage exists to the customer in this? In fact it is possible that before long cornflakes will go up in price to meet their advertising costs. It can be argued that advertising, in fact, increases costs.

2. Another disadvantage relates to the moral aspects of advertising. Advertising may persuade people to buy goods they cannot afford and therefore increase the problems of debt. Advertising may persuade people to buy goods which are harmful to them. Adverts relating to smoking and drinking could be said to come into this category. The use of 'sex appeal' to promote some products is questionable. To equate drinking and smoking with success with the opposite sex is a very doubtful exercise. Of course, as you know, the government does require tobacco manufacturers to publish a health warning with cigarette advertisements, and tobacco manufacturers cannot advertise cigarettes on TV.

Protecting Consumers Against Advertising

Because complaints have been made that some advertisements are misleading, offensive or sometimes morally wrong, the advertising industry has set up its own body to deal with them. The Advertising Standards Authority will investigate complaints relating to advertisements which are misleading or are against the British Code of Advertising Practice. Newspapers are very concerned about the standard of advertising and many of them lay down strict rules as to what they will accept.

See the extract opposite and read on overleaf.

MAIL ORDER ADVERTISING

British Code of Advertising Practice

Advertisements in this publication are required to conform to the British Code of Advertising Practice. In respect of mail order advertisements where money is paid in advance, the code requires advertisers to fufil orders within 28 days, unless a longer delivery period is stated. Where goods are returned undamaged within seven days, the purchaser's money must be returned. Please retain proof of postage/despatch, as this may be needed.

Mail Order Protection Scheme

If you order goods from Mail Order advertisements in this magazine and pay by post in advance of delivery, MIZZ will consider you for compensation if the Advertiser should become insolvent or bankrupt, provided:

1. You have not received the goods nor had your money returned; and
2. You write to the Publisher of MIZZ summarising the situation not earlier than 28 days from the day you sent your order and not later than two months from that day.

Please do not wait until the last moment to inform us. When you write, we will tell you how to make your claim and what evidence of payment is required.

We guarantee to meet claims from readers made in accordance with the above procedure as soon as possible after the Advertiser has been declared bankrupt or insolvent.

This guarantee covers only advance payment sent in direct response to an advertisement in this magazine not, for example, payment made in response to catalogues etc. received as a result of answering such advertisements. Classified advertisements are excluded.

As the above extract shows newspapers and magazines will actually offer compensation to readers who buy goods and services on the basis of an advertisement. You will have noted that this extract mentions the British Code of Practice.

We will assume that Home Exchange Ltd has not offended in any way and that its advertisements are acceptable to the various newspapers and magazines in which they are placed. The advertising campaign for Home Exchange Ltd is very successful and a great many requests are made to the company for details of the holiday scheme. The company is able to arrange a large number of home exchanges and John and Francesca can honestly say that their venture is successful. From the profits of the company John and Francesca decide to 'plough back' about 25 per cent but this still leaves 20p in the £1 for the three shareholders, John, Francesca and John's father; this 20p in the £1, known sometimes as the dividend (i.e. a share of the profits), is 20 per cent, which represents a very good return indeed. Since the demand for this type of holiday is so good John and Francesca can safely assume that the 'prices' of the holiday are about right.

4.3 AFTER-SALES SERVICE

John and Francesca realise that this is a first venture and they know that they must not rest on their laurels; one good beginning is not necessarily a recipe for continued success. Accordingly, each customer is sent a questionnaire on their return and they are asked for their reactions to the holidays and at the same time asked to make any suggestions for improvement. On the basis of the replies (over 90 per cent respond, a very good return) various improvements are made. The company, Home Exchange Ltd, is always anxious to improve the quality of its product and to listen sympathetically to any complaints. The success of a business often depends on the quality of its after-sales service; customers are pleased that, following their purchases, they are not forgotten but every attempt is made to assist them in their problems.

It is, of course, also important to make sure not only that existing customers are looked after but that attention is paid to market growth and, therefore, promotion must continue. Home Exchange Ltd is in its second year and has extended its advertising campaign; some use is now made of television advertising.

Exercise 3

1. What are the three purposes of advertising?
2. In a paragraph explain the circumstances in which advertising might increase the price of a particular brand of tea.
3. What do you understand by the term 'advertising media'?
4. What is the function of the Advertising Standards Authority?
5. Why do you think after-sales service is so important?

Activity

1. In the next few weeks try to think of: (**a**) examples of advertising that only persuade, (**b**) examples that persuade and inform, (**c**) examples of advertising that provide factual information.
2. What medium would you choose for advertising: (**a**) golf equipment, (**b**) a new make of packet soup, (**c**) a sale in a local shop, (**d**) a new novel?

4.4 MARKETING

We have taken Home Exchange Ltd to illustrate the subject of marketing which we summed up in the four *ps* – product, price, place, promotion. This is perhaps a simple method of remembering the key stages in marketing but in considering Home Exchange Ltd we developed these four aspects in more detail and identified:

1. market research;
2. product planning;
3. pricing policy;
4. marketing the product through advertising;
5. selling the product;
6. after-sales service.

It was clear that Home Exchange Ltd developed an effective market strategy. John and Francesca developed a particular marketing mix as it were. They somehow succeeded in combining the various ingredients in such a way that they achieved success. The mix of those ingredients is often called the 'marketing mix'. The idea of a marketing mix is summed up in Figure 4.2.

Figure 4.2 *The marketing mix*

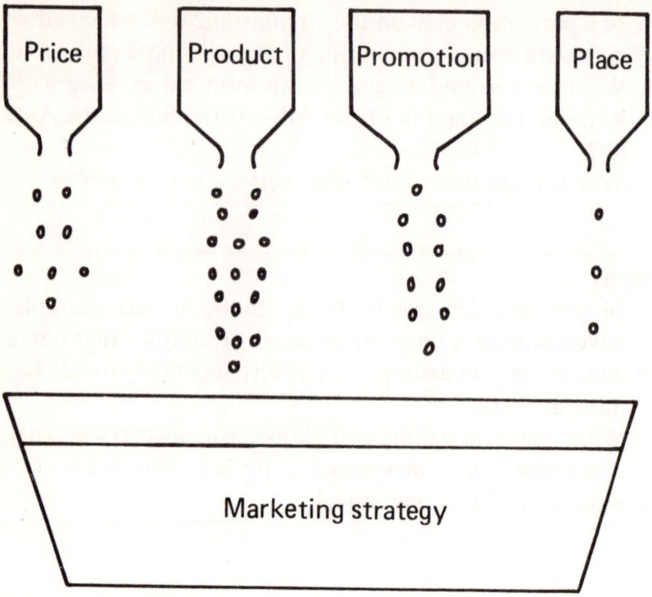

The balance of ingredients will be determined by the nature of the product. Thus a product which has high fashion content, e.g. teenage clothes, will be concerned very much with product development and keen promotion. Other goods, e.g. food, will be more concerned with price and ensuring that the goods are available to the public; place and price are the key ingredients.

If we think back to our example of Home Exchange Ltd, we can see that there was a heavy concentration upon the product, i.e. market research and careful product development price was an important issue but the place was not of great importance. It was felt that one office in Dover was sufficient for the distribution of the holidays. However, promotion through advertising was considered important.

> **Activity**
> Think of a new product which has recently come on to the market. Try to determine the marketing mix which might have been used.

Exercise 4

This chapter has been based upon the important subject of marketing which is concerned with all aspects of selling products or services from initial market research to sales promotion and after-sales service. You can learn a lot about this subject, particularly advertising, by being observant. Pay special attention to aspects of sales promotion during the next few weeks and see if you apply what you have learned from this chapter.

The following review questions are based upon Chapter 4. Try to answer the questions without reference to the chapter. If on checking your answers you find you have misunderstood some aspect of the work, read through that particular section again.

1. Why is initial market research sometimes known as desk research?
2. Explain what you understand by the term 'sampling the population'.
3. Explain the term 'product design'.
4. What considerations might an advertiser take into account when choosing media?
5. List three possible advantages of advertising.
6. List two forms of protection available to the consumer in respect of advertising.
7. Sometimes marketing is summed up in terms of the four *p*s. List the various stages when the four *p*s are developed further.
8. Which aspects do you consider important in trying to launch a product with a high fashion content?
9. Explain what you understand by the term 'marketing mix'.

If you wish to learn more about the subject of marketing, there are a number of good books available on this subject. Two books which provide a very good introduction are:

Douglas Foster, *Mastering Marketing,* Macmillan Master Series.
G. B. Giles, Macdonald and M&E Handbooks, *Marketing.*

DISTRIBUTION – RETAILING, WHOLESALING AND OTHER MARKETS

Distribution – retailing, wholesaling and other markets

You will remember that in Chapter 1 we looked at the expenditure of a family, the Percivals, and noticed that they spent their money on a range of goods and services which is probably fairly typical of families all over the country. These goods and services reach the consumer – the person who uses (consumes) the goods – through a process known as distribution or the chain of distribution.

Figure 5.1 shows the channels of distribution. You will notice that goods reach the consumer by one of a number of routes.

Figure 5.1 *Channels of distribution*

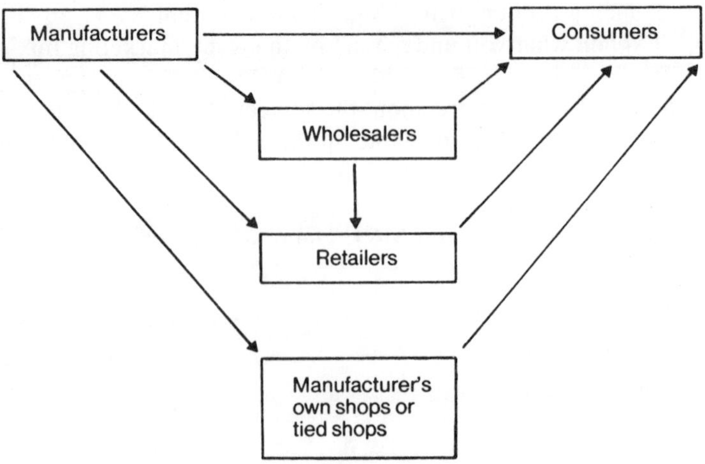

1. Some manufacturers sell direct to consumers and often advertise, inviting customers to send in a coupon which appears at the bottom of the advertisement. Rank Xerox and Cannon, producers of photocopying machines, and other office machinery often sell direct to the consumer.

> **Activity**
> See if you can find other examples of direct selling by manufacturers.

2. Some manufacturers sell direct to their own retail shops. Boots the Chemist is a good example of a large manufacturing firm which owns large numbers of shops.

> **Activity**
> See if you can discover other examples of manufacturers owning their own retail outlets. In some instances the retail outlet, although owned by the manufacturers, operates as a separate company and trades under a different name.

3. Some manufacturers sell goods to wholesalers who then sell them to retail shops.
4. In many instances, particularly in the case of the larger shops, the manufacturer bypasses the wholesaler and sells to the retailer directly. Sometimes retailers are tied to a particular manufacturer and can sell only one make of the product. Good examples of this are provided by public houses which can sell the beer of only one brewery. Sometimes one hears the term 'tied house' used to describe such pubs. Garages are often permitted to sell only one type of petrol.

In this chapter we will be dealing with distribution and will be considering in turn retailing, wholesaling and other types of markets.

5.1 RETAILING

Retailing is carried on by businesses which sell goods to the final consumer, and most retailing is done by shops. There are many different types of shops and retail outlets, as the following example shows.

Mrs Lynne Pullin has two children; she receives a weekly housekeeping allowance from her husband of £50 per week to which she adds £14.50 family allowance. Lynne has a part-time job and uses some of her wages to supplement the family budget. Her weekly income for spending on food, clothing, etc, is £80.

Lynne, in a typical week, would probably use most types of retailing establishment and by considering her spending we will be able to identify them.

Lynne spends about £45 per week on food and this is broken down as follows: every Friday she goes to the supermarket and spends about £25 on food of various sorts. She spends about £4 buying goods from a mobile shop which comes around her estate on Wednesdays selling bread, cakes and vegetables. On Saturdays there is a street market in Lynne's town and she usually spends about £10 on vegetables, fruit, cheese, etc. By about Monday Lynne usually has run out of some essential item and she finds it convenient to slip over to the local grocery shop where she spends about £6 a week. Most Thursdays, while the children are at school, she goes into town for the day with a friend and they usually spend some time in a large department store looking at clothes for the children and also have their lunch there. Lynne usually spends some money at the Mothercare shop on children's clothes and she also visits Woolworths, Marks & Spencer and Boots the Chemist.

Lynne buys some goods through a mail order firm since she finds it convenient to do some of her shopping at home with the aid of a catalogue. Lynne and her husband Reg cannot go out much in the evening because of their two young children so Reg often goes down to Kentucky Fried Chicken to buy some supper and he will often buy twenty cigarettes at the same time from a vending machine. Occasionally, if the Pullins want furniture or carpets for the house, they go to a discount store near the town.

At the end of the week Lynne finds she rarely has anything left of the £80. Lynne seems to use almost every type of retail outlet in her weekly shopping. It is important to consider each of these outlets in turn so that you can distinguish them and also understand the current trends in retailing.

Independent Retailer

You will remember that Lynne spent about £6 a week buying items from the shop across the road. These are usually owned by small businesses, often sole traders. Since they are small they cannot buy their goods in bulk and therefore cannot obtain them cheaply. Consequently, prices are often higher in small shops than large shops. Most people only use the small shop as Lynne does, for convenience, to buy those items which may have been forgotten.

The small shop is often conveniently placed and it is often open for much longer hours than the larger shops. The pattern for most people is to do the bulk of their shopping in large shops and obtain smaller or overlooked items in the corner shop.

Before the big increase in car ownership, families tended to rely upon the small corner shop for most of their requirements.

It is quite easy these days for people to travel to the larger shops. Many families have cars and can spend an hour or so in the local supermarket, meeting most of their requirements. This has meant that the small shop has declined in numbers. Britain was once known as the nation of small shopkeepers, but this is less true now. However, small shops still survive and they do so for the following reasons:

1. They provide a convenient service, i.e. the shop is just down the road.
2. They often have much more convenient hours of opening. Some shoppers prefer to deal with the local shop where they receive personal service.
3. Shopkeepers owning these small shops are often happy to exist even though their returns are small because they like being 'on their own'.
4. Small shops, because they know their customers, will often give credit and will put goods 'on the slate' as it is sometimes described.

Activity

1. During the next week or so see if you can compare the prices of items in small corner shops with those in the large supermarkets.

2. By talking to your family and friends see if you can find out what proportion of spending on food is carried out in small shops.

Exercise 1

1. Explain why a tin of beans may, in 1988, cost 25p in a supermarket and 37p in a small corner shop and why people are sometimes willing to pay the higher price.
2. Give five reasons for the survival of the small corner shop.

Multiple Shops

You will remember that Lynne did some of her shopping at Woolworths, Marks & Spencer and Boots the Chemist. These are examples of multiple shops. As the name suggests, these are shops operated by large companies with numerous (multiple) branches. Most large centres of population in the United Kingdom would have a Woolworths, Marks & Spencer and Boots branch. There are two types of multiples:

1. The multiple specialist shops which specialise in the sale of a fairly narrow range of goods. Freeman, Hardy & Willis, 'K' Shoes or Mothercare are examples.
2. The multiple variety chain store. These sell a variety of goods. Woolworths, British Home Stores and Littlewoods are examples.

In the past few years, stores which have been regarded as specialist have increasingly come to be seen as variety chain stores. Marks & Spencer, which used to concentrate upon clothing, is now selling a much wider range of goods including foods, wine, cosmetics and books. Boots, once a specialist pharmacy (chemist) multiple, now sells records, books and stationery.

Multiple shops can buy their goods in bulk because they are bought for many branches and, because of this, discounts can be obtained which can be passed on to the consumer. Policies on pricing, staffing, etc., are often made centrally and advertising can be done centrally, giving local branches the opportunity to advertise in the most expensive media such as television. Multiples have grown rapidly in the last ten years, not necessarily in the number of outlets but in the amount of turnover. By 'turnover' we mean the total value of sales, usually expressed as an annual figure.

Activity
There are many examples of multiple stores both of the specialist and variety chain type. When you are next in a large town look around and see how many examples of these stores you can find.

Departmental Stores

You will remember that Lynne's weekly trip into town involved a visit to a departmental store. A departmental store has been described as 'a number of shops under one roof' and in fact each department specialises in a particular range of goods. Such shops were very popular at the beginning of the century and catered for the more prosperous classes. Selfridges and Harrods are good examples of stores which were established in the prosperous West End of London. However, most departmental stores have nowadays to provide for a much wider section of the population and in most the 'exclusiveness' of former years has disappeared. Many departmental stores are part of a large chain such as Debenhams, John Lewis or House of Fraser. In some cases it is difficult to recognise that they are a part of a chain if they have kept their former names. An advertisement from the House of Fraser set out the following stores which come under the ownership of this group but still retain their former names. Goodwill has been built up in an area and when stores are taken over it is often better to keep the former name.

HOUSE OF FRASER (All the stores listed here are part of the House of Fraser Group.)

Army & Navy	Basildon, Bromley, Camberley, Chichester, Eastbourne, Epsom, Gravesend, Guildford, Hove, Kingston, Lewisham, Maidstone, Newport IOW, Tunbridge Wells, Victoria.
Barkers	Kensington
Binns	Blackpool, Bridlington, Carlisle, Darlington, Doncaster, Dumfries, Grimsby, Harrogate, Hartlepool, Hull, Lincoln, Middlesbrough, Newcastle, Scunthorpe, South Shields, Sunderland
Cavendish House	Cheltenham

David Evans	Cwmbran, Swansea
D. H. Evans	Oxford Street, Wood Green
Dingles	Bournemouth, Bristol, Dorchester, Exeter, Falmouth, Helston, Newton Abbot, Penzance, Plymouth, Salisbury, Torquay, Trowbridge, Truro, Yeovil
Howells	Cardiff
Jollys	Bath
Kendals	Manchester
Rackhams	Altrincham, Birmingham, Bradford, Cirencester, Leamington Spa, Leicester, Sheffield, Shrewsbury, Skipton, Wolverhampton
Arnotts	Airdrie, Ayr, Banff, Bellshill, Dundee, East Kilbride, Elgin, Falkirk, Glasgow, Greenock, Hamilton, Inverness, Irvine, Kirkaldy, Paisley, Wishaw
Frasers	Aberdeen, Edinburgh, Glasgow, Kilmarnock, Perth, Stirling

Debenhams was taken over in 1986 by the Burton Group but it is most likely that the name will not change, though you may notice certain changes in the way the shops are organised. A development in many departmental stores is for "shops within shops"; in Debenhams for example you may find:

Dorothy Perkins	Top Man
Principals	Top Shop
Samuels	British Telecom

This trend has been furthered with the recent takeover of Debenhams.

Activity
When next you visit a large town visit the departmental stores to see if you can see other examples of this trend towards departmental stores operating 'shops within shops'.

The big advantage that a departmental store has is that it can offer the shopper the opportunity to do all his/her shopping under one roof and even in many cases have lunch during shopping. Departmental stores offer a variety of credit facilities, for example through the use of account cards. An example is shown below.

Cooperative Retail Societies

In the last chapter we discussed briefly the origins of the Coop. Most of the shops would be considered to be multiple chain stores, sometimes being specialist shops and sometimes multiple variety chain stores. In some large towns they are departmental stores. There have been enormous changes in organisation of the cooperative retail societies in the last fifteen years or so.

1. Many more experienced and well-paid managers have been recruited so that the societies might compete with other retail establishments.
2. To gain the advantage of large-scale bulk buying many of the local societies have amalgamated. In 1967 there were 625 separate societies; in 1987 there were 100 separate societies.

> **Activity**
> Find out the name of the local society, if any, operating in your area. See what types of shop are being operated by the society.

Supermarkets and Hypermarkets

Lynne, as you will remember, did her shopping on Fridays at a supermarket. Supermarkets are usually in the control of multiples, e.g. Tesco, Gateway, Sainsbury, Safeway, Asda, although it is possible for an independent retailer to open a supermarket. The distinguishing feature of a supermarket is its size, *not* the type of ownership.

A supermarket has floor space of at least 186 square metres. The growth of supermarkets in the past ten years or so has been due to a number of factors:

1. They usually stock a wide range of goods so that, once in, the shopper can obtain all requirements.
2. The goods are on display and are selected by the customer, therefore resulting in less labour being required with a corresponding saving in costs and therefore prices.
3. Prices are often also low because goods can be bought in bulk at a discount.
4. Supermarkets stock only goods with a quick turnover, i.e. goods which sell well. Supermarkets concentrate on stocking the minimum but never running out. This is a delicate balance and requires the use of well thought out stockkeeping methods. This policy, however, saves costs and ensures that the goods are always fresh.

The hypermarkets, which are beginning to become popular in this country, are very large shops with over 2500 square metres of floor space. They are usually situated outside large towns with good facilities for parking. Hypermarkets started in France and many people go from Britain to hypermarkets in Calais, Boulogne and Dunkirk. The first hypermarket in the United Kingdom was situated in Caerphilly in Gwent but since that time a number have been established.

Voluntary Retail Chains

An independent retailer cannot obtain the benefit of bulk buying and often has to buy small quantities at high prices from the wholesaler. In order to try to reduce prices many independent retailers have organised themselves into groups such as Spar and Mace. Orders for goods are placed through the group and higher discounts can be obtained. It is also possible for the independent retailer to contribute to advertising by the group. You may have seen examples of Spar or Mace advertising on television.

By joining a group the independent retailer hopes to retain all the advantages of the small independent retailer but with much lower prices. It is difficult to assess how successful this movement has been but what evidence there is would suggest that it has played its part in slowing down the rapid decline of the small independent retailer.

Exercise 2

1. What is the difference between a multiple specialist store and a multiple variety chain store? Give two examples of each.

2. What is the distinctive feature of a departmental store?

3. Give two possible reasons why the decline of the cooperative retail societies has been halted.

4.(a) Give a definition of (a) a supermarket, (b) a hypermarket.

(b) Give several reasons for the growth in importance of supermarkets.

5. Explain how some independent retailers have tried to fight the competition of the supermarkets.

Other Types of Retail Outlet

You will no doubt remember that Lynne did some of her shopping using other types of retail outlets from those which we have considered.

Mail Order

This type of buying has grown rapidly in recent years. The attraction for many is that shopping can be done in the comfort of one's own home by selecting from colourful and attractively produced catalogues. The other major attraction is that goods can be obtained on credit. Usually the instalments are spread over twenty weeks or, for more costly items, thirty-eight weeks. The firms running these mail-order businesses, e.g. Kays, Freemans and Littlewoods, are really wholesalers – they organise large warehouses and a shop is not necessary. However, there are other costs involved:

1. One only has to look at a catalogue to realise how expensive they are to produce.

2. Since all the business is by post the firms have to incur high postage costs.
3. Agents who run 'clubs' as they are sometimes called are paid 'commission', i.e. so much in the £ for all orders obtained and this is a cost which has to be borne by the business.

Mail order retailing accounted for 3.5 per cent of total retailing in 1988.

Retailing Under Franchises

There has been a marked increase in this type of business, where the retailer sells one type of product or service under licence to the producer. Examples include take-away food businesses, such as Wimpy and Kentucky Fried Chicken. The company trains the retailer, helps him with advertising and will often provide the shop premises fitted out in a distinctive and easily recognisable style. There has also been a growth in franchise shops for the provision of services, e.g. Prontaprint for printing and reprographics and Bonusprint for photographic services are examples of this development. Newspaper, sweet and tobacconist shops are sometimes run under franchise. Two examples are Forbouys and Martins.

Vending Machines

Improving technology has meant that reliable vending machines can provide an increasingly wide range of goods, from cigarettes to packaged meals. The major advantage of this type of outlet is that it never closes and does not need constant staffing. On the other hand these machines are prone to vandalism because they are not supervised and of course if they are to be acceptable they must be in good operating order.

Discount Stores

There has been a steady increase in discount stores. Discount stores are really large warehouses run by wholesalers but increasingly open directly to the public. Only a few staff have to be involved in running these discount stores and as their name suggests they can offer their goods at low prices (discount). Discount stores are a feature of the furniture and carpet trades. Allied Carpets, which frequently advertises on TV, is a good example of such a discount store.

By using the example of Lynne we have examined most types of retail outlet. Retailing plays an important part in our daily lives because it is the retailer who supplies the consumer with goods and services. He is the last link in the chain. What then are the major functions of the retailer?

1. *Retailers break the bulk of goods into saleable portions.* The word 'retail' originally meant to cut again or, in other words, to buy goods in large quantities and sell them in small. Shoppers usually buy in small quantities, but manufacturers obviously want to sell in large quantities.
2. *Retailers often have the function of putting goods into a saleable state.* The butcher will often buy the whole animal and then offer joints of meat to his customers.
3. *Retailers make goods immediately available to customers.*

> **Activity**
> When next you are in a grocery shop look at the range of goods and identify the vast number of places, both in this country and abroad, from which the goods come.

A retailer saves shoppers from having to go physically to obtain the goods from the manufacturer. The retailer provides the goods at a place where the customer wants them.

4. *The retailer measures consumers' preferences.* Since the retailer is in constant contact with the consumer he can tell which goods are required and which are not. In fact, the retailer must know this because otherwise he will start to stock goods which he cannot sell. This is an important service both for the consumer and for the manufacturer: (a) the consumer knows that retailers will stock what they want; (b) manufacturers can ensure that they produce products which will be demanded.

> **Exercise 3**
> **1.** Give two reasons for the growth of mail-order business in recent years.
> **2.** Mail-order firms have certain high costs: what are they?
> **3.** Why can discount stores offer their goods so cheaply?
> **4.** In what three ways might a retailer retailing under franchise be assisted by the supplier?
> **5.** State briefly four functions of the retailer.

Changing Nature of Retailing 1971–88

Mention has been made earlier of the changes that have taken place in retailing.

1. There has been a large increase in the amount of trading by *large retailers*.
2. There has been a corresponding *fall in the number of small shops*. In fact, during the period there was a 43 per cent reduction in the number of small shops.
3. There has been a marked increase in the number of shops both large and small that have gone over to *self-service*.
4. A number of shops which would once have been described as multiple shops have become *variety chain stores*.

> **Activity**
> Think for a moment about the distinction between the terms 'multiple shops' and 'variety chain stores' and try to remember some examples of this trend.

Although there has been a considerable reduction in the number of small shops, official statistics from the Government's Business Statistics Office reveal that 29 per cent of the total turnover in retailing is from what are called single outlet retailers.

5. To try to combat the decline in trade experienced by the small independent retailer, there has been an increase in the number of *small independent retailers linking themselves to wholesalers in groups* such as Mace and Spar.
6. *Cooperative societies,* after experiencing a good deal of decline, have prospered again following new policies to try to deal with some of the problems, particularly those caused by societies which were too small.
7. There has been an increase in *mail-order trading* and also a large increase in *discount stores*.
8. Another feature has been the change in the nature of *departmental stores* as they have tried to attract a much bigger share of the population.

Probably the outstanding trend in retailing has been the increase in trade of large-scale retailers. Companies such as Tesco, Gateway, Sainsbury, Halfords, W. H. Smith, Menzies, Burton and Boots have all seen their share of the retail market increase. This would suggest that there are quite considerable advantages in large-scale operations. The leading mixed retail businesses as at 1988 are:

Marks & Spencer (turnover £4336m)
Boots
F. W. Woolworths
The John Lewis Partnership
House of Fraser
W. H. Smith & Sons
Storehouse Group (including British Home Stores)

The leading food retailers are:

Sainsbury (270 stores; turnover £5232m)
Tesco (337 outlets; turnover £4948m)
Asda
Gateway
Argyll Stores
Safeway
Kwiksave

Turnover refers to the amount of stock that is sold – it is the same as sales.

Economists have long recognised that size is often associated with lower costs and certainly it would seem that retailing is no exception to this. The following example will help to explain some of the advantages of size.

Advantages of Large-scale Retailing – Tesco

Tesco is a well-known retailer, having food supermarkets in most cities and towns in the UK. In recent years it has also opened a number of stores, usually side by side with the supermarkets, known as 'Home 'n' Ware'. If we examine for a few moments Tesco food-stores we will be able quickly to see how they can achieve low costs which can be passed on to the customer in the form of lower prices.

Bulk Buying
Because Tesco plc buys goods for large numbers of stores it can gain valuable discounts from the manufacturer. In other words it can buy the goods more cheaply than would be the case with smaller orders – thus it has the advantage of bulk buying.

'Own Branding'
You will often find in a Tesco store goods bearing the 'Tesco' mark. Manufacturers will often *package* goods specially for a large retailer provided they can be assured that it is a large order. These goods will often be sold more cheaply than the goods bearing the manufacturer's own trade-mark. Most of the large retailers do this.

> **Activity**
> When you are next in a large store see if you can find an example of own branding. It might be interesting to compare the prices of the two types of goods, i.e. the retailer's own brand and manufacturer's brand.

Sometimes retailers will ask a manufacturer to *produce* goods especially for the retailers and then will sell under its own brand name. The well-known 'St Michael' products are produced by manufacturers especially for Marks & Spencer. Provo, a British Home Stores trade-mark, and Keynote, a Littlewoods trade-mark, are other examples. You may be able to find further ones.

Specialist Buying
Because Tesco plc has large numbers of stores it can employ buyers who visit the various manufacturers to make sure they buy goods which are of good quality and at the best possible price.

Self-service
Because the majority of Tesco stores are self-service the group save on labour costs since staff are required mainly for stocking shelves and at the check-outs. It is not necessary to deal with each customer personally. From the customer's point of view this also has advantages; he/she can examine and choose the goods at leisure.

New Technology
A large organisation such as Tesco plc can afford to install modern aids to make retailing more efficient. Computers are becoming particularly effective in stock control. Sales can be analysed and the right goods can be always available. You will have noticed new symbols appearing on goods which look like a series of lines. These symbols allow the price of goods to be identified by passing them under a scanner at the check-out and thus should improve efficiency. This system has become widely used in large supermarkets.

This computerised system allows a more efficient check-out and avoids the need to ring up each item. It also allows more efficient stock control because each till is linked to a computer which records the sale of certain commodities and indicates where stocks are low. It also allows the store manager to see at a glance those products that are selling well and those that are not.

Large Turnover
Large retailers such as Tesco can often sell at lower prices because they can take advantage of quick turnover, i.e. they can gain the benefit of sheer volume of sales.

Examples
Shop A is a small independent retail shop. Its total volume of sales at cost is £3000 per week and the mark-up is 25 per cent i.e. £750.

Shop B is a large multiple shop. Its total volume of sales at cost is £300 000 and its mark-up is 20 per cent i.e. £60 000.

By 'mark-up' we mean the value added to the cost of buying the goods; e.g. shop A bought the goods for £3000 and sold them for £3750, while shop B bought the goods for £300 000 and sold them for £360 000. Shop B can add a smaller mark-up because it can sell many more goods. The small retailer cannot afford a low mark-up because he sells fewer goods and must make what he can on the smaller volume of sales. If we add this advantage to the fact that the goods are often bought more cheaply from the manufacturer by the large retailer then it is not surprising that goods in supermarkets, etc. are often so much cheaper than those sold by small retailers.

Disadvantages of Large-scale Retailing

1. Many shoppers like *personal service* and the small independent retailer often gains by being able to provide this. He can deal with his customers individually.
2. Large-scale retailers tend to site their shops in shopping areas. They cannot provide the *'round the corner' service* which the small trader can. Although the large shops have recently experimented with later opening hours they cannot really match the smaller shops for *flexibility of opening hours.*
3. If a shopper wants *specialist* goods which are not in great demand, he may not find them in the large retail establishments. For example *small specialist shops* provide a service in such goods as antiques, musical instruments, certain types of books. You can probably think of many other examples.

4. The large shops which are often organised on a self-service basis have to accept quite considerable losses arising from *pilfering and shoplifting*. Despite the introduction of security systems, the large multiples still lose large sums of money as a result of pilfering.

Exercise 4

1. Give four examples of advantages of large-scale retailing.
2. Give four examples of disadvantages of large-scale retailing.

5.2 WHOLESALING

Roy Goldman owns a general store situated in a busy holiday resort in the South of England. Roy sells a wide range of goods including newspapers, magazines, confectionery, tobacco and the full range of groceries. Although the shop is a very busy one, particularly during the summer holiday season, Roy does not stock large quantities of any one type of good and this means that he obtains few of his goods direct from the manufacturer. In fact, most of his orders are placed with wholesalers. You will remember from page 64 that the wholesaler occupies a place between manufacturer and retailer and is therefore sometimes known as a 'middleman'. Roy deals with wholesalers in a number of different ways; in some cases, particularly for tobacco, cigarettes, sweets and chocolate, he places his orders with wholesalers' representatives who visit his shop from time to time. For other goods he will visit wholesale warehouses, select what he feels will sell well and then place orders. Increasingly Roy has been going to cash-and-carry warehouses where he presents his card to show that he is a genuine retailer customer and then selects his goods. As the term 'cash-and-carry' suggests, he pays for the goods and takes them away on the same day. Roy often uses Wednesday afternoon, his half-day closing day, to collect these goods and visit his other wholesalers.

Wholesalers have come in for criticism because some argue that they increase costs of goods since they occupy yet another stage in the process of goods reaching the consumer. However, although there has been a decline in the number of wholesalers, as manufacturers deal increasingly with retailers direct, they still play an important part in the process of distribution.

The Wholesaler's Service to the Manufacturers and Retailers

Retailers may wish to order goods from large numbers of manufacturers and this would surely be very time-consuming both for the retailers and the manufacturer. By channelling orders through a wholesaler the retailer needs to contact only one source for most of his goods.

Figure 5.2 shows the reduction in the number of contacts which result from the presence of a wholesaler.

1. By selling a lot of goods to one source (see Figure 5.3) the manufacturer can save:

   (a) transport costs;
   (b) administration costs.

Each order involves paperwork and this of course will be saved if fewer orders are necessary.

Figure 5.2 *How wholesalers save transport and administrative costs*

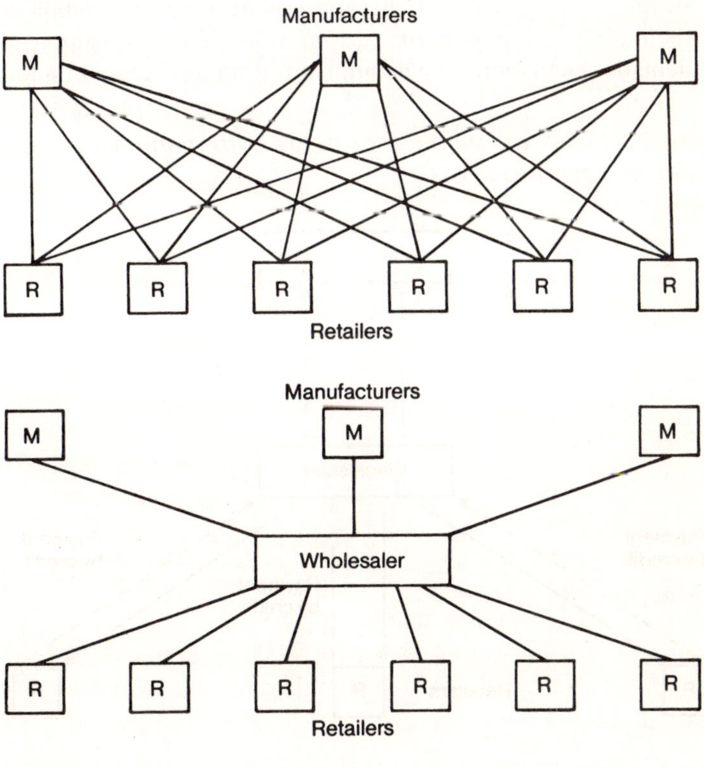

2. As pointed out earlier, the wholesaler stores his goods in warehouses. These are expensive in terms of rent and labour and these costs are saved by the manufacturer.
3. The wholesaler can take some of the risks from the manufacturer. Goods are sometimes produced which go quickly out of fashion. Often it is the wholesaler who takes this risk, sometimes being left with stock which has gone out of demand.
4. Wholesalers also help manufacturers and retailers with cash problems. Manufacturers often want their money quickly so that they can buy materials for new batches of goods. If they sold directly to small retailers they might have to wait because the small retailer often requires some credit, e.g. perhaps one month. Wholesalers may assist manufacturers by paying quickly for large supplies but then giving credit to retailers, as shown in Figure 5.3.
5. The wholesaler can buy goods from manufacturers throughout the year even though demand is 'seasonal'. For example, to return to Roy Goldman, he buys toys and Christmas cards for the Christmas period, but manufacturers produce these all the year round and supply them to wholesalers who have the task of storing them for sale at the appropriate time. The wholesaler then plays an important part in smoothing out supply and demand fluctuation. The manufacturer can produce continuously

Figure 5.3 *How the wholesaler helps both manufacturer and retailer in 'cash problems'*

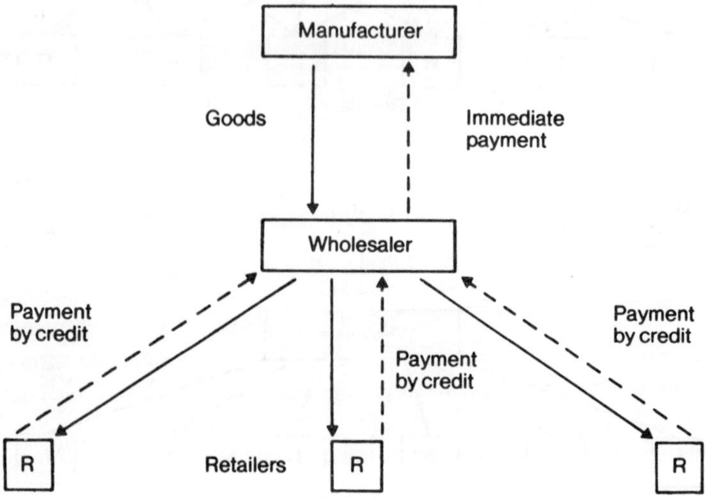

and the retailer does not need to store goods for long periods. Sometimes the situation is reversed: supply is seasonal but demand is regular throughout the year. Much of the fruit grown in England is harvested at a certain time of the year and then tinned. Large quantities are produced and the wholesaler will take these large quantities, selling them to retailers at regular intervals (see Figure 5.4).

6. Wholesalers also play a large role in preparing certain goods for sale. The wholesaler will receive goods in 'bulk' and then break the bulk down to saleable quantities. In some cases he will have to process the goods. Tea wholesalers are involved in blending; some wine wholesalers are involved in bottling.

Figure 5.4 *How a wholesaler can assist with seasonally demanded and seasonally produced goods*

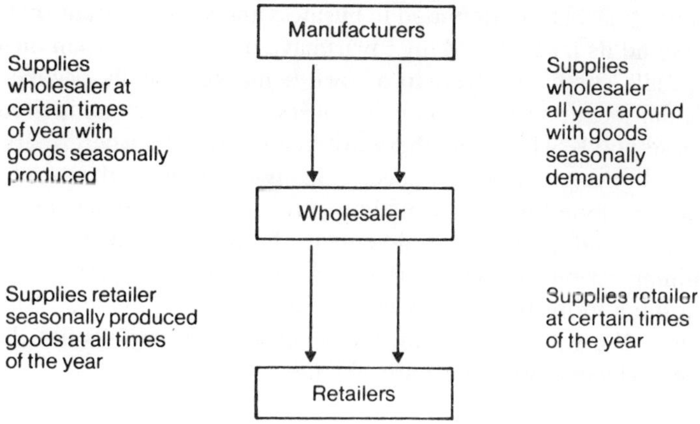

Is the Wholesaler Justified?

The wholesaler as shown in Figure 5.1 provides another link in the chain but, as we have seen, he performs important functions for the manufacturer and retailer. He is paid for these services, though, and these payments add to costs. In recent years there has been a decline in the number of wholesalers but as manufacturers have increasingly taken over their functions they have had to bear costs such as storage, dealing with retailers, increased transport.

Exercise 5

1. Why is a wholesaler known as a 'middleman'?
2. Give one reason why the wholesaler is in decline. A clue to the answer may be provided by reference to the trends in retailing.
3. Explain the term 'cash-and-carry'.
4. Give one example each of goods which are: (a) produced regularly but demanded seasonally, (b) produced seasonally but demanded regularly.
5. Explain in a sentence how the wholesaler can save manufacturers transport and administrative costs.
6. Explain in a sentence how the wholesaler can assist the manufacturer and retailer in the problems of cash.

5.3 OTHER MARKETS

The term 'market' is often used in business and it is important that we understand its meaning. Many towns have market days when buyers and sellers come together. In a town a market usually occupies a particular location where sellers set up stalls and buyers are invited to purchase goods. However, there are many instances where markets exist and buyers and sellers never actually meet each other – all the business is done by an intermediary, someone who comes between the buyer and seller; a 'middleman'. In this section we will be examining various types of market, remembering always that markets are nothing more than places where buyers and sellers are brought together. We will consider not the small general markets but those markets which serve a specialist need.

Stock Market

Frank and his wife Angela have for some time held shares in a public company. They wish however to obtain money from sale of the shares in order to purchase a car so they decide to sell the 1 000 shares that they hold. Frank goes to see a stockbroker, who agrees to sell their shares. The stockbroker arranges for the shares to be sold on the Stock Exchange. There are a number of stock markets in the United Kingdom, the largest by far being the London Stock Exchange. At the Stock Exchange it is likely that stockbrokers with shares to sell will come into contact with stockbrokers who wish to buy, and fortunately Frank's stockbroker sells the shares to a stockbroker acting for Mr and Mrs Ted Harris, two pensioners who wish to invest some of their savings. We will be considering the Stock Exchange in greater detail in Chapter 7.

'Futures' Market

HFC (Coffee Blenders) plc is a large company supplying coffee to a large number of retail and catering establishments. The company buys all its coffee at the London Commodity Exchange, which is a market dealing with a wide range of commodities including coffee, rubber and vegetable oils. HFC is anxious to buy coffee for delivery in December but wants to take advantage of the low prices existing in September. The company then buys coffee at the London Coffee Exchange for delivery in December. This is known as a 'futures' market and of course there is an element of risk in this because if the price of coffee falls drastically by December then HFC will make a loss. HFC could agree to sell the coffee at a fixed price in December to its customers and therefore the company would have 'hedged' itself against the possibility of losses.

A futures market is a market where goods are ordered at the present price but delivered later; in other words, the present price is guaranteed.

Hedging means trying to cover your risk by another deal. Sometimes you hear the expression 'hedging one's bets', which really is the same principle.

Freight Market – the Baltic Exchange

Leawood Exporters plc, a UK company, wishes to send a consignment of machinery to Kenya (East Africa) and also a consignment of jewellery to Australia. In the first case Leawood wishes to use sea transport and in the second case air transport. Both arrangements can be made at the London-based Baltic Exchange which houses a number of markets:

1. The freight market deals with finding cargo space on ships; i.e. it is a place where the sellers of the space are brought together with the buyers of the space.
2. The air freight market provides a similar service for air freight.
3. A grain futures market.
4. An oil and linseeds market.

Insurance Market

Tudor House Engineering plc wishes to insure some very expensive computerised machinery. To obtain the best possible deal an insurance broker is approached; the broker introduces the company to a number of insurance possibilities with different companies. This is an example of yet another market, the insurance market, where buyers of insurance, e.g. Tudor House Engineering plc are brought into contact with sellers, the insurance companies. We will deal with insurance in more detail in Chapter 8.

Other markets include the Bradford Wool Exchange, the Liverpool Cotton Exchange, the fresh produce markets in London such as Smithfield (meat), Billingsgate (fish) and New Covent Garden (fruit and vegetables). They all have one thing in common; they provide a place for buyers and sellers to come together.

Activity
Try to think of other examples of specialist markets. Television news sometimes gives examples of foreign exchange dealings on what is called the foreign exchange market.

Exercise 6
The following questions are based upon the work in Chapter 5. Try to do the questions without reference to the chapter. If on checking your answers you find you have not understood any aspect, go over that section again.

1. Where might you find a market for air freight, wheat and cargo space?
2. Explain what you understand by futures.
3. Give a definition of a market.
4. Give two examples of the way in which a wholesaler might smooth out demand and supply fluctuations.
5. Why are customers willing to go on paying high prices for goods sold by small independent retailers?
6. Give one example of a small independent retailing group.
7. In a year shop X sells goods to the total value of £40 000; the cost of the goods is £30 000.
   (a) What is the value of the annual turnover?
   (b) What is the average mark-up percentage?
8. Give two methods of 'own branding' used by retailers.

9. The small independent retailer has improved his share of the total retail market in the period 1971–88. True/false?

10. List three possible advantages of the small independent retailer.

CHAPTER 6

FINANCE

6.1 BALANCE SHEETS, AND PROFIT AND LOSS ACCOUNTS

Frank Bennison is employed as a lorry driver working for a firm which transports goods all over the country. Frank has always been ambitious to run his own business and an opportunity arises when, following the death of his father, Frank is left a sum of £48 000. Frank buys two lorries and rents garage space and a yard near his home. He takes on one employee as a lorry driver and sets up in business as Bennison (Haulage). Because the prices which Frank quotes are competitive his new firm does well in its first year of trading. Frank is aware that he must keep the books up to date, not only because of tax but also because it is important that businesses always have accurate information available so that they can see how they are doing.

The Balance Sheet

Frank is particularly fortunate because his wife Angela has done a college course in bookkeeping and accounting and she keeps his books for him. Every year Bennison (Haulage) prepares a balance sheet. A balance sheet is a statement which shows a business how it stands financially. The balance sheet contains two lists as shown in Figure 6.1. The *assets*, that is all the items that the business owns, and the *liabilities*, all the items that the business owes. Figure 6.1 is the opening balance sheet, showing when Bennison (Haulage) started in business. Bennison (Haulage) assets include the two new lorries, various pieces of equipment, e.g. a desk, a typewriter, loading gear, spares, tarpaulin, and cash in the bank. The total comes to £48 000 which exactly equals the liabilities. The term liabilities needs perhaps further explanation. You will remember that Frank invested his

£48 000, which his father left him, in the business. The business thus owes Frank the £48 000 and thus we say it is a liability.

Liabilities		*Assets*	£
Capital	48 000	Two lorries each at 18 000	36 000
		Equipment for the garage and yard	6 000
		Cash in the bank	6 000
	48 000		48 000

Figure 6.1 *Opening balance sheet, Bennison (Haulage), 1 February 1988*

At the end of the first year of the business a second balance sheet is prepared which is arranged exactly as the first, i.e. liabilities on the one side, assets on the other. (These days many balance sheets are arranged in vertical form but they are easier to understand in the more traditional horizontal form, liabilities on the left, assets on the right.) Figure 6.2 shows the balance sheet following the first year of trading.

Liabilities			*Assets*		
	£			£	
Capital	48 000		Lorries	36 000	
Profit	18 000		*less* Depreciation	3 360	32 640
	66 000		equipment	6 000	
less Drawings	8 400	57 600	*less* Depreciation	600	5 400
Creditors		9 600	Debtors		7 200
Rent/rates/ electricity		4 800	Cash in bank		26 760
		72 000			72 000

Figure 6.2 *Balance sheet, Bennison (Haulage), 1 February 1989*

Let us look first of all at the *liabilities*. They include all that which is owed by Bennison (Haulage) at the time the balance sheet is drawn up. The opening capital of £48 000 is owed to Frank; the business has made a profit of £18 000 and from this Frank has drawn £8400. In other words Frank has drawn from the business £8400 during the course of the year for his own living expenses. This leaves £9600 profit which is added to Frank's original £48 000. The profit really belongs to Frank and is therefore said to be 'owed' to Frank. At the time the balance sheet was drawn up £9600 was owed for diesel fuel and several repairs to the lorries. It is listed as 'creditors', which means the firm to which the money is owed has given Bennison (Haulage) credit. Finally the list includes rent, rates and electricity bills outstanding, i.e. £4800. The total liabilities are £72 000.

On the asset side is included the lorries – the original £36 000 reduced to £32 640. If the business tried to sell the lorries it would not receive £36 000 for them, and in balance sheets a 'depreciation' figure is included. Depreciation means the amount by which the article has fallen in value during the period. In our balance sheet the calculation has been £1 680 per year per lorry for ten years, when they could be sold for scrap for £1 200 each. You will notice that £600 has been estimated for the depreciation on the equipment which is also part of the assets of the company. At the time the balance sheet was drawn up several companies owed Bennison (Haulage) for jobs that had been done and this amouted to £7200. The item has been listed as 'debtors', i.e. those who owe the business money. Finally, the figure of £26 760 represents cash in the bank, in other words, money owed by the bank to Bennison (Haulage).

Exercise 1

1. Which of the following items are liabilities and which are assets?

XYV (*Clerical Services*)

Opening capital	£30 000
Profit	£10 000
Debtors	£12 000
Equipment	£8 000
Cash in bank	£6 000

2. If a firm buys a typewriter for £1 500 and it is itemised as £1 200 in the following year's balance sheet, what is this loss known as?

3. Why is a business's profit known as a liability?

4. Draw a simple balance sheet for Pel (Hairdressers) from the following information:

Opening capital	15 000
Hairdressing equipment	7 500
Cash in bank	5 000
Furniture	2 500

Profit and Loss Account

It would appear from the balance sheet that Bennison (Haulage) has done quite well; but for Frank to find out exactly the level of profit that has been made he would need to draw up what is called a profit and loss account. This account is often referred to as a trading profit and loss account since it relates the profit and loss position after a period of trading. Figure 6.3 shows the trading profit and loss account for Bennison (Haulage) at the end of the first year of trading.

Costs	56 000	Revenue from	
Gross profit	30 000	haulage business	86 000
Rent/rates/ electricity	10 000	Gross profit	30 000
Net profit	20 000		
	30 000		30 000

Figure 6.3 *Trading profit and loss account, Bennison (Haulage), for year ending 31 January 1989*

You will see that in the period from 1 February 1988 to 31 January 1989 the business obtained £86 000 from customers for whom it carried goods (haulage). However, in order to operate its lorries the business had to pay out £46 000 for fuel, etc. for the vehicles, and £10 000 wages to the one employee. The difference between the revenue £86 000, and the cost of running the lorries, £56 000, is the gross profit, i.e. £30 000. For a business therefore the gross profit is sales (revenue) minus costs.

Exercise 2
If a shop takes £50 000 in one year but it has to pay £30 000 for its stock what is its gross profit?

However, as you can see. Bennison (Haulage) is involved in additional costs. The rent and rates of the garages and yard have to be paid and there are also electricity charges – these amount to £10 000. If we subtract the £10 000 from the gross profit of £30 000 we arrive at what is called net profit, i.e. net of all costs.

Thus net profit is gross profit minus all other costs, which in this case comes to £20 000.

Exercise 3

Curtis Bros is a small hairdresser's shop. After a year's trading its position is as follows:

Sales	£60 000
Cost of stock	£40 000
Rent and rates	£5 000
Electricity	£3 000

Calculate the gross profit and the net profit earned by the business.

Bennison (Haulage) has made a net profit of £20 000. An accountant would say that his profit of £20 000 represented a return on capital invested of

$$\frac{20\ 000}{56\ 000} \times 100 = 35.7 \text{ per cent}$$

35.7 per cent is a high rate of return. However, in economics it would be said that £20 000 was not really the true rate of profit. The economist would ask how much Frank would have obtained as a lorry driver working for an employer? And how much would £56 000 invested bring? Let us assume that Frank would have earned £10 000 per year from his job and that he could have invested £56 000 at 10 per cent, i.e. £5 600. Then by not opening up the business Frank would have obtained £10 000 + £5 600, i.e. £15 600. The economist would say that Frank's true profit is £4 400. This distinction between the accountant's view of profit and the economist's view is an important one. Many small businesses operate at what really is a negative true profit if you take into account what they might have earned elsewhere and the likely result of investing their money in shares, for example.

This may indeed be one of the reasons why still so many small businesses continue. For many the challenge of working on one's own is very tempting.

Exercise 4

1. Define gross profit.
2. Define net profit.
3. Explain in a sentence the difference between the accountant's view of profit and the economist's view of profit.

6.2 EXPANSION OF THE BUSINESS

Frank Bennison has been very pleased with the way his business has prospered and he feels he would like to expand. He has had to turn away quite a lot of business during the year and he feels that he could make even more money by buying two additional lorries and also buying a yard, storage area and garages which have become vacant near his home. The cost of this expansion, however, is quite considerable. The two lorries would cost £20 000 each, i.e. £40 000, and to buy the yard, etc. would cost another £40 000. Frank has to find £80 000 in order to make the sort of expansion he desires. In this section we will be considering the various ways in which a business can obtain the funds to expand its operations.

Ploughing Back

A business can expand by ploughing back its profits. This means it uses the profits to buy new equipment or premises or whatever else may be needed to expand. In the case of Bennison (Haulage) we have seen that out of the £20 000, Frank drew £8 400 for his own living expenses and therefore the £11 600 remaining would not allow him to make much expansion.

Hire Purchase

Bennison (Haulage) could purchase the two lorries by means of hire purchase, i.e. Frank could pay a deposit on each of say 20 per cent (£4 000 each) and then pay for the lorries by instalments. This would involve the business in interest payments. The finance company could charge a rate of interest on the transaction. This rate of interest represents a cost to the business.

> **Activity**
> Try to find out the rate of interest which might be charged by a hire purchase company for a vehicle. You will probably find that it is quite high.

Mortgage

Bennison (Haulage) could possibly buy the yard by means of a mortgage; i.e. a finance company or a bank might be prepared to advance the money on security of the property. This means that the company or bank lending the money keeps the ownership documents (the deeds) of the property and, if there is a default in payment by Bennison (Haulage), the property could be sold to pay the debt.

A mortgage is an arrangement whereby money is advanced on the security of property. A business taking out a mortgage will have to pay interest. If the yard, storage area and garage is bought with a mortgage, then, assuming that a deposit of £5000 is paid, if the interest rate is 12.5 per cent, Bennison (Haulage) would be paying £4375 interest per year or £365.58 per month on a loan of £35 000.

Bank Loan

Bennison (Haulage) can go to the bank for a loan, but again interest will be charged.

> **Activity**
> Try to find out the rate of interest charged by banks for loans to business.

It is possible for businesses to obtain some relief on interest paid. Businesses pay tax on their profits but it is possible for a business such as Bennison (Haulage) to obtain tax concessions on purchases of capital equipment such as lorries. At the end of each year accounts, sometimes known as a tax return, must be made to the tax inspector who may agree to certain expenses incurred by the business being set against profits. It is possible, therefore, for Frank to offset some part of the rate of interest by obtaining these allowances.

> **Activity**
> Go along to your nearest Inland Revenue (Tax) office and try to obtain some information on the way in which tax is assessed for the small business. You may be able to obtain a booklet which explains the system.

Leasing

Bennison (Haulage) could lease its lorries; i.e. it would rent the lorries from a finance company which will buy them from the supplier. Leasing, however, is quite expensive. For a £20 000 lorry it is likely to be as much as £100 per week.

Activity
You will often find advertisements for leasing in newspapers. Try to find out the cost of leasing a van or a lorry from these adverts.

Exercise 5
Freelink Engineering is a small engineering company. It buys five lathes for £30 000. To do this it takes out hire purchase for £25 000 at 10 per cent per annum. It buys a small factory for £60 000 taking out a mortgage of £50 000 at 12.5 per cent per annum. Calculate the total annual interest charge on these two items of expenditure.

Setting up a Partnership

Frank might be able to expand his business by taking on several partners who could provide the capital which he needs for expansion. We learned in Chapter 2 of the method by which a partnership might be set up and clearly this could be a means of obtaining additional finance. However, the disadvantage of this method for Frank is that he would lose complete control. Since the other partners were putting in their money they would be likely to want a say in the running of the business, and this is the price that Frank would have to pay. Would he want expansion at the cost of the loss of independence?

Forming a Company

Frank could also expand by forming a company and then inviting people to invest in shares in the company. If Frank obtained his £80 000 by the sale of shares then he might no longer have the largest shareholding and therefore might lose control of the business. However, formation of a company is one way of obtaining capital for expansion. In Chapter 2 we learned how companies were formed and also the difference between a private and a public company.

Exercise 6
State the difference between a private and a public company.

6.3 COMPANY FINANCE

In this section we will be dealing with the various types of shares and other sources of finance available to companies. The following example will help to illustrate how a company obtains funds.

Lifeguard plc is a public company in the North-West of England which produces deodorants, perfumes, soaps and a wide range of other toiletries. Its capital is made up as follows:

Ordinary shares	£1 000 00 of £1 shares
Preference shares	£500 000 of £1 shares at 10 per cent
Debentures	£500 000 £1 debentures at 8 per cent

Ordinary Shares

Lifeguard plc has one million £1 ordinary shares. These ordinary shareholders are often known as the 'true risk' bearers because when the profit is being shared out they rank last behind the debenture holders and preference shareholders. If the company should go into liquidation, or fold up, to use another popular term, then the ordinary shareholder would be in the most risky situation because, when the company's assets were being shared out, the ordinary shareholders would again rank last.

Ordinary shareholders are entitled to a vote at the annual meeting which companies must hold, however. Each £1 share in Lifeguard plc which is an ordinary share will carry one vote.

An ordinary shareholder receives a share in the firm's profits (if any). This share, known as a dividend, is the amount declared by the directors. After the interest has been paid to the debenture holders and preference shareholders a dividend will be declared, usually expressed as a percentage. Thus if Lifeguard plc declared a 10 per cent dividend then each shareholder would get 10p per £1 share.

Preference Shares

As the name suggests, anyone holding this type of share will gain preference over the ordinary shareholder when the profits are being distributed. The preference shares in Lifeguard plc are 10 per cent and these will have to be paid before any dividend is declared. Preference shareholders also come before the ordinary shareholder when the company folds up. Preference shareholders do not have a vote.

Usually preference shares are *cumulative;* this means that if the company does badly one year and cannot pay its preference shareholders their 10 per cent, or cannot pay the full amount, then the arrears are paid the following year before the ordinary shareholders are paid.

A Share Certificate

If someone is a shareholder in a company this means that they share in the ownership. As proof of ownership shareholders will receive a share certificate. A copy of a share certificate appears in Figure 6.4

Figure 6.4 *A share certificate*

Certificate 1479 *1000 shares*

Lifeguard plc
(Incorporated under the Copmpanies Act of 1948 and 1967)

This is to certify that Philip Gardener of 14 Lower Street, Canterbury, Kent, is the registered holder of 1000 Ordinary Shares of one pound each, fully paid in the above company subject to the Memorandum and Articles of Association of the Company.

Given under the Common Seal of the company on the ....15...... day of MARCH.1989

No transfer of these shares or portion therof can be registered until this certificate has been deposited at the regisitered office of the company.

Debentures

Debentures are *not* shares but are loans to the company. A holder of a debenture is like a creditor to the company. In other words he is owed money by the company. In our example interest of 8 per cent must be paid to debenture holders whether profit is made by the company or not, and if interest is not paid then the debenture holder can force the company into liquidation, i.e. to fold up. We will deal with liquidation in more detail on page 121.

Example Now that we understand the distinction between the various types of shares and debentures let us assume that at the end of a particular year's trading Lifeguard plc makes a profit after tax of £310 000.

It first has to pay its debenture holders: 500 000 debentures at 8 per cent (£40 000). It then pays its preference shareholders: 500 000 preference shareholders at 10 per cent (£50 000). This leaves £220 000. The directors are not obliged to distribute all the profits to the ordinary shareholders; indeed often it is decided to use some of the money to plough back. You will remember we met this phrase on page 93. If we assume £100 000 is ploughed back, used for example to buy two new machines, then there is £120 000 for distribution to the shareholders, i.e. a dividend of 12p in the £, of 12 per cent.

Exercise 7

1. Why is a preference share so called?
2. The share of the profits received by an ordinary shareholder is known as a . . . .
3. A debenture holder is a part owner of the company. True/false?
4. What expression is used to explain the process whereby a business uses some of its profits for expansion?
5. Calculate the dividend of the ordinary shareholder in the following circumstances:

   John Paget (video) Co. Ltd has made a profit of £5 000
   The company has 1000 £1 10 per cent debentures
   3000 £1 10 per cent preference shares
   5 000 £1 ordinary shares
   The directors decide to plough back £3 000.

6.4 HOW A COMPANY OBTAINS ADDITIONAL FINANCE

In Chapter 2 we touched briefly upon how a company raises money through issuing new shares. In this section this will be explained more fully by reference to the following example.

United Book Supplies plc, a large publishing company, wishes to expand its operations but requires additional finance to do so. In fact, it wishes to raise an additional £2m. We have already learned that one way of doing this is to plough back some of its profits but this will not provide sufficient funds. The company therefore decides to raise extra money by offering two million £1 shares for sale to the public. United Book Supplies plc, as its title indicates, is a public company and therefore can sell its shares freely to the public.

Issuing new shares is a very common method of raising additional finance and in this section, using this example, we will show the various ways by which a company can sell its shares to the public.

1. *The prospectus* United Books plc could invite the public to buy shares by advertising by means of a prospectus. A prospectus, just like a college school prospectus, is a description of what the company is engaged in; its likely 'prospects'. At the bottom of a prospectus is a form which applicants can complete stating how many shares they wish to buy.
2. *Offer for sale* United Books plc could alternatively have sold its shares to a merchant bank which would then invite the public to buy them by means of an advertisement known as an offer for sale. The merchant bank will charge for the service and their charges will be the difference between what they buy the shares for and what they sell them for, e.g. the merchant bank may buy the shares for 90p each knowing that the shares can easily be sold for £1 each. More and more companies are using this method rather than doing the job themselves.

   A company doing the job itself or a merchant bank will try to make sure that it is not in a position where shares remain unsold by persuading various financial organisations to 'underwrite' the issue; i.e. a bank may agree to take 500 000 £1 shares should they remain unsold.
3. United Books plc might make what is called a '*rights issue*'. That means it will ask its existing shareholders if they wish to buy additional shares by offering them the right, for example, to buy one share for every four held. This represents a relatively inexpensive way of raising finance.
4. United Books plc may sell some of its shares directly to what are called *institutional investors*. These include insurance companies, trade unions, pension funds, unit trusts and investment companies. An insurance company will wish to make profits for its policyholder and thus will invest the premiums which policyholders pay in companies which it regards as likely to give good returns.

Activity
Although you may not be an investor in a company directly, think of the various ways you may be investing in a company indirectly.

You will remember that United Books plc have issued two million £1 shares. It is most likely that the issue would have been quoted in the Stock Exchange; this means that the Stock Exchange would report that the issue was available. The Stock Exchange, however, *does not* sell new shares, as we will see in the next chapter. The expression 'listed on the Stock Exchange' is sometimes used.

Shares, like any other commodity, will vary in price according to the demand for them. If investors, both individual and institutional, feel that United Books plc is a good company to invest in, there will be a big demand for the shares and the price may be pushed up beyond £1. If shares are sold above their value they are sold 'above par'; if they are sold below value they are sold 'below par', and if United Books plc's shares are sold for £1 they are being sold 'at par'.

Exercise 8

1. Give three examples of institutional investors.
2. When a merchant bank agrees to buy 50 000 of a company's new issue of £1 shares if they are not bought, this is known as . . . .
3. If £1 newly issued shares are sold for £1.20 this is known as 'below par'. True/false?
4. If a merchant bank takes up all the issue they will invite the public to buy the shares by means of an . . . .
5. Where existing shareholders are given the chance to buy extra shares this is known as a rights issue. True/false?

Exercise 9

The following review questions relate to the whole of this chapter. Try to answer these questions without looking back at the chapter. If when you have checked your answers you find you have misunderstood any part then reread the particular section.

1. What is a balance sheet?
2. When a person invests £20 000 in a business which he opens why is this regarded as a liability?
3. Money owed to a creditor by a business would be known as an asset. True/false?
4. Valerie Plaxton (Secretarial Services) is a small business which at the end of a year of trading made £20 000 net profit. The owner, Valerie, had invested £6000 in the business (the £6000 had formerly been invested at 10 per

cent) and she earned before opening her business £8500. What is her true rate of profit and why does this differ from net profit?

5. What do you understand by the term 'mortgage'?

6. How can a business get some tax relief on interest payments it has to make?

7. What does 'plc' after a company name mean and what does it signify in respect of company shares?

8. What do you understand by the term 'cumulative preference share'?

9. An ordinary shareholder with say 1000 £1 shares in a company may make a profit in two ways; explain the two ways.

10. What does it mean when you hear that a company's shares have been 'listed'?

CHAPTER 7

THE STOCK EXCHANGE

In the last two chapters we looked at business finance and also at personal finance and in both chapters there is mention of the Stock Exchange. In this chapter we will deal with the Stock Exchange in more detail particularly taking into account the changes that have been introduced by what has been called the 'Big Bang'.

The Stock Exchange does not exist for the purpose of buying and selling new shares. It is the market where buyers and sellers of existing shares come together. The following example may help to explain the functions of the London Stock Exchange.

Susan Bennet has 500 shares in Tesco which she decides to sell in order to obtain the cash for a very expensive holiday. She bought the shares when they were priced at 350p per share but they are now selling at 400p. Susan knows this because she regularly looks at the share prices in the Saturday papers.

David Walters has some savings which he wishes to invest in shares and his stockbroker advises him that shares in Tesco are likely to be a good investment. David instructs his stockbroker to buy shares for him and Susan instructs her broker to sell her shares in Tesco. David lives in Kent and Susan lives in Derbyshire, they do not know each other but fortunately the Stock Exchange is a market where buyers (David) and sellers (Susan) come together. They do not of course meet directly but they do so by means of their stockbrokers. Susan has told her stockbroker she expects to get around 400p per share, that is 500 × 400 p = £2 000 altogether and this just happens to coincide with the amount that David wishes to invest.

Activity

Shares are quoted on Saturdays in such newspapers as The *Times, Guardian, Independent.* See if you can find the present price of the following shares:

Barclays, Imperial Chemical Industries, Sainsburys, Woolworth, Trust House Forte, Royal Insurance, GEC.

The shares are usually quoted in pence unless they are over £10 per share and companies are grouped e.g. you will find the above under the following groups: Banking, Chemicals, Food, Drapery & Stores, Hotel and Caterers, Insurance and Electrical.

7.1 HOW SHARES CHANGE HANDS ON THE STOCK EXCHANGE

You will no doubt have heard the expression the 'Big Bang' which was used to describe the changes that have taken place on the Stock Exchange recently. The old method whereby shares were bought and sold by 'jobbers' has been dismantled and direct dealing is possible by brokers. In fact the Stock Exchange has become much more modern in its approach and there has been a large increase in the use of computers and advanced methods of communication. A summary of the technical changes which have taken place is on page 105.

Susan's stockbroker contacts a large investment house and indicates that she wants to sell shares. David's stockbroker works for a firm with a London office who deal on the Stock Exchange and he tells his London office that his client wishes to buy shares in Tesco. It quickly becomes apparent through the computer network that there are Tesco shares for sale and these are bought.

David now has 500 shares in Tesco and Susan has £2000. They both will be involved in paying a commission to their respective brokers for making the arrangements. Both Susan and David will receive a contract note summarising the deal. In due course David will receive a share certificate from Tesco and will receive a share in the profits (a dividend). The system is summed up in Figure 7.1.

7.2 THE 'BIG BANG' AND STOCK EXCHANGE CHANGES

Here is a summary of the main technical changes introduced to the Stock Exchange at the 'Big Bang'.

Figure 7.1 *How shares are bought and sold on the Stock Exchange*

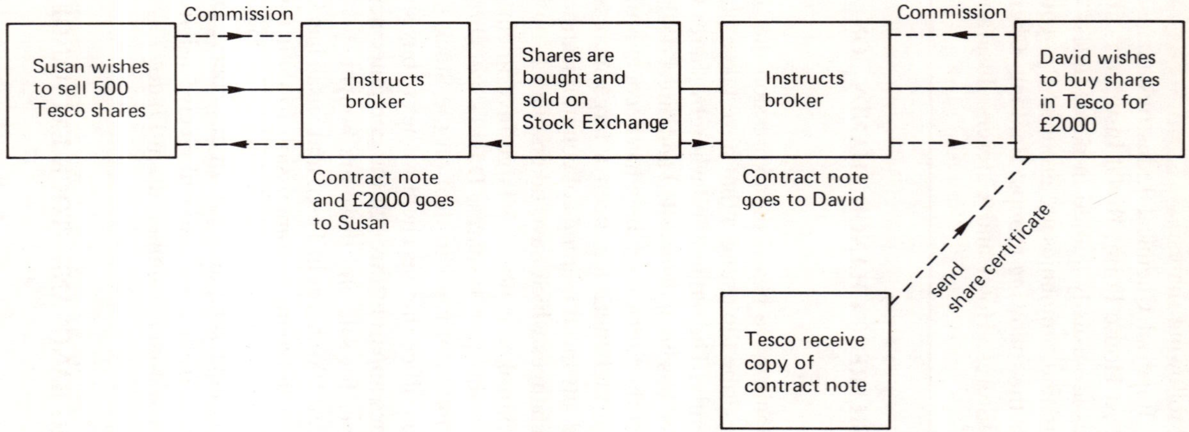

1. The abolition of the scales of minimum commission, i.e. no lower limit was set. Members became free to charge their clients commission on a negotiable basis. This introduced much more competition whereby members could compete on the basis of their charges as well as the quality of the service provided.
2. There was no longer a separation of member firms into jobbers and brokers. Under the new system firms are simply broker/dealer and are able to act as either agency brokers representing their clients in the sale or purchase of shares or to act for themselves buying and selling shares on their own account. Members are however still obliged to trade at the best possible price for his client at all times.
3. As you have probably seen on television, the market has become increasingly electronic. To deal with the 'Big Bang' market the Stock Exchange has introduced and successfully developed a terminal based quotation system called the Stock Exchange Automated Quotations (SEAQ).

   Dealers now enter their buying and selling prices onto the SEAQ from terminals within their own offices. SEAQ then puts together composite (a summary) pages of these prices for display at the Dealers/Brokers' offices using the Stock Exchange's own ViewData network.

   Trading takes place over the telephone or on one of the Stock Exchange's trading floors. It is estimated that over 95 per cent of trading now takes place by telephone. Stock Exchange trading always previously conducted on the trading floors is changing considerably.

The Stock Exchange has seen quite considerable changes since 27 October 1986 when the changes were introduced and the hope is that it will, through a more modern approach, be able to compete more effectively with the other two main centres – New York and Tokyo.

Exercise 1

1. When did the 'Big Bang' occur?
2. Name the other two main share centres besides London.
3. What profit has Susan made between buying her shares and selling them?
4. Give two technical changes introduced by the 'Big Bang'.

7.3 THE IMPORTANCE OF THE STOCK EXCHANGE

There is no doubt that the Stock Exchange plays a very important role in the commercial life of the country.

1. The Stock Exchange does not deal in new issues of shares but will allow a company a stock exchange quotation, as it is called. The Stock Exchange will only do this when it is quite sure that the company is reliable.
2. Many people only buy shares because they know they can sell them when they want to. The Stock Exchange is a market for secondhand shares and because investors know there is such a market they are willing to invest.
3. Investors are protected by Stock Exchange rules. Companies dealing on the exchange must disclose full information and strict rules of conduct are applied.
4. Because insurance companies, trade unions, pension funds, investment and unit trusts deal on the Stock Exchange it allows many people to benefit from business's prosperity. Insurance Companies, trade unions, pension funds, investment and unit trusts are sometimes known as 'institutional investors' to distinguish them from individual shareholders.
5. The number of people investing in shares in the UK is growing rapidly. The Stock Exchange aids this process.
6. The Government benefits from the Stock Exchange because government securities are bought and sold on the Stock Exchange, using exactly the same procedure as explained in relation to Susan and David. If Susan had bought government Gilt Edged Stock as it is called and wished to sell she would do it in exactly the same way. The Stock Exchange is a market for secondhand government stock not new issues. People invest in the government because they know they can sell their stock on the exchange therefore the Stock Exchange assists the government to raise money.
7. The Stock Exchange deals in foreign shares and then allows investors to invest in foreign ventures. Over 50 per cent of the London Stock Exchange dealings are in foreign companies.

Activity

Write to the Stock Exchange and try to obtain some of the excellent explanatory leaflets. It is also possible to visit the Stock Exchange and if you are planning a visit to London in the near future then see if you can include a visit.

CHAPTER 8

INSURANCE AND BUSINESS INSOLVENCY

8.1 INSURANCE

Anyone who starts his or her own business takes certain risks. It may be that the demand for the particular goods or service offered by the business falls and the business starts to make a loss or the business property may be damaged by fire or some of the business goods may be stolen. Business is risky but fortunately some of the risks can be protected against by means of insurance. In this chapter we will be considering the principles of insurance, showing what risks are insurable and those that are not and also looking at the insurance market. The following example will be used to explain some of these aspects.

Marlene Ward has for some time worked as an assistant in a department store; she has always been in the furniture department in the soft furnishing section selling curtains, chair coverings and bedding. Marlene, however, has been anxious for some time to start her own business and she buys a soft furnishing shop in a small but busy country town in Derbyshire. Marlene has calculated that her stock, i.e. curtains, cushions, floor coverings and bedding, is worth about £50 000 and the value of the property which she has bought is about £110 000. Marlene knows the risks involved in business and she approaches an insurance company, Securities plc to see if they will insure her against the risks of damage to or loss of her property and stock, i.e. total value £160 000.

Stages in Arranging Insurance

1. Securities plc will send Marlene a form known as a proposal form on which she will give details of the property and stock she wishes to insure.

2. Securities will then work out how much it will charge Marlene for taking on this risk. The company will look at their records to find out what the 'probability of loss' is in connection with this sort of property. The insurance company has calculated that it will have to pay out the equivalent of a total loss of one business in every four hundred insured properties of this type. Thus, if one thousand such properties are insured, there would be an equivalent total loss of two and a half businesses. If each business is worth £160 000, therefore, the total amount to be paid out would be £160 000 × 2.5 = £400 000. The company will divide 400 000 by the number of such businesses on its books, i.e. 1000 to obtain the figure of £400. Obviously the insurance has to meet costs of running the company and will add so much for this, say £100. It will quote to Marlene a *premium* of £500 per annum. The premium is the cost of the insurance. So for a payment of £500 Marlene can rest assured that if her property and stock is lost through fire, for example, she will be able to claim from Securities plc.

   Securities is able to offer what is a fairly low premium because it has 'pooled the risks', i.e. all the furnishings shops on Securities' books have paid into a central pool and this central pool has been used to compensate those businesses unfortunate enough to suffer losses. Figure 8.1 illustrates the 'pooling of risk' principle.
3. Marlene will receive from Securities plc an 'offer', i.e. the insurance company will insure her property and stock for a payment (premium) of £500 per annum. If Marlene accepts this then the insurance company will draw up an agreement which they will send to Marlene by means of a document known as the policy.

   This insurance agreement is in fact a contract between Marlene and the company. In all contracts there must be something given by both parties; i.e. Marlene gives the £500 premium and the insurance company takes the risk.

Exercise 1

1. Calculate the insurance premium which is likely to be charged by an insurance company which has 100 people each taking out insurance for a risk which totals £1000 and where the probability of total claims made on the insurance company is £5000, or 5 per cent, and where the administrative costs per policy are £10.

2. What is the purpose of a premium?
3. Insurance companies takes on a number of risks; this is known as . . . . . .

Figure 8.1 *Pooling of risks*

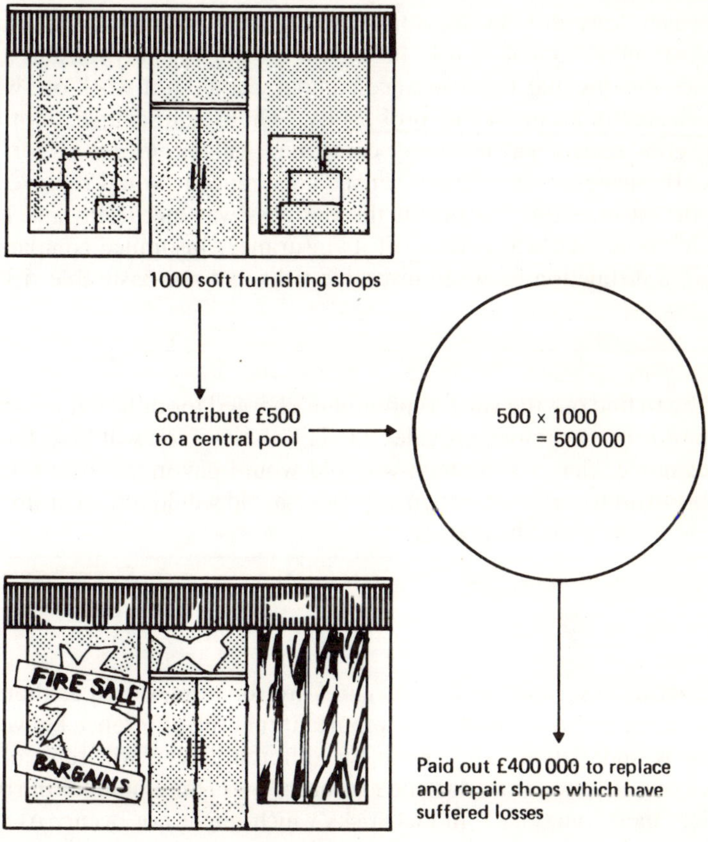

Activity

1. Try to obtain a proposal form from an insurance company to examine the type of questions asked.
2. If you have an insurance policy look at it to see the way in which the conditions are laid out.

Insurable and Non-insurable Risks

It is likely that Marlene's insurance policy was a 'comprehensive one', insuring her against all sorts of risks, e.g. fire, flooding, burglary, theft, dishonest staff, claims made by the public for accidents in the shop. These are all insurable risks because the insurance company can calculate the 'probability of risk' and therefore, as our example showed, can quote a premium which relates to the degree of risk. However, certain risks are non-insurable. A business cannot insure against failure to make profit because there are so many reasons and causes for this that the insurance company could not work out with any degree of accuracy the 'probability'. There is, of course, another very good reason why insurance companies will not insure this sort of risk. If business people could get such insurance it would remove an important incentive because if the business was inefficient and lost money it could always claim off its insurance. Insurance companies make a distinction between insurable risks and non-insurable risks.

> *Activity*
> Try to find out the various premiums charged for different risks; motor-car insurance provides good examples. You will find, for example, that a seventeen-year-old would pay more to insure his two-litre sports car than a forty-year-old would pay to insure his 1.3 litre family saloon.

Insurance and Assurance

The terms 'insurance' and 'assurance' are sometimes used as though they mean the same thing. It is important that the difference between them is understood. To explain the difference, you will remember from our example that Marlene's insurance was for a number of risks – fire, theft, burglary – in fact, risks which might not occur. At the same time as taking out her insurance Marlene decided to take out an endowment/life policy. For a premium of £47 per month Marlene could get a sum of £30 000 at the age of sixty, or this amount would be paid to her husband if she died before reaching the age of sixty. Marlene, of course, will either reach the age of sixty or die before that time. They are two events, one of which will definitely happen. The term 'assurance' is used for life and/or endowment policies because it relates to events which will happen. In other words, the insurance company is assured that one or other of the events will occur and the premiums are worked out on this basis. The older a person is the higher the premium is likely to be.

The Principles of Insurance

All insurance agreements have certain principles built into them and we will use our example again to illustrate the four main principles.

Utmost Good Faith

If insurance companies are going to make a proper assessment of the risk involved they have to be in full possession of the facts relating to that risk. Marlene would have to complete a proposal form which would ask certain questions about the property and stock she wished to insure. Marlene would have to answer these questions truthfully but she would also have to give information about anything else she thought might be relevant. For example, if Marlene sold paraffin in her shop then it would be essential that she stated this because this increases the risk of fire. If Marlene thought the insurance company would not find out that her soft furnishing shop was also selling paraffin and therefore said nothing about it, then if the shop was damaged by fire, Securities plc might not pay out. This principle is known as the principle of utmost good faith or to use the legal term, *uberrimae fidei.*

If Marlene wished to take out life insurance she would have to give details of her health, etc. If Marlene engaged in dangerous sports such as parachuting or gliding she would be obliged to inform the insurance company because, as we have learned, the insurance company needs to assess the risk before it can quote a premium.

Insurable Interest

It is possible to insure against a risk only if you would suffer some loss if that event occurred. Clearly if Marlene's shop was damaged by fire she would lose and therefore it is said she has an insurable interest. If Marlene tried to insure a friend's shop she would not be able to because she has no interest in her friend's shop. She would not lose anything if the friend's shop was damaged. The rule relating to insurable interest was introduced in the eighteenth century to prevent criminals insuring other people's lives and then committing murder to claim the insurance. As you can see this is now impossible because of the principle of 'insurable interest'.

Indemnity

If you think for a moment about the basic purpose of insurance, it is to put the insured person into the same position as he was before the loss occurred. If burglars entered Marlene's shop and got away with stock and money to the value of £4000, then Marlene would claim that amount from her insurance company. It is not intended that a 'profit' should be made from insurance; thus there would be no point in Marlene insuring her property and stock for more than its value. If Marlene decided to insure for £200 000 and the true value was £160 000 then it would be £160 000 she would receive if her property and stock were destroyed. However, it is equally important not to be *under-insured;* thus if Marlene decided to save on premiums and insure her business for only £80 000 and it was completely destroyed, she would receive only £80 000. The 'indemnity' principle is illustrated in an example from car insurance. If Marlene bought a Metro for £6200 and two years later, following an accident, it was a 'write-off', then Marlene, provided she was insured comprehensively, would be compensated; on the principle of indemnity, she would receive only the present secondhand value, i.e. how much she would have to pay to buy a similar car, say £4900.

The principle of indemnity cannot be applied to 'life insurance'. Clearly it is impossible to put a value on loss of life or, for that matter, personal injury. A widow who receives insurance following her husband's death would probably regard the money as small compensation for the loss of her husband.

There are certain insurance policies whereby the insured can get new for old so that if he loses a particular item he can replace it by buying a new item. This sort of arrangement is not usually available for motor car insurance.

Subrogation

Connected to the principle of indemnity is that of subrogation. If an insured person receives full compensation (indemnity) for his loss, any other money received belongs to the insurer. For example, if Marlene's shop was gutted by fire and she received full compensation from Securities and then discovered some stock which had not been too badly damaged and decided to hold a sale which realised £1000, the £1000 would legally belong to the insurer (Securities plc); this is known as 'subrogation'. The insurer takes the place of the insured; in our example Securities takes the place of Marlene.

Contribution

This is also connected to indemnity and can be explained by the following example.

Marlene is a very cautious person and decided to insure her property and stock with two insurance companies. Securities plc and Safesure plc. If, following the loss of her property and stock, she made two claims, i.e. 2 × £160 000, a total of £320 000 would represent a 'profit'. To prevent this, the two insurers (Securities and Safesure) would share the compensation, i.e. £160 000, and this sharing is known as the principle of contribution.

Proximate Cause

Insurance companies will normally provide cover for losses suffered which are a *direct result* of the event happening. If Marlene's business was destroyed by fire the company would pay out money for the loss. If Marlene had taken out 'consequential loss' cover she would also receive compensation for loss of trade during the time her business could not function. However, if, through the worries caused by the fire, Marlene became ill, she could not claim for this because the insurance company would argue that Marlene's illness was not a direct consequence of the loss.

Average Clause

We have already mentioned the problem caused by being under-insured. If a person owns a house worth £100 000, but it is insured only for £50 000, then, if the house is totally gutted by fire, he will be able to claim only £50 000. However, not only would he lose if the house was completely ruined, but if the fire caused partial damage, say £30 000, the insurance company would apply the average clause: i.e. his insurance cover is only

$\frac{1}{2}$ or $\frac{\text{£ }50\,000}{\text{£}100\,000}$ therefore he would be able to claim only $\frac{1}{2}$ of £30 000,

i.e. £15 000. This is known as the average clause and will be applied when the insured is under-insured.

Exercise 2

1. Failure to make profits is an insurable risk. True/false?
2. Why is life insurance sometimes called assurance?
3. All information about the risk to be insured must be given in a proposal form for insurance. This is known as . . . .
4. Is it possible to insure a friend's house against fire risk. True/false?

5. Explain the term 'indemnity'.
6. If you insured your new car for £5000 and a year later it was involved in an accident which caused it to be a complete wreck would you get £5000 compensation from the insurance company. If not why not?
7. If you insure your property with two insurance companies what would happen in the event of a claim?
8. Explain the term 'subrogation'.
9. If a business could not operate because of fire damage it could get insurance cover for loss of trade. This is known as . . . .
10. An antique worth £10 000 is insured for £5000. It is damaged and the repair costs £500. How much wili the insurance company pay out? Explain why it will not be £500.
11. Why will the premium on life insurance be higher the older the insured is?

Types of insurance available to a Business

Fire Insurance

Most businesses will take out insurance to cover themselves against fire. Fire insurance will also include losses due to flood, burst pipes, explosions, etc. In some cases so great is the damage caused by fire, etc. that the business cannot continue trading. It is possible in these circumstances to take out insurance to cover oneself against what is called 'consequential loss', i.e. losses as a consequence (following from) the fire.

Accident Insurance

Liability Insurance A business will usually insure against claims made by employees who may be injured during their work and also against claims made by the public. For example, Marlene's shop is in the main street of a small town and during one week she meets the following problems.

1. One of her assistants is injured while removing some heavy curtain material from the shelves. The assistant decides to claim against Marlene.
2. A passer-by slips badly outside Marlene's shop due to loose masonry on the shop front. The passer-by decides to sue Marlene.

3. A customer in Marlene's shop is injured when some boxes stacked in a corner fall over. The customer claims compensation.

Marlene could obtain insurance cover to pay out on the risks described. In the first instance she could take out an employer's liability insurance and, in the other two cases, she could take out a public liability insurance which covers her against claims made by the general public, which would include customers or passers-by.

Personal Accident Marlene could take out a personal accident insurance policy which would cover her if she was unable to work due to a personal injury.

Property Insurance Marlene could insure all her property against accidents including burglary and vandalism. Thus she would insure her car, shop and stock.

It is possible for one premium to cover a whole range of risks such as the ones described above; this is known as 'comprehensive insurance'.

Fidelity Guarantee Insurance

A business often has to take on employees to engage in various tasks, some of which may involve handling money or valuable stock. Although most employees are honest some businesses have found, to their cost, that a dishonest employee can result in considerable losses. It is possible under a fidelity guarantee insurance to cover this sort of risk. Usually, however, insurance companies will insure only up to a set percentage; generally not more than 80 per cent. Thus, if a dishonest employee misappropriates his employer's property to the extent of £1000, the employer, if he has a fidelity guarantee insurance, will be able to claim only £800.

Life Insurance

There are two types of life insurance.

1. *A whole life policy* provides for a sum to be payable on the death of the insured. The premium charged for such a policy depends of course on the degree of risk, i.e. the age of the insured and his health.
2. *An endowment policy* provides for a lump sum after a period of years, e.g. 25 years, or at death, which ever event comes sooner. Because the insurance company can invest the premiums it receives (see page 99) it can pay profits on such policies, and

often the endowment policy is with profits. This represents a useful way of saving and provides a helpful lump sum to the insured.

> **Activity**
> It is possible to buy a house with the benefit of an endowment mortgage. Try to find out from a building society how this works.

A holder of an endowment insurance policy can surrender the policy, i.e. give it up, after a period of time and he will be entitled to a 'surrender value'. Most insurance companies give nothing if the 'surrender' is during the first year.

> **Activity**
> Newspapers carry advertisements about endowment policies. Find out the relationship which exists between age, premium and size of the lump sum payment.

Household Insurance

Just as a business can insure against a wide range of risks, so also can an ordinary householder. It is possible under a 'comprehensive policy' to insure against fire, flooding, theft, burglary, personal liability.

Marine Insurance

This is a specialised form of insurance which relates to ships. Most marine insurance is dealt with in this country at Lloyd's of London (see below). Some of the terms relating to marine insurance can be best explained by reference to an example.

Stuart & Harman plc owns a number of merchant ships. One of its ships, the *Canterbury*, is taking a consignment of machine tools from London to Rio de Janeiro (Brazil) and the company wishes to make sure that it is fully insured against all risks. The company will therefore take out the following marine insurance.

Hull Insurance
This relates to the ship itself and covers the owner for loss or damage at sea to the vessel and its fixtures; by fixtures is meant the equipment belonging to the ship, e.g. steering gear, lifeboats.

The insurance cover can be made for the voyage, i.e. from London to Rio, which would be a 'voyage policy', or it may be taken out for a period of time, e.g. one year, so that the ship is covered for perhaps two or three different voyages. This is known as a 'time policy'.

Cargo Insurance
This is insurance relating to the cargo itself. If the machine tools in our example are lost or damaged during transit then the owner, i.e. the person in Rio who has purchased the machine tools, is fully compensated.

Freight Insurance
Stuart & Harman plc would normally be paid in advance for shipping the mahcine tools to Rio. If for any reason the company cannot deliver the goods the freight charges must be repaid. Freight insurance will compensate the shipowner for his loss of revenue.

Shipowner's Liability
Stuart & Harman plc in the course of its voyage to Rio by the *Canterbury*, might have to meet various claims, e.g. injuries to the crew, collisions with other ships, damage to the berths at the various docks (at Rio or London). These claims can be met from a shipowner's liability policy.

The Insurance Market

In Chapter 4 we learned that markets were merely means by which buyers and sellers could come together.

A business requiring insurance can go direct to one of the numerous companies offering insurance, such as Norwich Union, Commercial Union, Prudential, Eagle Star, Legal & General. A business wishing to obtain the most competitive rates of insurance, however, will often go to an insurance broker. An insurance broker is a middleman operating between the insurer (the company) and the insured (the businessman). The broker will take a commission for arranging insurance; because he is a specialist he knows the market well and he can find the best rates for his client. Often, of course, the broker receives commission from the company with which he places the insurance and consequentially he may provide his services free to his clients. Even where the insured does pay the commission, however, the competitive rates in the premium will usually more than compensate him.

Lloyd's of London

Lloyd's is a specialist insurance market whose members undertake insurance. It is important to remember that Lloyd's is not an insurance company but merely a place where insurance cover may be obtained. The best way of explaining how Lloyd's operates is by means of an example.

Bristol Shipping plc has just purchased a large ocean-going liner which it has named SS *Avonia*. The value of the vessel is £35 million. The company wishes to insure this vessel for its first year of voyaging.

1. The company approaches a broker who tries to obtain cover on the best terms.
2. The broker will approach Lloyd's underwriters and will present them with a 'slip' showing the amount of cover required and the period. He then seeks the best deal for his client. The underwriter will 'underwrite' (insure) a proportion of the risk, say £10 million, and will indicate the premium. Other underwriters will then sign the slip, e.g.:

Underwriter A	£10 million	for 1 year	at £2 000
Underwriter B	£5 million	for 1 year	at £1 000
Underwriter C	£5 million	for 1 year	at £1 000
Underwriter D	£15 million	for 1 year	at £3 000
Total insured	£35 million	Total premium	£7 000

The premium in total would be £7 000 and the policy is prepared and signed by all four underwriters who have each agreed to accept a proportion of the risk.

Exercise 3

1. Insurance against dishonest employees is called . . . . .

2. In a sentence explain the terms (a) 'cargo insurance' and (b) 'freight insurance'.

3. What is the main difference between whole life insurance and endowment insurance?

4. What is the term given to describe the members of Lloyd's who take insurance risks?

Figure 8.2 *The insurance market*

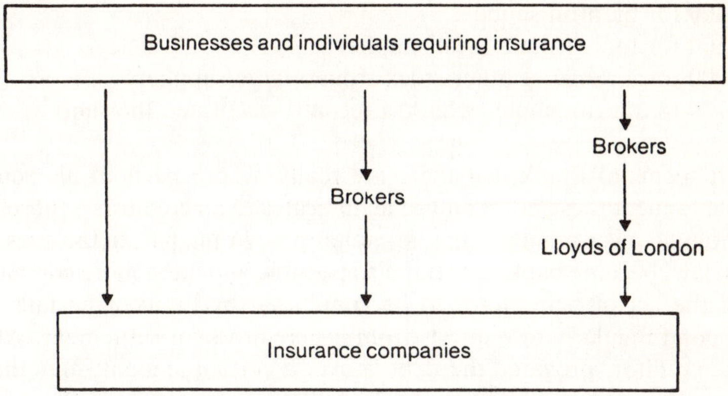

8.2 BUSINESS INSOLVENCY

It is not possible for a business to take out insurance for 'failure to make profits'. There are two reasons for this: first, insurance companies could not work out the possible frequency of this eventuality and therefore could not quote a premium; secondly, if businesses could take out this sort of insurance, it might encourage a carefree attitude by the businessman himself. However, many businesses cannot make profits, and so serious are the losses sometimes that the business has to be ended. This situation is known as business insolvency. 'Solvent' means having enough money to survive; 'insolvent' therefore, means the opposite. When a business or partnership cannot meet its debts it may go bankrupt. However, companies never go bankrupt when they cannot meet their debts; they may go into *liquidation*.

It is not necessary in this book to go into detail on the subject of bankruptcy and liquidation but it is useful to have some knowledge of the process.

Bankruptcy

Frank Jones runs a small DIY shop on the outskirts of Torquay. For the first two years of the business things went well but in the last couple of years trade has gone down and Frank finds that he is getting increasingly into debt. In fact, his position is becoming serious, as the figures below indicate:

Debts owed
£500 for rates to Torbay local authority
£400 for paraffin supplies
£1500 for tools from a local supplier
£2000 for a range of other stock from a large supplier
£700 to a local painter who has recently decorated the shop

It seems to Frank that there are really no prospects of his being able to meet these debts and so he indicates to all creditors – those to whom he owes money – that he cannot pay. Frank has, in the eyes of the law, become bankrupt. It is also possible and often more common for the act of bankruptcy to be committed by Frank if he fails to respond regularly to requests from his creditors for settlement. Any one creditor, provided the debt is over a certain amount, may then present a petition to the court asking that a 'receiving order' is made out against Frank.

Frank's affairs will now be in the hands of an official receiver and he will deal with all matters relating to the business. Notice of the receiving order is published in two newspapers: the *London Gazette* and a local paper. The notice is a warning to other traders not to deal with Frank because Frank is prevented from disposing of any of his assets.

Frank will be asked to attend a public examination where all his financial and business affairs will be closely looked at and, if it seems that he could not pay these debts, he will be declared bankrupt.

Usually at this stage much of the business and stock will be sold and as much as possible will be paid back to the creditors. It is likely that they will not be paid in full and will receive a share of what is left, e.g. 50p in the £. The painter in our example would get only £350 instead of £700.

One of the problems facing Frank because he is a sole trader and thus has unlimited liability is that some of his personal property may be sold to help pay his debts.

Frank will now be a bankrupt until he gains a discharge from the court. Discharges are only granted under certain conditions.

Activity
See if you can find any examples of bankruptcy notices in the local newspapers.

The example of Frank was related to a small independent trader but it could equally have applied to a partnership.

Company Liquidation

Companies do not go bankrupt but may be forced into liquidation. Liquidation means simply to turn the company's assets into liquid-money form so that the creditors may be paid. In these circumstances the company is wound up, i.e. its existence comes to an end. The process of liquidation will be explained by the following example.

West Country Bakers Co. Ltd is a small bakery company in Gloucester. It supplies bread and cakes to a large number of shops in Gloucestershire and some parts of neighbouring Worcestershire and Wiltshire. In the past few years trade has fallen off as more and more shops have turned to the large bakeries for their supplies, and the compny finds that it is falling heavily into debt. Several debts have remained unpaid, despite a number of reminders, for several months.

A bill for flour and other baking supplies from a large flour supplier	£9 200
The half-yearly rent for the premises to Gloucester Property plc	£3 800
A repair bill for work on one of the bakery ovens	£1 900
A petrol bill for its two delivery vans, to Weston Garages	£3 760
Electricity charges	£2 400
A bill for a typewriter for the office owed to Gloucester Office Supplies Ltd	£1 340

Several of these creditors, e.g. Gloucester Property plc which is owed £3 800 and Gloucester Office Supplies which is owed £1 340, may request the court that West Country Bakery Co. Ltd be wound up, i.e. that its affairs be brought to an end. If the court is satisfied that the debts, which amount to £22 400, cannot be paid then it will appoint an official receiver whose job it is to examine the affairs of the company and to wind it up; in other words to bring the company's affairs to an end. The official receiver will then liquidate the company. That is, he will try to convert the company's assets, i.e. the machinery, the vans and other equipment, into money. There are some circumstances where the official receiver will try to keep the business going but in the majority of cases he will liquidate it or sell it as a going concern. In 1986 a chain of shops known as Reject China went into liquidation but the official receiver was able to obtain a buyer and obtain the money rather than sell all the assets. Let us examine the stages by which this process of liquidation is achieved.

1. All the assets are sold; we will say that the vans fetch £2200 each, the secondhand bakery machinery is sold for £2600 and other equipment for £1600. This gives a total of £8600.
2. The company has £1600 in the bank.
3. Its stock, i.e. bakery provisions, flour, comes to £1000.
4. Some companies will have shareholders who are not fully paid up and this money can be used; e.g. if in every £1 share only 75p has been paid then the official receiver can call for the additional 25p per share. We will assume that the company's shares are all paid up or fully paid up.

Having sold the assets the total realised is £11 200 and this will be used to pay the creditors. However the total debt is £22 400, therefore the creditors will receive only 50p in the £.

Exercise 4
If 50p in the £ was declared how much would Westons Garages obtain?

We have described the compulsory winding up of a company which resulted from the inability of West Country Bakery Co. Ltd to meet its debts. It was wound up as a result of a request from creditors. A company may decide to wind itself up because it wishes to discontinue business or amalgamate with another company. This is known as voluntary winding up.

Activity
Newspapers often carry stories of companies being wound up and in recent years a large number of companies have been forced out of business. Try to find examples.

Exercise 5
Try to answer the following review questions without reference to the chapter. If when checking your answers you find that you have not understood any particular topic, re-read the section.

1. What is the payment made to an insurance company known as?
2. Explain why it is not a good use of money to over-insure a risk.

3. If a risk is under-insured then any payment made by an insurance company will not be full value of the loss. This is known as . . . .
4. If a business insures against fire and loss of trade due to the fire what is the insurance against loss of trade known as?
5. What do you understand by the term 'surrender' of an endowment insurance policy?
6. Members of Lloyd's are known as . . . .
7. If a small business cannot pay its debts the creditors may seek an order from the court; what is this known as?
8. Bankruptcy notices must be advertised in newspapers; in which newspapers must they appear?
9. When a company's assets are converted into liquid form this is known as . . . .
10. A company is wound up only when it cannot meet its debts. True/false?
11. If all the shareholders have paid for their shares in full the company's shares are said to be . . . .

CHAPTER 9

BANKING SERVICES AND BUSINESS

In Chapter 8 we considered insurance and learned that it is a very important service to business in that it enables the businesses to take away some of the risks and place them with an insurance company. In this chapter we will be considering the ways in which banks assist businesses and we will use the example of one business to illustrate this.

Pine Furniture Co. Ltd is a small but growing private company which was started by the present managing director, Marc Holburn. Marc started as an independent sole trader and business grew up so that he formed a company. The company now produces pine furniture for a number of furniture shops and also supplies its own shop which is situated in a beautiful part of the Cotswolds and so attracts a lot of tourist trade. Like most businesses, Pine Furniture Co. Ltd has a bank account. The company has its bank account with the Midland Bank, Broadstone.

9.1 FUNCTIONS OF THE BANK

1. Many of Pine Furniture Co. Ltd's customers pay for their goods by cheque and the Midland will handle the cheques for the company, making sure that the money related to these cheques is paid into the company's account.
2. The company has to pay for materials for its furniture. It also has to settle bills in relation to deliveries. This can be done easily by means of cheques, drawn on the company account to suppliers.
3. The shop belonging to Pine Furniture Co. Ltd also takes a lot of cash and for security reasons the company does not wish to leave large amounts of cash lying around the premises. It regularly banks it, therefore, often using the night safe facilities. The

company has a key to the bank's night safe and money can be dropped into this in special bags if the bank is closed.

4. Pine Furniture Co. Ltd has five employees and these are all paid by direct transfer to their bank. The following are the amounts:

   Mr Taylor £180 — Mr Davey £190
   Mr Jennings £240 — Mrs Cohen £150
   Mrs Evans £150

   This represents a total of £910. Marc Holburn, the managing director, can instruct his bank to pay the employees these amounts and the bank will credit the accounts of the employees as indicated by the company and will debit (take away from) the company's account.
5. If Pine Furniture Co. Ltd wishes to get a loan from the bank then the bank after looking at the application might grant the company a loan or an overdraft. We will be considering the difference between the two types of loan on page 134.
6. There are a whole range of other functions which the Midland Bank may provide for the company; for example:
7. If the company is involved in exporting then the bank will assist in this.
8. The bank will arrange insurance.
9. Cash dispensers are available at most main branches of banks so that customers can draw cash when the banks are closed by using a special card.

9.2 TYPES OF ACCOUNT

The Midland Bank can offer Pine Furniture Co. Ltd a number of different accounts.

Current Account

This is an account which as its name 'current' suggests involves movement. In fact it is an account which can be used by the company to pay into and draw out of. The bank will allow holders of current accounts a cheque book and cheques can be used to settle bills. A cheque is, as we will see on page 127, an order to the bank to debit (take from) the current account. A current account does not normally pay interest, in fact, the bank will normally make charges for its services and the charges will vary:

1. The greater the number of transactions on the account the higher the charges; i.e. if our company pays out a lot of cheques then this will increase its charges.
2. The greater the balance of money in the account the lower the charges.
3. A number of banks have abolished charges on current accounts provided the account stays in credit.

Thus if our company keeps a large balance of money in its current account and there is not much movement, i.e. few cheques drawn on it, then the charges will be low.

A holder of a current account will receive from time to time a statement which is a summary of what has happened to the account during a particular period. It records the payments in and the payments out. A businessman can use the statement to check the payments that have been made to and from the business. With a current account Pine Furniture Co. Ltd will also receive a paying-in book for use when paying in money to the bank.

Deposit Account

Pine Furniture Co. Ltd could have a deposit account. Cheques cannot be used with a deposit account and deposit accounts do provide interest. If our company keeps £1000 in the deposit account for a period of time, let us say six months, it will get interest. If the interest rate is 5 per cent per annum it will receive £25, i.e. £1000 at 5 per cent = £50 per year, but for six months £25.

Budget Account

It is possible for a company or individual to open a budget account. This really is an account to allow you to spread your bills over a year by regular monthly payments. It is used particularly by families to settle their regular bills, and the following example will illustrate this type of account.

John Hartley has an account with Lloyds Bank. He opens a budget account besides his current account and uses this budget account to pay all household bills. First of all he adds up all his bills for a year and his calculations suggest the following:

Gas	£600
Electricity	£400
Rates	£400
TV rental	£200
Telephone	£200
	£1 800

By transferring £150 per month to his budget account to make £1 800 in the year John can pay all these bills and the bank will allow him to overdraw (draw out more than he has in the account) provided he uses the budget account only for these items. This type of account is sometimes called a Home Management Account.

Exercise 1

1. The bank pays interest on a deposit account. True/false?

2. If someone wishes to draw money out of the bank while the bank is closed they can use a . . . .

3. Explain the term 'direct transfer'.

4. What monthly payments would someone need to pay into his budget account if his annual bills amounted to £600?

5. From time to time a holder of a current account will receive a summary of what has happened to his account; this is known as a . . . .

6. Current account holders may pay bank charges; the level of these bank charges depends upon two factors; what are they?

9.3 CHEQUES

When a person writes a cheque he is ordering his bank to transfer money from his account to someone else's. Let us assume that Pine Furniture Co. Ltd receives a cheque from a customer for £120 for a small pine table which is on sale at the shop. Mrs Gardener is on holiday from Kent and so pays by means of a cheque drawn on her account at the National Westminster, Ashdon, Kent.

The cheque, which appears in Figure 9.1, is an order to the National Westminster at Ashdon to pay Pine Furniture Co. Ltd £120. There are three parties involved in a cheque:

Figure 9.1

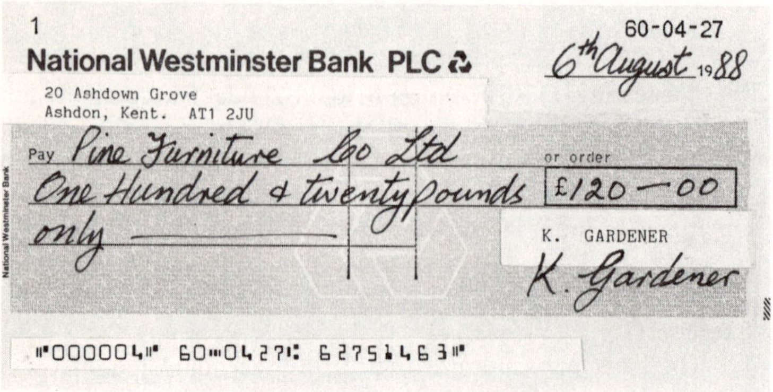
1
60-04-27
National Westminster Bank PLC
6th August 1988
20 Ashdown Grove
Ashdon, Kent. AT1 2JU
Pay Pine Furniture Co Ltd or order
One Hundred & twenty pounds only
£120—00
K. GARDENER
K. Gardener
National Westminster Bank
⑈000004⑈ 60⑉0427⑆ 62751463⑈

1. *The drawer* – the person drawing the money out, i.e. the person who makes out the cheque, in this case Kate Gardener;
2. *The drawee* – the bank which is being ordered to pay the money, National Westminster Bank;
3. *The payee* – the person to whom the money is being paid, Pine Furniture Co. Ltd.

There are a number of features on a cheque:

1. The figures at the bottom are the code relating to the account. It is Mrs Gardeners' account number.
2. The figures in the top right hand corner are the branch code number, i.e. the number of Ashdon, Kent.
3. The amount to be paid must be in words and numbers and if these differ in any way the bank will not pay out.

Clearing of Cheques

Pine Furniture Co. Ltd will take this cheque for £120 and together with other cheques that have been received will put them into the bank, which you will remember is the Midland Bank, Broadstone, Gloucestershire. The cheques are sent to Midland's head office. Any cheques drawn on other Midland branches will be sent from the head office to the branch concerned, but all other cheques, i.e. Barclays,

National Westminster and Lloyds, will go to the clearing house. If when all the cheques are listed the Midland Bank owes Lloyds money, it will pay Lloyds by means of a Bank of England cheque which is drawn on a deposit held at the Bank of England by the Midland. All the banks hold deposits with the Bank of England. This process, summed up in Figure 9.2, is known as 'bank clearing'. The process usually takes three days. The cheque then goes back to the National Westminster in Ashdon and this will be the end of the journey as far as the cheque is concerned. All that will remain to happen is for Kate's account to be debited.

If, however, for any reason Kate does not have sufficient money in her account to cover the cheque and she has not made any arrangements with her bank for an overdraft, then the cheque would be sent back to the Midland, Broadstone, with the words 'refer to drawer' stamped on it or sometimes merely 'R/D'. This is really an indication that the bank should send the cheque to Pine Furniture Co. Ltd who will then refer to the drawer, or in other words get in touch with Mrs Gardener, indicating to her that her bank has refused to 'honour' the cheque. If this happens Pine Furniture Co. Ltd's account will not be credited by £120. Sometimes the expression is used that the cheque has 'bounced'.

Figure 9.2

K. Gardener drawn on
National Westminster cheque for £120
↓
Pine Furniture Co. Ltd.
↓
Midland Bank, Broadstones
↓
Head office of Midland
↓
Central clearing
↓
Head office National Westminster
↓
National Westminster, Ashdon
K. Gardener's account debited by £120

Dishonouring of Cheques

We have already learned of one situation where the bank will 'dishonour' (not pay out) on a cheque. If there are insufficient funds in the account of the drawer then the bank may dishonour the cheque and mark on it 'refer to drawer'. There are several other situations in which the bank may dishonour the cheque.

1. The drawer might stop the cheque, i.e. instruct his/her bank not to pay out on it. Thus Mrs Gardener could instruct her bank not to pay out the £120 and provided she did this before the cheque was cleared then the National Westminster, Ashdon, would not pay out on it.
2. If the drawer has incorrectly written the cheque so that the words, i.e. one hundred and twenty pounds, do not coincide with the figures 120 – if for example Mrs Gardener had put 86 – then clearly the bank will not be sure what was intended and will not honour the cheque.
3. If the cheque is out of date – if the date when the cheque is presented by the payee is six months later than its date, it will not be honoured. For example, if Pine Furniture Co. Ltd presented the cheque in August 1989 then it would be out of date and not honoured.
4. Finally, if the bank discovers that the drawer has died or become bankrupt then it will not honour the cheque. If they were aware that Kate had died before the cheque was presented to her bank they would not pay out.

Exercise 2

1. List the five reasons for which a bank may stop a cheque.
2. Michael who has an account at Barclays pays a cheque of £40 to Janette whose account is at Lloyds. Name the drawer, drawee and payee in the above situation.
3. What does 'refer to the drawer' mean? Under what circumstances might a bank write this on a cheque?
4. How long does cheque clearing usually take?

Cheque Crossings

If you look back to the diagram of the cheque on page 128 you will notice that it has two lines drawn vertically across it. This crossing means that the cheque must be paid into an account. A bank will never pay cash from the counter if the cheque is crossed. Thus in our example Pine Furniture Co. Ltd would have to pay the cheques into its account. If someone receives a crossed cheque and he has no bank account then he can ask someone who has an account to cash it for him but he must endorse it, i.e. sign it on the back. The person who accepts the cheque will then pay it into his account.

Cheques which are not crossed are known as open cheques, which means that the bank will pay out cash on them.

Our cheque made out by Mrs Gardener has an ordinary crossing on it; it is, however, possible to have special crossings. Two types of special crossing are shown in Figure 9.3.

Figure 9.3

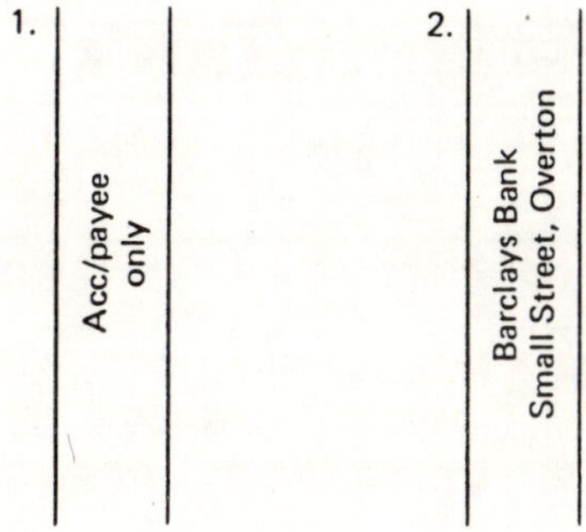

The first crossing, (1), on which is written 'Acc/payee only', means that it can be paid only into the account of the payee. This, of course, prevents the cheque being wrongly used if it goes astray.

The second crossing, (2), 'Barclays Bank, Small Street, Overton', means that the cheque must be paid into the bank named. A business having several accounts might wish that payments made to it are made to the account at a particular place.

Before we leave the subject of cheques it is important to understand the purpose of a cheque card. Many shops these days will not accept cheques unless they are supported by a cheque card. Banks now issue to their current account customers cheque cards. If the number on this card is written on the back of the cheque, provided the cheque is for £50 or less, the bank will guarantee that it will be 'honoured', provided it is correctly filled in. In other words the Midland Bank will not refuse to pay out even though the account holder has not sufficient funds in his account to meet it. Obviously this protects businesses which are concerned about customers whom they do not know.

An example of a cheque card is shown below. In some cases the bank cheque card also doubles up as a cash dispenser card. The Midland Bank, for example, uses one card for both purposes. Used as a cash dispenser card the account holder would need to know his/her PIN number (PIN stands for 'personal identification number'). The account holder inserts his or her card into a cash dispensing machine and if the PIN number is correct then money (up to a maximum amount per day) can be drawn.

> **Activity**
> See if you can spot examples of notices in shops which indicate that payment by cheque can be made only if the cheque is supported by a cheque card.

9.4 METHODS OF PAYMENT USING THE BANK

We have already learned that a cheque is a useful way of paying money, in fact, it is used extensively in the UK and in terms of the toal value of transactions it is far more important than notes and coins. However, there are other ways by which money can be paid using the services of the bank, as the following example will show.

Pine Furniture Co. Ltd has the following bills to pay:

1. A bill for water to the Severn-Trent Water Authority for £240.
2. A bill for £80 which is a monthly hire purchase charge.
3. A regular payment to the Small Business Association of £90 per annum.

4. A payment of £200 for a new woodworking machine, which the supplier will not deliver until paid.

1. Bank Giro

The company can pay the first bill by means of bank giro credit which is a credit transfer system by which Pine Furniture can pay its water bill through the bank and save the cost of posting.

2. Standing Order or Banker's Order

Pine Furniture could pay its £80 hire purchase charge by asking its bank to make the payment for it. This is known as a standing order, which means an order which remains for the period of time specified or until such time as it is cancelled by the account holder. Clearly this has advantages; it saves the cost of posting and it means that Pine Furniture cannot forget to pay.

3. Direct Debit

This could be used for the £90 payment. It is like a standing order, i.e. an instruction to the bank, but the amount can vary. If the subscription was raised then the Small Business Association would directly debit Pine Furniture's account for the amount in question.

4. Banker's Draft

You will note that the supplier supplying the woodworking machine wants his money before delivery. You will remember that a cheque takes three days to be cleared. It is possible for Pine Furniture to ask its bank to prepare a banker's draft for £900. A banker's draft is really exactly the same as money because it does not need to be cleared; the receiver knows that he does not need to worry about the payer's credit worthiness. A good example of the use of a banker's draft is when a house is bought; the deeds (the property ownership documents) will not normally be transferred to the buyer until the seller (or his solicitor) has a banker's draft for the outstanding money.

Exercise 3

1. If someone wishes his bank to make regular payments for him he can use two possible methods. What are they?

2. A bank's credit transfer system is known as . . . .
3. What does a crossing 'acc/payee only' mean?
4. Crossed cheques may be paid only into a bank account. True/false?
5. A banker's draft takes three days to clear. True/false?
6. How can a shop ensure that a cheque for £35 will be 'honoured'?

9.5 BANK CREDIT

We have considered most of the services available from the bank to its creditors. We did mention on page 125 that it was possible to obtain credit from the bank, as the following three examples will illustrate.

Diana Clapham Fashions is a ladies' clothes shop. The owner, Miss Clapham, often finds that she has to pay for stock, i.e. dresses, skirts, coats, etc., before she has enough money in her account. She therefore asks her bank, Lloyds, to grant her overdraft facilities of £1000; she wants the bank to allow her to 'overdraw' up to a maximum of £1000, in other words to spend more than she has. If the bank agrees to this request then Miss Clapham will pay interest on the amount she has overdrawn; she will pay interest on £1000 only when she has gone to the maximum.

This is a good way of borrowing money, particularly if money is being paid in regularly, because unlike the ordinary loan interest is charged daily on the amount outstanding.

For example, if the interest rate on the overdraft is 10 per cent per annum and the situation is as follows:

Day 1	£750 overdrawn
Day 2	£1000 overdrawn
Day 3	£300 overdrawn (i.e. £700 paid in)
Day 4	nil overdrawn (i.e. £300 paid in)

The interest charge would be for the three days when there was an overdraft:

Day 1	20p
Day 2	27p
Day 3	8p
Day 4	nil
Total	55p

Birkett Bros (Builders) wish to buy some new equipment, total cost £1000. Bob Birkett goes to the bank, Lloyds, and asks for a loan. The bank manager looks at Bob's business and decides to grant him a loan of £1000 at 10 per cent for two years. The total interest charge is £200 and Bob will be paying that rate of interest even though in the second year he has only £500 but interest of £100 to pay off. Getting a loan is much more expensive than an overdraft, but banks will not usually grant overdrafts for specific items, only for day-to-day trading.

The law requires the bank to state the actual payment rate (APR) and although there is not a formula for converting a flat rate (10 per cent in our example) to APR the rough rule of thumb is flat rate × 2+ 1 per cent ∴ 10 × 2 = 20 + 1 = 21 per cent.

John Adams runs a small computer agency and has to travel around the country quite a lot. He does not like to take too much cash with him and he uses his credit card as much as possible. This allows him to pay for hotels, petrol, meals, etc. There are various types of credit cards available. Barclays Bank, TSB and the Bank of Scotland use a Visa card. The other three banks, Midland, National Westminster and Lloyds, use Access. John has a Midland account and thus uses Access. Every month he will receive a statement from Access showing the amount outstanding, the interest charge and the minimum payment due. An example of an Access and a Visa card is shown below. The rate of interest at present (1988) charged by Visa and Access is 1.75 per cent a calender month, that is 21 per cent per annum.

Exercise 4

1. Suppose business A borrows £1000 by means of a bank loan for one year and business B borrows £1000 by means of a bank overdraft for one year. Both are at 15 per cent interest; why might total interest payments paid by each business differ?
2. Name three banks that use the Access network.

Banks are offering businesses and personal customers more and more services. The Bank of Scotland has advertised widely their HOBS (Home and Office Banking Service) system whereby a businessman or personal account customer can, by means of a home computer linked to the bank's system, instruct his bank to effect all sorts of transactions which will be recorded in his own office or home. Barclays introduced 'Connect' in 1987 and Midland, National West-

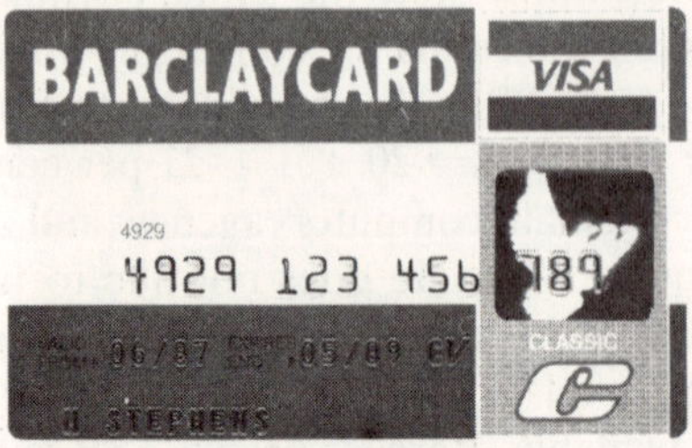

minster and the Royal Bank of Scotland introduced 'Switch' in 1988. Both systems operate so that customers, on presentation of their cards, can pay for their goods or services and have their bank current accounts automatically debited. An example of a Connect card is shown above and Switch is available where you see the logo shown below.

> **Activity**
> Think of any other credit card systems apart from Access and Barclaycard. Try to find out how American Express differs from Access and Barclaycard.
>
> Try to get explanatory leaflets so that you can find out more about 'Connect' and 'Switch'.

Exercise 5
Answer the following review questions without reference to the chapter but if after checking your answers you find that you have not understood any section read over that section again.

1. Many employees are paid their wages directly into their bank accounts. How can firms do this?
2. Bank charges are always paid on a deposit account. True/false?
3. A budget account holder is never allowed to overdraw his account. True/false?
4. What does the term ‘payee’ mean?
5. How could someone get money on a crossed cheque if he did not have a bank account?
6. Payment may be made by cheque provided the cheque is supported by a cheque card. What does this mean?
7. What is the difference between a standing order and a direct debit?
8. Banks will usually grant overdrafts for purchase of equipment. True/false?
9. Calculate as near as possible the APR on a flat rate loan of 16 per cent per annum.

CHAPTER 10

PERSONAL FINANCE

In the last chapter we considered business finance and looked at some of the ways in which a business could obtain finance for its operations and for expansion. In this chapter we will consider personal finance, that is how individuals might borrow money or how individuals might lend money to earn interest. In Chapter 1 you will remember we considered the case of the Percival family and how they used their income to the best advantage as they saw it. In this chapter we will consider the Boyden family.

Richard Boyden is a manager of a large retail shop and earns £16 500 per year. He is married to Julia who works as a secretary to a solicitor and she earns £6500 per year. Richard and his wife live in the South East of England near their parents. Richard's father, Robert, has just retired and has to make certain decisions about how to invest his retirement lump sum gratuity of £45 000. Using this family as an example we will be looking at the various ways in which individuals can obtain credit and the various ways in which they can make investments.

10.1 BORROWING

Building Societies

Richard and his wife have recently bought a house for £45 000 and like most first-time buyers they certainly could not pay cash and therefore took out a mortgage of £30 000 from the Halifax Building Society. Richard and Julia own the house which is situated at 15 Beaumont Close, Maidstone, Kent but the Halifax Building Society has an interest in it.

Richard and Julia must pay interest on this loan of £30 000. The interest rate is 9.8 per cent per annum. Richard and Julia have what is called an endowment mortgage which means that over a period of, let us say, 25 years they pay interest on the £30 000 and pay back the £30 000 at the end of the period when their endowment insurance matures and is paid out. Richard and Julia will need to pay monthly to the Halifax the sum of:

$$£2940 \text{ (interest)} + \frac{2940}{12},$$

that is, a monthly sum of £245.

The government is anxious to encourage home ownership and interest on up to £30 000 is subject to tax relief. This means that at present (1988) Richard and Julia will pay £2 940 less 25 per cent = 2205.25, that is a monthly payment of £183.75. Their monthly repayments will be reduced therefore by £61.25 [25 per cent is the present (1988) standard rate of tax, see Chapter 14].

> **Activity**
> Our figures have been based upon a 9.8 per cent rate of interest. This was the rate for new buyers in April 1988. These rates vary from time to time. Visit a building society and find out the present rate of interest. Banks also will give mortgages. Go to your bank and find out what is available.

> **Exercise 1**
> Calculate the monthly interest payments on a mortgage of £22 000 assuming a 10 per cent rate of interest and a tax relief of 25 per cent, that is a net rate of 7.5 per cent.

Types of Mortgages

Richard and Julia are quite sensible with their money and before buying their house they have an appointment with someone from the Halifax who explains to them the difference between a repayment mortgage and an endowment mortgage.

The Repayment Mortgage

The building society advance the £30 000 and the borrowers, Richard and Julia, would pay back the interest less tax relief but also something off the advance. It is sensible to take out a mortgage protection insurance so that if Richard or Julia should die before the 25 years the full repayment is made.

The Endowment Mortgage

In this case only the interest less tax relief is paid. Richard and Julia take out an insurance which will pay out at least £30 000 after 25 years to pay off the advance. It is likely that extra money will be earned known as cash surpluses. If Richard or Julia should die before 25 years then the insurance would come into effect immediately.

More and more people are taking advantage of this endowment option and the Halifax show Richard and Julia the figures on the computer's VDU and then give them a print out.

```
InView                              22-Apr-88 13:41
                    NORWICH UNION

For: MR & MRS BOYDEN
Male 27 nb n/s          Female 27 nb n/s
Mortgage Amount £30000      Term 25 years
                        Repayment Endowment
Net Rate                   7.350%    7.350%
B/S Payment                221.33    183.75

Life Premium                 4.80     39.30
 Monthly Total             226.13    223.05

  ILLUSTRATIVE MATURITY BENEFIT
With Profits Sum Assured NIL          10320
Assumed Annual Bonuses   NIL          19680
     Mortgage Repaid                  30000
  ILLUSTRATIVE CASH SURPLUS
Annual Bonuses           NIL           4948
Guideline Total          NIL          14662

  0 Requote 3 Low Start
  5 Select Company 9 Halifax Mtge Prot
```

A4 **HALIFAX BUILDING SOCIETY**

You can see from the print out that the interest is calculated after tax relief i.e. 9.8 per cent less 25 per cent = 7.35 per cent. You can also make comparisons between the 2 options. Note that these figures are for April 1988 and may change. Make sure you keep up to date.

Bank Loans, Credit Sales and Hire Purchase

Richard and Julia decide to buy a new car and they decide on a Ford Fiesta at £6250. Richard trades in his present car for £3250 and needs to find £3000. There are a number of possible options open to him.

1. He could draw on his savings.
2. He could seek a bank loan.
3. He could obtain finance from a finance company, e.g. Mercantile Credit.

We will assume that he decided against option (1) and wishes to consider borrowing the money.

Bank Loan
Richard and Julia have an account with Barclays Bank. Richard goes to the bank and is offered a bank loan over three years at 15 per cent per annum. This would mean that Richard would need to pay £3000 + £1350 interest, over the three year period.

Exercise 2
Calculate the monthly repayments to be paid by Richard.

Although the rate of interest is 15 per cent per annum, in the second and third years it is of course much higher and over the full period of the loan the actual rate of interest is therefore higher than 15 per cent. Banks and finance companies have by law to quote the actual interest rates. These are quoted as APR – annual percentage rate.

Richard could alternatively go to a finance company and garages usually have links with companies such as Mercantile Credit, Lloyds Bowmaker, United Dominion Trust.

Finance companies will offer a credit or hire purchase arrangement. If Richard decides on a credit arrangement then he will receive as it were a loan for £3000 repayable over a fixed term, usually three years. In April 1988 Mercantile Credit were quoting 15 per cent per annum (APR = 31 per cent). Whether this would be better than a bank loan would depend upon the rate of interest. The Ford Fiesta would become Richard's and would not belong in any way to the finance company.

A hire purchase agreement will be similar in terms of repayments but the car would remain the property of the finance company and would be hired to Richard. If for any reason Richard did not pay his instalments the company could seize back the car. In a credit arrangement under no circumstances would the finance company seize back the car.

Exercise 3
There are three basic differences between a credit arrangement and a hire purchase, see if you can remember them.

Car manufacturers anxious to boost their share of the market will often offer very attractive interest rates. The advertisement below is from Vauxhall and shows the rates offered to purchasers of the 1 litre Nova three-door hatchback. This also is a good example of advertising with attempts to both persuade and inform. You will note that the APR (the average percentage rate) is quoted.

Activity
Assume that you wish to borrow £1500 to buy a car. Find out the difference in interest between a bank loan from a finance company and a loan from a car manufacturer's credit arrangement.

Credit Cards

Many people these days have credit cards, i.e. Access, Visa, American Express, to name a few. Richard has a Visa card. Customers of Barclays Bank, Trustee Savings Bank (TSB) and the Bank of Scotland can obtain a Visa card. Richard's account is with Barclays and he has a Visa card.

Midland, National Westminster and Lloyds are part of a similar scheme known as Access.

Let us see how the Visa credit card system operates. Richard has a credit limit of £500 in other words he can only be in debt to a maximum of £500. Richard often uses his card to buy petrol and he

Above is the Nova 1 litre three-door Hatchback.

To the right, a selection of tempting take-away terms.

As you can readily see, a 40% deposit and weekly payments of £23.59 will place you comfortably inside a new Vauxhall Nova.

And that's just one of the ways in which our special low-cost finance scheme works.

12·8% APR.

There's a flexible variety of other ways and means available for selection. And the package that suits you best can be applied to any of the 14-model Nova range.

(From a two-door Saloon to a five-door Hatchback.)

So visit your Vauxhall dealer soon or call 0800 400 479 free of charge for the complete Factfile details.

The offer ends however, with the end of June.

It may seem that time's on your side but it's smart to get motoring right away.

NOVA			
Typical Examples: NOVA 1·0 3-Door Hatch	4·9% Finance **9·7% APR**	6·5% Finance **12·8% APR**	6·5% Finance **12·8% APR**
Repayment period	24 months	36 months	36 months
On the road price	£5,131.99	£5,131.99	£5,131.99
Minimum deposit (Cash or trade-in)	20%	20%	40%
	£1,026.40	£1,026.40	£2,052.80
Interest charges	£402.33	£800.49	£600.37
Monthly repayments†	**£187.83**	**£136.28**	**£102.21**
Equivalent weekly	£43.35	£31.45	£23.59*
Total credit price	£5,544.32	£5,942.48	£5,742.36
Customer saving**	**£459.84**	**£492.84**	**£369.36**

VAUXHALL. ONCE DRIVEN, FOREVER SMITTEN.

VAUXHALL IS BACKED BY THE WORLDWIDE RESOURCES OF GENERAL MOTORS. PRICES SHOWN CORRECT AT TIME OF GOING TO PRESS. CALCULATIONS INCLUDE ESTIMATED COST OF NUMBER PLATES, DELIVERY AND 6 MONTHS ROAD FUND LICENCE. †£10 OPTION TO PURCHASE FEE IS ADDED TO FIRST PAYMENT. **CUSTOMER SAVING COMPARED TO THE CREDIT PROVIDERS 10.5% INTEREST (21% APR) IN FORCE IMMEDIATELY PRIOR TO 1ST JANUARY 1988. THIS OFFER IS SUBJECT TO APPROVAL AND REGISTRATION WITHIN THE PERIOD 1ST APRIL TO 30TH JUNE 1988. WRITTEN DETAILS AVAILABLE FROM GMAC, WESLEY HOUSE, 19 CHAPEL STREET, LUTON LU1 2SE WHO PROVIDE THE CREDIT FACILITIES.

can use his card to obtain cash either from the bank or a cash dispenser. In the latter case he needs what is called a PIN number (personal identification number).

Each month Richard will receive an account from Visa showing his transactions. The system operates so that he can pay the outstanding amount in full, e.g. £350 or he can pay the minimum stated 5 per cent of the outstanding debt, i.e. £17.50. If he pays the minimum then interest will accrue at the rate of 1.75 per cent per month (1988). If he pays the maximum then no interest is payable. (An example of an account is shown below.) However, if he draws cash then he will have to pay interest from the time of the cash advance until he pays off the outstanding amount. The current (1988) rate for a cash advance is 1.50 per cent per month. If Richard uses his Visa card to draw £30 then he will pay interest at 1.50 per cent i.e. 45p.

BARCLAYS BANK. Visa Centre. Northampton NN1 1SL

Name
R T BOYDEN
Account No.
4560 7205 9905 2231

Statement Date
16 March 88

Date	Reference	Description	Amount
		Balance Brought Forward	£250.00
15 March	S7DFXN2E	Payment Received – Thank you	40.00
		Interest at 1.75%	3.70
			213.70
12 Feb	0013B1MV	BR Maidstone West	30.00
12 Feb	002MW5FW	Detling Self-service, Maidstone	40.00
18 Feb	001TBF38	Voucher for 200FF Pierre Lamont, Calais	20.00
21 Feb	002MV1FD	Cash Advance Barclays Bank, Maidstone	40.00
21 Feb	002MV1FD	Handling Charge at 1.50%	0.60
4 March	001TBF38	F. W. Woolworth, Maidstone	20.70
10 March	00A1PEG	Marks & Spencer, Canterbury	20.00

Your credit limit	You can spend	You need only pay	to reach us by	Your present balance
£500	£115	£19.25	10th April	£385

You will note that it is possible to use the Visa card in France and indeed also in many parts of Europe.

Access works in exactly the same way but American Express works differently, the whole outstanding sum becomes payable immediately. The other difference is that American Express customers have to pay an annual subscription.

Exercise 4

1. Calculate the minimum payment on an Access account of £250
2. What are the two differences between Access/Visa and the American Express system.
3. Name three banks associated with Visa.
4. Name three banks associated with Access.

Budget or Charge Cards

Richard and Julia also have a British Home Stores Card known as a BHS Storecard. Many retail shops operate budget card systems similar to BHS‹ You saw an example of these types of cards on page 71. There are basically two systems.

1. The customer pays a fixed monthly charge and credit is allowed up to 24 times the monthly payment i.e. for £20 per month £480 credit.
2. The customer pays a minimum of £5 per month or 5 per cent of his/her outstanding debt. This is similar to the Visa/Access system.

Richard and Julia, who both have BHS Storecards have decided on option 2. Interest is payable on outstanding amounts.

Activity

See if you can find out the rate of interest chargeable on:

1. An Access debt.
2. A Debenhams' or Marks & Spencer debt.

Advantages and Disadvantages of Credit Facilities

It is easy to obtain loans of the various kinds described and there is a worry that convenience of obtaining credit facilities will lead people into debt they cannot deal with.

Remember credit costs money and it is possible to make comparisons between the costs of various types of credit. Credit, however, allows people to 'enjoy now and pay later' and the credit and budget card system provides a convenient, reasonably secure way of making purchases without the need to carry money around with you. Cards are being introduced in a large number of situations and some people argue that we are moving towards a cash free economy.

One very new development is the system of computerised banking introduced by a number of banks. Presentation of a card to a retailer will allow the retailer to debit the customer's account. This, of course, is not credit but is another development of the card system taking advantage of computer technology. This facility is now available from most of the banks.

The various credit developments described here are of course of considerable importance to businesses. There seems little doubt that the growth of the credit card system has had a considerable effect in boosting the levels of retail sales. Retailers have good reason to feel grateful to the 'flexible friend' as the advertisement often calls credit cards such as Access.

Activity

1. Write to Access in Southend-on-Sea and Visa in Northampton to find out more about the operation of the two cards.
2. Try to find out the difference in interest payments charged by:
   (a) Access, (b) Visa, (c) Debenhams, (d) Marks & Spencer, (e) Chargecard.
3. Compare these interest rates with the rates charged by a bank for a personal loan.

10.2 **LENDING**

Let us now turn to lending. Many people have savings and they wish to make the most of these. You will remember that Richard's father, Robert Boyden has £45 000 to invest. There are many ways he could consider investing this. He will need to weigh up various factors.

1. Does he want security for his money or is he willing to take some risk?

2. Does he want to tie up his money for some time or does he want to obtain it at short notice?
3. Does he want to invest in assets which have growth potential?
4. Does he want a regular income from his investment?

Let us then look at several possibilities.

Building Societies

Investment in building societies is very safe but does not result in a very good return. Remember the greater the risk the greater the chance of a good return. Interest payable by building societies varies according to the type of investment and also with the general rate of interest. At this moment (April 1988) rates are quite low.

The Halifax Building Society offer the following rates (All are net of tax):

Card Cash Account	4 per cent
Deposit	3.75 per cent
Regular Saving	5 per cent
High Interest Account	£ 2000+ 6 per cent
	£ 5000+ 6.50 per cent
	£10000+ 6.75 per cent

The interest is quoted net of tax and you will often see the gross figure quoted.

There is little chance of the Halifax Building Society going into liquidation and Robert's money would be quite safe in such an investment.

Activity
Try to obtain details of the present rate of interest paid by any building society by obtaining a brochure from the local office.

Exercise 5
Assume Robert had invested £10 000 in the High Interest Account what would his annual rate of return be.

You will have noticed that rates offered by building societies vary:

1. Higher rates are offered to higher investment.

2. Higher rates are offered if you are willing to keep the money with the Building Society for a fixed period.

You will have noticed, too, that withdrawals are quite easy with the increasing use of cash dispenser machines. Building Societies are now able to offer a range of financial services and this may well make building society investment even more attractive.

Investment in Shares

Robert could, of course, buy shares. We have already seen that there are two types of shares – new issues and existing shares. Many people invested in new issues when buying British Telecom, TSB and British Gas shares. The biggest market, however, is in existing shares and purchasers of shares may gain in two directions:

1. Dividends (a share in the profits) are paid from time to time.
2. Share prices like other prices go up and down and the fortunate investor is the one who bought when the price was low and sold when it was high.

During 1988, to take one example, the Body Shop's shares fluctuated between 260p per share to 925p per share.

> **Exercise 6**
> If Robert has invested £10 000 of his savings in Body Shop when the price was 260p what would he have sold the shares for if he sold at the highest price.

This particular gain is spectacular and an investor would have needed to have bought and sold at the right time. The present price of shares in Body Shop is 610p. Quite a considerable change and as you can see, just as you might gain, you can also lose. If you bought at 960p for example, but had to sell at 610p. The gain made by Robert in his Body Shop share dealing will be subject to a tax known as the capital gains tax which will be referred to in Chapter 16.

Shareholding has become very popular in the UK and the present (1988) government is anxious to promote this. Recent sales of shares in British Telecom, TSB, Britoil and British Gas boosted interest and you will remember considerable amounts of money was spent on advertising. In 1984 there were two million shareholders in the UK, this has grown to nearly ten million and is still rising.

The recent change in the Stock Exchange described in Chapter 7 has aided the small investor. However, the investor will need to pay a fee known as commission. The average fee (1988) is 1.65 per cent. Thus on £10 000 Robert would pay £165 + VAT. An investor can go to his bank but a bank's fees are similar. Banks will use their own brokers. One advantage of using a stock exchange broker or a bank's broker is that if the broker's company should fail then some compensation is available.

Activity

The Times, the *Telegraph*, the *Independent* and the *Guardian* produce share lists on Saturdays. Over the next three or four months follow the fortunes of the following companies:

Sainsburys	(Retailing)
Trusthouse	(Leisure)
Tottenham Hotspur	(Leisure)
George Wimpey	(Building)
Body Shop	(Retailing)
GEC	(Electrical)

The companies are usually listed in groups and you will find them mentioned under the headings suggested.

An example of an entry is as follows, which relates to April 1988.

	Price	+ or −
Storehouse (British Homestores, Habitat and Mothercare)	285p	+12

This shows that 285p was the price of Storehouse shares and during the week they had gained 12 pence.

Unit Trusts

Robert could invest in what are called Unit Trusts. The system operates as follows: the Unit Trust management invests in a wide range of shares and therefore each unit is made up of different shares. Commercial Union for example are at present selling units at 52p per unit and investors are offered three types of unit trust:

1. CU Income Inc. – investment in UK equities (shares).
2. CU UK & General Fund – this is a fund which as the CU puts it attempts to create a stable balance between capital growth and income.
3. CU Worldwide Inc Fund – this fund seeks out spectacular growth potential in worldwide investment.

Commercial Union claim that investors who invested in their Prime Life UK Equity Fund 45 months ago achieved a 151.65 per cent growth.

> **Exercise 7**
> Assume growth is 150 per cent over three years and Robert invests £10 000 of his savings in 1988, what will his investment be in 1991?

Unit Trusts can of course go down and the manager will deduct a fee. On a £10 000 investment for Commercial Union there is a 5 per cent fee plus 1 per cent + VAT per annum. In the first year Robert would pay £500 plus £115. Unit trusts are likely to be very popular and recently we have seen the introduction of PEP – Personal Equity Plans – which are unit trusts.

> **Activity**
> All four major banks offer PEP. Go into one of your local banks and see if you can find out more details.

10.3 INVESTMENT MANAGEMENT

Often investors, rather than wishing to deal with the complex financial world themselves, will place their funds with investment firms who for a fee will manage investment. The investment manager will invest in what he regards as the most lucrative but will also be mindful of security.

An example of such a fund is Framlington's European Fund. This fund claimed a growth from February–December 1986 of 44 per cent, that is 50p–72p.

Before Robert invested his money with an investment company the would wish to know that the company was reliable. Investment companies often boast membership of the Financial Intermediaries Brokers and Managers Regulatory Association (FIMBRA) and as a result of changes in the law all dealers in securities must now be members of FIMBRA or another self-regulatory body approved by the government's Securities and Investment Board, or approved directly by the government's Securities and Investment Board, otherwise they are breaking the law.

However, e.g. the crash of the Canterbury based Macdonald-Wheeler Invesment Group, in 1986 does not inspire great confidence in the FIMBRA organisation and the feeling of the investors in the unfortunate Macdonald–Wheeler company is that FIMBRA will need to prove itself much more if it is to gain the confidence of the small investor.

Exercise 8

Assume that Julie Evans invested £5000 in a unit trust buying units at 50p each.

1. Calculate her gain if the units rose in a year by 130 per cent.
2. Calculate the charges she would pay to the unit trust assuming 5 per cent initial fee, 1 per cent per annum + VAT.

Exercise 9

The following review questions relate to the whole of Chapter 10. Try to answer them without reference to the text. If when you have checked your answers you find you have misunderstood any part then reread that particular section.

1. Calculate the monthly interest repayment on an endowment mortgage of £25 000 assuming an interest rate of 10 per cent.
2. Jack Richards has a mortgage of £10 000, he pays 11 per cent interest
   (a) What are his monthly interest payments?
   (b) How much tax relief will he get (assume 25 per cent standard rate tax)?
3. Maureen Johnson takes out a loan from her bank of £10 000 at 15 per cent for two years, what is the rate of interest in the second year?

4. Rachel Prince buys a stereo stack system for £500 by means of a credit agreement. She loses her job and the credit firm recovers the goods. Is this legal?

5. What is the difference between a Visa card and an American Express card?

6. You have £10 000 to invest. Assume you buy or invest

(a) £2500 worth of 50p unit trusts
(b) £2500 in a High Interest Account with Halifax
(c) £2500 in J. Sainsburys shares
(d) £2500 in a high interest account with the bank

Calculate your gains or losses in a year where:

(a) 75 per cent increase in value in the unit trust
(b) $6\frac{3}{4}$ per cent net interest with Halifax
(c) J. Sainsburys shares fell from 400p–350p
(d) 5 per cent net interest in the bank account

7. Name the recent organisation set up by the government to protect investors.

CHAPTER 11

TRANSPORT AND COMMUNICATIONS

11.1 TRANSPORT

Fortrex plc is a large public company which produces lifting equipment, including fork-lift trucks. It has customers all over the UK and is developing a large overseas market, especially in Africa, India and the Far East, Fortrex's main factory is in Swindon, Wiltshire, but it also has other offices and depots in Leeds and London. The company uses all available means of transport both to obtain materials for its products and to distribute its finished product. The directors of the company and its managers have to do a good deal of travelling, both in this country and abroad. The particular mode of transport which the company uses will depend upon several factors:

1. *Economy* – A company like Fortrex knows that costs of transport are added to costs of production and, therefore, they try to keep costs down as much as possible. Cost is an important consideration when choosing a method of transport.
2. *Speed* – It is often important to transport goods or employees as quickly as possible. Speed can be a key factor in choosing a method of transport, therefore. However, the quickest method may be the most expensive, so the factor of economy must be balanced against the need for speed.
3. *Convenience* – This is a vital factor. Some businessmen choose fast Inter-City rail because it carries them from the centre of one city to the centre of another. However, goods may often be moved by road because they can be transported from one place to another directly, without the need for off-loading on to other vehicles.
4. *Regularity* – Some companies use a particular type of transport because it is regular and reliable. Ships, planes and trains operate

to regular scheduled timetables and companies therefore rely on this.

Let us return to our company, Fortrex plc to see how these factors influence its choice of transport.

Rail Transport

Fortrex plc uses rail transport for several of its services. Managers always travel by Inter-City express from Swindon to London. The company also uses rail transport to send some of its manufactured items to its depot at London. There are clearly advantages and disadvantages attaching to rail transport:

1. Travelling speed is often good because trains can travel more quickly than road vehicles and are not held up by traffic congestions. Fortrex plc's office is in the centre of London, near Baker Street, and the Inter-City express from Swindon terminates nearby at Paddington.
2. Sending goods to London by rail can cause delays. The goods have to be loaded on to vehicles to reach Swindon station and off-loaded again at London. These additional loadings create additional costs. Sometimes delays are caused by problems on the railway, such as signal failure. It is difficult to find alternatives routes when rail services are disrupted.
3. There has been in recent years a large increase in the cost of rail travel. Although a train operated by two employees can carry much greater loads than a fleet of lorries, there are other costs involved. The railways in Britain employ a large number of staff, which, together with the enormous cost of maintaining the track, creates difficulty for rail services in competing with road transport.
4. Although Fortrex uses rail for sending employees and goods to London it does not do so for journeys to Leeds, its other depot. This is because of the time factor. Railways run according to schedules and it would be difficult, for example, to travel from Swindon to Leeds for a lunchtime meeting. A car journey is likely to be much quicker. Timetabling does entail rigidity whereas a car is much more flexible.

Developments in Rail Transport

Containerisation

The difficulties created when goods have to be transferred from lorries to trains at both ends of their journey led to the introduction of special containers. These containers, which look like huge boxes, can be loaded from lorries directly on to purpose-built rail wagons. When the containers reach their destination, they can be loaded directly on to a lorry.

Special Transporters

British Rail can provide special wagons for particular types of loads, such as cars, oil, grain and chemicals.

Parcel Deliveries

British Rail operates a Red Star parcel service, whereby parcels are transported by passenger train. This is a fast and efficient service for businesses but its disadvantage is that the service is available only from certain stations and parcels have to be collected from the station of destination.

Activity

Compare the cost of using the Red Star parcel service of British Rail with sending a parcel by the GPO.

Exercise 1

1. Name the four factors which a businessman might consider when choosing a particular form of transport.
2. Explain why rail transport is very convenient for passengers travelling between large cities.
3. Give two reasons for the high cost of rail travel.
4. List three ways in which British Rail has tried to increase its share of transport business.

Road Transport

Fortrex plc uses road transport for some of its business. It provides its salesmen with cars to enable them to visit their customers. Materials are delivered to its Swindon factory by road and finished products are transported to markets in Britain and to sea ports, ready for export to overseas destinations.

The road network in Britain has been greatly enlarged since the 1950s; the growth of motorway links between major cities has been especially marked. The number of railway lines has been considerably reduced during the same period.

Activity
Try to find an example of a railway line in your area which has been closed in the last twenty years.

Advantages of Road Transport

1. Goods being transported can be off-loaded at their final destination. A person travelling by car can go directly to his destination.
2. Road transport offers flexibility. A Fortrex employee who needs to travel to Leeds can leave when he likes, without being tied to train times or having to plan for rail connections.
3. Exceptionally large single loads, which the railway service cannot take, can be carried by road.
4. Road transport is generally cheaper since the cost of road maintenance is lower than that required to keep the railway service in running order.

Disadvantages of Road Transport

1. Travel time is longer – motorways are geared to fast-moving, traffic but congestion of vehicles slows down even the speediest of drivers.
2. Trains are better equipped to carry bulk loads. One train might transport a very large load of dangerous chemical, for example, which would involve the use of twenty lorries. Bulk transport by rail is cheaper and safer in such circumstances.
3. The *social costs* of road traffic – pollution, noise and expenditure on traffic control, for example – are considerable.

Internal Air Transport

There has been an increase recently in the use of air transport by some of Fortrex's executives. The company has chosen faster air travel for several of its sales meetings in Edinburgh. Fortrex's site at Swindon gives it quick access to Heathrow Airport and executives can leave in the morning, attend an afternoon meeting at Edinburgh and be back home for the evening. This speed is not possible by rail transport. Against this, however, airports are sited away from city centres, making it necessary to obtain transport into the cities.

Alongside the increase in recent years in the use of internal air transport, several British domestic airports have been developed to take large intercontinental flights. Manchester Ringway Airport, for example, provides a direct service to Europe and the USA.

Exercise 2

1. The number of miles of railway track has increased dramatically in the last thirty years. True/false?
2. What do you understand by the term 'social cost' in respect of road transport?
3. Because of the development of motorways, inter-city transport by road is by far the quickest method for passengers. True/false?

Transport to other Countries

Fortrex plc has developed a large export trade for its equipment, both to Europe and to Africa, India and the Far East. Sea transport is used for the export of goods but the company uses air transport to carry staff abroad.

For trade with Europe, Fortrex uses a combination of road and ferries, using ports such as Dover (Kent), Felixstowe (Suffolk) and Immingham (Humberside). These ports have installed sophisticated equipment for handling containers, and lorries can off-load containers for rapid unloading in the European ports of France, Holland, Belgium and Denmark.

For exports to Africa and India, Fortrex plc uses Southampton and London, though Liverpool and Glasgow are also major ports for general cargo traffic.

Fortrex has sales representatives in Africa, India and the Far East who travel back to Britain by fast jets. Air transport between Europe and other continents has almost completely replaced sea transport for passengers. Most people travelling by sea do so for pleasure and most such voyages start from Southampton.

Fortrex will also export smaller spare parts for its equipment by air transport.

Channel Tunnel

A development which is likely to introduce quite a considerable change in the building of what is called a fixed link between this country and France. This tunnel will utilise the shortest route between England and France which is on the Kent coast between Dover and Folkestone. The tunnel is being built by a consortium (group) of French and British companies known as Trans Manche Link (TML). It is a rail tunnel but designed so that vehicles will be able to drive easily onto the regular trains at the terminal at Ashford (Kent). The effect upon the channel ports is difficult to assess but the advantages of a tunnel have been suggested as:

1. It will be open 365 days a year and not affected by weather conditions.
2. It will not affect shipping in the channel since it is below the sea.
3. Fast trains will run between London, Paris and Brussels which will make the air routes somewhat less competitive.
4. The tunnel will be financed by private money and not from government resources.

Activity
Try to find out and compare the costs of travelling by air, road and rail between (a) Manchester to London, (b) Newcastle and London, (c) Cardiff and Birmingham.

Exercise 3
Which form of transport would you use for each of the following?

1. Coal from Newcastle to an electricity power station near London.
2. Expensive jewellery from London to Manchester.
3. Which company is building the Channel Tunnel?

11.2 COMMUNICATIONS AND NEW TECHNOLOGY

All business relies upon communications – it is necessary to communicate with suppliers and customers and businesses require methods which are economical, accurate and efficient. Increasingly new technology is being introduced into business communications.

Telecommunications

Telephone
Businesses rely upon telephone services now provided by British Telecom. Telephones have the advantage of immediate contact and

many businessmen feel that speaking to a customer or supplier on the telephone is more useful than writing letters. The disadvantage of the telephone is that there is no written record of conversations. Direct contact can now be made to most parts of Britain and, increasingly, to many other parts of the world through a system known as STD (subscriber trunk dialling) and IDD (international direct dialling) which enables a caller using a code followed by the number to ring directly. It used to be necessary, to make other than local calls, to ring the exchange and ask for your call. To dial Bristol, for example, the code 0272 is used followed by the number.

Activity
Try to find out if it is possible to telephone the following cities through STD/IDD: Madrid, Lagos, Sydney, Belgrade.

Most larger businesses have installed a system of internal phones so that communications within the company are improved.

There is, of course, a considerable increase in the use of car phones and a businessman 'on the road' can contact head office to see if there are any messages or instructions he ought to be aware of. The radio-pager system which indicates a message is a cheaper option than the car telephone.

The major supplier of telephone systems is British Telecom which is now a public company in the private sector. A number of other private sector companies are now in the market for the supply of equipment, e.g. Merlin, but in a number of cases the equipment must be approved by British Telecom.

Teleprinters
Large firms often use teleprinters, which may be privately owned or alternatively provided by British Telecom and known as Telex. A caller will type his message on to a special machine and this will be simultaneously typed on a similar machine at the required destination. Contact with another telex subscriber is made by dialling their telex number. The advantages of such a system are:

1. A written record is provided.
2. It overcomes the time problem between countries.

For example, if Fortrex wishes to Telex one of its customers in Bombay, it could do so in the afternoon in the United Kingdom (evening in Bombay), and the message will be awaiting the staff at Bombay when they arrive the following morning.

This method of sending messages is expensive, the cost depending upon the length of the message.

Activity
See if you can find examples of Telex names and addresses. They are often printed together with the address of firms on headed notepaper, invoices, delivery notes, etc. Find out also how the radio pager system works.

British Telecom has introduced a *Teletex* system which allows a business person to send an A4 page of text in less than ten seconds. When the letter, for example, arrives at its destination it can be stored and then retrieved at the receiver's convenience and printed and/or displayed on the visual display unit. Note we have used the term Teletex, do not confuse this with *Teletext*, which refers to Ceefax and Oracle services provided by the broadcasting authorities.

A recent development is called Fax whereby documents or photographs can be sent to a destination by being fed into a special machine known as Bureaufax systems.

Another interesting development provided by British Telecom is one where business people can hold conferences despite being in different locations. The service known as Contravision provides studios in cities where sound and vision is linked up so that discussions can take place as if all those attending the meeting were in the same room.

Activity
Go to your nearest British Telecom office or showroom and try to obtain a leaflet or leaflets describing the range of services offered. These are changing and being developed all the time.

Those of you who have been to France will perhaps have noticed how advanced their telephone system is. In Paris the telephone directory has been abolished and subscribers are linked to a very sophisticated computerised system which can locate telephone numbers very quickly indeed.

Postal Services

The Post Office offers a range of services.

Ordinary Letter Post

There is in Britain a two-tier system. First-class post, which is more expensive, is intended to be delivered the day after posting. Second-class post is slower. Automation has been introduced into the service and the use of post codes, e.g. 'DA14 7BT', allows the automatic sorting of letters and therefore a more efficient service.

Recorded Delivery Service

This is a system whereby letters on receipt must be signed for. If, for example, a company sends a reminder to a customer that money is owed and wishes to make sure that the reminder was delivered, it can use this method of checking. The Post Office charges an extra fee for this service.

Registered Post Service

This is a method by which valuables or money can be sent by post. The Post Office will pay compensation, up to a certain amount, if the package is lost.

Freepost

A system which enables a business to attract customers by encouraging them to reply to offers without incurring postal charges. The business will have paid a deposit to the Post Office before sending out the envelopes or cards which customers must use to take up the offers. The word 'FREEPOST' will be set out in the address to which offers must be returned and the Post Office will deduct all postal charges incurred from the deposit paid. A similar system to the freepost system is the business reply system.

Express Delivery

For an extra charge an express service can be used whereby a letter is sent in the ordinary way but a messenger delivers it from the Post Office to the destination. For example, if Templet plc wishes to send a letter to Bury in Lancashire by this method, the letter will arrive at the postal sorting office at Bury and then will be delivered personally. An alternative method is to use Railex, whereby the letter is sent by the first available train and then delivered by messenger.

Other services which the Post Office mail service provide include parcel delivery services and air mail for speedy service overseas (all letters to European destinations are sent by air).

The increasing use of computers in business has resulted in another service being offered by the Post Office. This is known as DataPost and is used for delivering computer data. Packages are collected from the sender at an agreed time and delivered the next morning.

The Post Office and Competition

A number of businesses use other organisations for parcel and letter delivery. In London a number of firms offer courier services often using motor cycles. A number of firms offer nationwide and world-wide delivery services. This competition is causing the Post Office to think about the quality of its services and whether it can guarantee 'next day' first-class letter delivery.

Computers and Word Processors

Computers are being used more and more in businesses because they are machines which can provide businesses with quick, accurate and efficient information. Our company, Fortrex plc, has already got a number of its functions computerised.

1. All the Fortrex secretarial staff are trained as *word processor* operators and they type on these machines. Word processors are merely computers which are programmed (organised) to process words. They allow letters to be stored and amended without the typist having to retype the letter.
2. *Accounting.* Fortrex has completely computerised its accounting system. Customers are sent invoices, statements and demand notices by computer. The company's accounts can be produced quite easily using this system.
3. *Payroll.* Records are kept of hours worked, sickness, tax, etc on all employees. Fortrex employees receive pay advice slips printed by the computer and their salaries are paid into the bank.
4. *Stock Control.* Fortrex can keep a record of all its stock both of finished products and raw materials.
5. Fortrex has a *management information system* so that managers can have up-to-date information on the company to make decisions much more reliable.

Computers carry out five types of operation.

1. *Accessing data from a user* – this is usually done by the user tapping in the information on the keyboard. This is known as input.

2. *Supplying data to a user* – the user might ask for information and this is produced on the visual display unit (VDU).
3. *Processing data* – this can involve sorting and selecting, making calculations or even making simple decisions.
4. *Storing data* – this is stored in the memory but also on what are called floppy discs.
5. *Communicating data between computers in a network* or over longer distances using telephone or satellite links.

The three charts in Figure 11.1 show

Figure 11.1

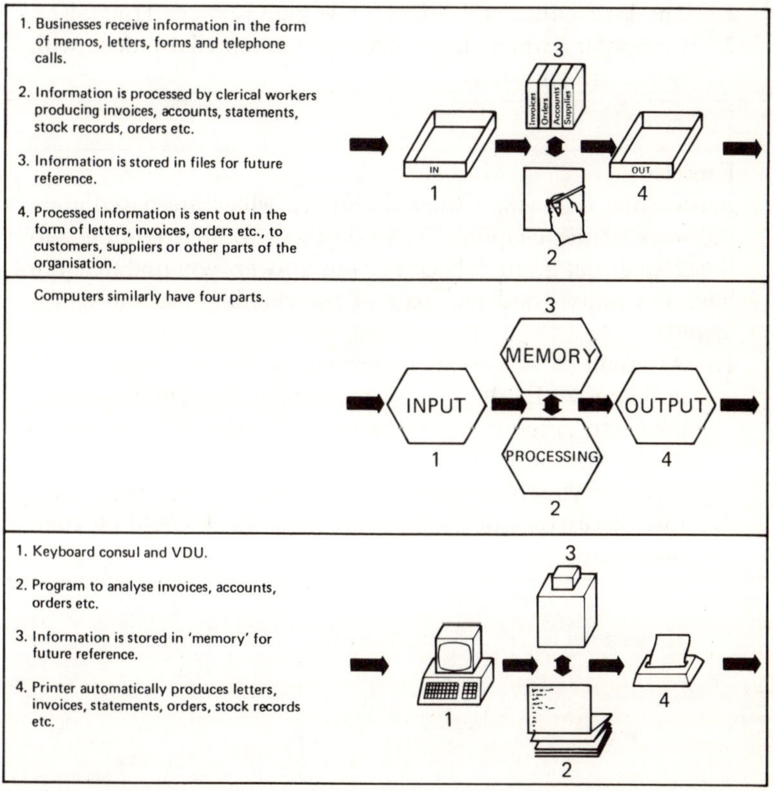

1. A business system in four parts.
2. A computer system in four parts: input, processing, memory, output
3. The actual system

It is not possible here to examine in detail the work being done by computers and word processors, but it is an important and very rapid development. Many developments are taking place and a good deal of progress has been made in voice recognition which would make it unnecessary to even use the keyboard.

Activity
See if you can find examples of word processors and computers being used in business.

Exercise 4

1. The Post Office still offers a telegram service. True/false?
2. Computers which have been programmed to deal with words are known as . . . .

Exercise 5
Answer the following review questions, which are based upon the work of this chapter. Try to do them without reference to the chapter but if after checking your answers you find that you have not understood that part of the chapter read through it again.

1. Armfield plc is a company producing watches and is based in Glasgow. Explain the factors which the company might take into account when choosing its form of transport to destinations in the South of England.
2. List five types of postal service provided by the Post Office.
3. List three types of business function which could be computerised.

CHAPTER 12

INTERNATIONAL TRADE

Very few countries can exist just using goods and services which they produce themselves, and therefore it is necessary for countries to trade with each other. This trading between countries is known as international trade. Britain, for example, cannot produce such materials as copper, gold and uranium, nor foods like oranges, lemons, tea and coffee, to name but a few, and it therefore has to import copper from Zambia, gold and uranium from South Africa, oranges and lemons from Spain and Israel, tea from India, coffee from Brazil. Britain, however, is a manufacturing country and exports goods such as vehicles and machinery to other countries. As you know, Britain is now a large producer of oil and some of this is exported. Britain also imports goods which it does produce; in recent years there has been a large increase in the imports of cars into Britain from Japan, Germany, Sweden, Italy and France. This is because often these countries are able to produce cars more cheaply than Britain and increasingly foreign cars are gaining a reputation for greater reliability.

Thus *imports* are goods coming in from another country and *exports* are goods going out. When a country imports goods, money is spent, but when a country exports goods, money is earned. Countries are involved in international trade for the following reasons:

1. Some countries have certain natural advantages which allow them to produce more of certain goods than they need, while other countries – e.g. the UK, in the case of oranges – do not have the natural conditions or resources needed to produce those goods.
2. Countries concentrate upon what they can do most efficiently. Although wheat grows in Britain, for example, nevertheless Britain exports manufactured goods in exchange for wheat

because it is more advantageous to use resources in manufacturing rather than growing wheat. Some what is grown in the UK, but not all UK demands are met by home-grown wheat and it is necessary to import wheat from countries such as Canada.

3. A country will use its surplus of one produce to buy other products. Thus a country like Kuwait could not possibly use all the oil it produces so it exports a good deal of its oil to pay for imports that it requires.

12.1 BALANCE OF PAYMENTS

Britain's balance of payments figures, which are published regularly, are a statement of the country's financial transactions with the rest of the world. They resemble a national cash book.

Figure 12.1 shows the balance-of-payments figures for a recent year.

Figure 12.1

Current account	*£m*
Visible trade	
Exports	78 051
Imports	80 162
Visible balance	−2 111
Invisible	
Credits	42 623
Debits	36 910
Invisible balance	+5 713
Current balance	+3 602

Visible Trade

You will notice from Figure 12.1 that there was a visible balance of £2111 million. 'Visible' trade means goods, i.e. tangible things that can be touched or seen: so the UK imported £2111 million more in goods than it exported.

Britain exports mainly manufactured goods, goods which have been made and assembled. Examples of British exports include machinery, motor vehicles and engines. The total value of exports was £78 051 million. British imports, i.e. goods coming into the UK, totalled £80 162 million. Britain imports raw materials for its industries – copper, timber and iron, for example. The UK also imports foodstuffs such as cereals, fruits, butter, meat. In recent years there has been a large increase in the import of manufactured goods into the UK, as pointed out earlier. Motor-cars are a good example of this: almost half of all the new cars bought in the UK are foreign. Another example is the import of motor-cycles: Japan, with such well-known makes as Kawasaki, Suzuki and Yamaha, has now a virtual monopoly in the sale of motor-cycles in the UK. In fact the large increase in the import of manufactured goods into the UK has been a cause for concern, as British manufacturing industry finds it increasingly difficult to compete with foreign manufacturers. As you can see the UK visible balance was in deficit, i.e. a minus figure.

Invisible Trade

Invisible trade means the trade in services, i.e. not goods which can be seen or touched. Invisible imports are such things as British people going abroad for their holidays. British people booking air flights with foreign airlines, the payment of British soldiers stationed in West Germany. A foreign company may own businesses in the UK and as the profits and interest payments are paid out this represents an invisible import.

Figure 12.2

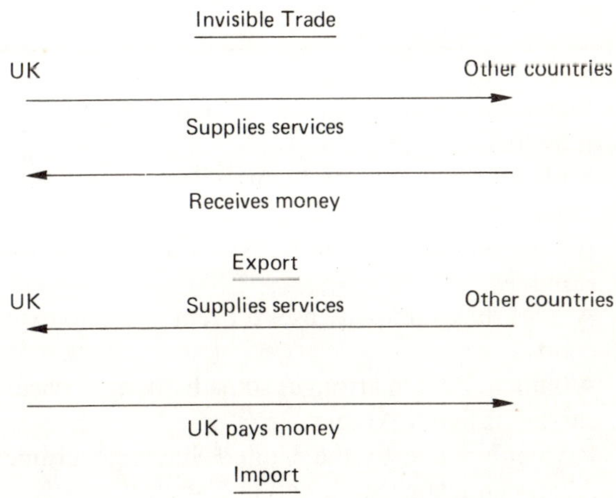

An invisible import then is something which is not tangible, i.e. not a good, and causes money to go out of the UK. If someone books a flight with Lufthansa, the German airline, Germany will receive the money. It is possible to identify an invisible import by the flow of money. If money is going out of the UK then for the UK this will be an import.

The UK had a favourable current balance. Although it had a deficit on its visible trade, i.e. £2111 million, this was more than made up for by its surplus on the invisible trade, i.e. £5713 millions.

If we add the two together: Visible Balance – £2111m + Invisible Balance + £5713, we get an overall balance of £3602 million.

Invisible exports are services for which the UK receives money. If any American spends a holiday in the UK, money will come into the country. The UK is very much the insurance centre of the world and many foreign companies take out insurance with British insurance companies. The UK also provides banking services for many countries and these services are paid for. Shipping and air services are provided by British merchant ships and British airlines. An invisible export results in money coming into the country. If a foreign shipping company insures its vessels with Lloyd's of London then the premiums are paid into the UK, i.e. an export. It is possible to identify an invisible export by the flow of money. If the money is flowing into the UK then for the UK this will be an export.

In the example you can see that Britain exported more invisibles than she imported. In fact the *invisible balance* was + £5713 million, i.e. exports exceeded imports by £5713 million.

Exercise 1

1. The difference between the export and import of goods is known as the . . . .
2. Which of the following are (a) invisible exports, (b) invisible imports?
   - **(a)** A London businessman books a flight on Air India to Bombay.
   - **(b)** A Yorkshire company uses a French ship to export its goods.
   - **(c)** A bank in Britain arranges some banking services for a citizen of Saudi Arabia.
   - **(d)** Payments made by the United States government to American troops stationed in Cambridge, UK.
3. When the visible and invisible balances are totalled, the result is what sort of balance?

> **Activity**
> Each year the government's statistical office produces a summary of the balance-of-payments accounts. Try to obtain a copy from your library so that you are able to see the up-to-date position.

The balance of payments summarises all the income received and all the payments made by a country. It also records movements of capital, e.g. if a British company invests money in an overseas undertaking this will be recorded. The figures in Figure 12.1 show only the *current* balance and for this year it was favourable. If a country has a favourable balance it can use it to increase its reserves of foreign currency or to repay loans it may have had to make in the past. The world bank, known as IMF (International Monetary Fund), will make loans to countries in difficulty but these have to be repaid. A country's reserves can also be used for times when the balance is not favourable or at these times a country can borrow from IMF or from another country's central bank.

If a country is in debt it can:

1. draw on its reserves
2. borrow from another country usually a central bank
3. borrow from the International Monetary Fund (IMF).

Countries cannot, however, go on doing this and like a person in debt it is necessary for a country to put its own house in order.

12.2 PROTECTION AND FREE TRADE

When a country is finding that imports are affecting its own industries – e.g. imports of foreign cars into the UK are having an adverse affect upon home car manufacturers – then there will be some people who argue that protection be given to the country's industries by stopping imports. There are others who say that the best policy is free trade and if industry cannot compete effectively then it ought not to be protected. There are several ways of imposing protection.

1. *Tariffs (or custom duties)* – An extra charge is put on to the imported goods so that when they go into the shops they are dearer.

2. *Quotas* – Only a limited amount of a particular good may be imported. Some argue that a quota should be put on Japanese cars.
3. *Subsidies* – This is a method by which the home producer is given money so that he can price his goods more cheaply to compete with foreign goods.

12.3 EXPORTING

In Chapter 11 we learned that Fortrex plc was a large exporter of lifting gear including fork-lift trucks. The company has built up quite a lot of trade with various countries and it has used a variety of methods to sell its goods abroad.

1. Fortrex plc sells some of its products to France using buying agents. These are agents employed by French firms resident in the UK whose job it is to buy goods for export to France.
2. Export houses. Some products are sold to export houses, which are merchants who specialise in exporting. The benefit of dealing with such organisations is that they will handle all the documentation involved in foreign trade.
3. Overseas exporting agents. For its trade with India and Pakistan, Fortrex deals with overseas agents, which are firms based in these two countries and which specialise in importing. Clearly one advantage of this sort of dealing is that the agent, usually being an agent of that country, is very familiar with the conditions in that country.
4. Because of its strong links with Nigeria, Fortrex has helped to finance the building of a factory which produces lifting gear in Lagos. The factory, owned by Nigerians, produces the goods according to Fortrex's specification, and when they are sold a proportion of the profits (royalties) go to Fortrex. This is known as licensing. The foreign company produces the goods under licence.
5. Most of Fortrex's export trade, however, is done by its own well-organised export department. The company has a number of salesmen based overseas and these are linked to its export department.

Export Documentation

When a company exports goods overseas it is necessary for it to prepare various documents in respect of the goods. In this section we will be dealing with these documents briefly and we will use the following example to explain the various procedures.

Bill of Exchange

Fortrex plc has received an order from a German company, Deutz GMBH of Dortmund, for the supply of goods to the value of £50 000. Deutz GMBH requires a certain amount of credit, which is often the case in export trade. The usual practice is for the exporter – Fortrex plc – to draw up a bill of exchange like the one shown in Figure 12.2.

Figure 12.3

£50 000

Fortrex plc
Swindon
Wiltshire
UK
1 February 1988

Ninety days after sight pay Midland Bank, High Street, Swindon the account of Fortrex plc 4243692 the sum of fifty thousand pounds.

Signed ....

P. Newman
Director
Fortrex plc

Deutz GMBH
Dortmund

A bill of exchange is an order in writing addressed by one person (or company) to another person (or company) requiring the person or company to pay at some specified time a certain sum of money. In our example it indicates that the £50 000 be paid within ninety days. When Deutz receives this bill of exchange and when it has received the bill of lading, the company will accept the bill of exchange. Because the bill of lading is the document which gives ownership of the goods, it will usually be sent to a bank in Dortmund and will be released only when the bill of exchange is accepted. The bill of exchange is then sent to the exporter's (Fortrex plc's) bank.

The exporter can do one of three things:

1. He can wait for ninety days, after which Deutz will pay into the Midland Bank.
2. He can ask the bank (Midland) to pay him the money straight away, i.e. the bank will discount the bill, pay Fortrex £50 000 less interest and then collect when the ninety days fall due.
3. If Deutz is not a well-known firm the bank may not be willing to discount it and Fortrex will need to go to a specialist acceptance house. These houses have a good knowledge of overseas buyers and, for a fee the acceptance house will accept the bill, i.e. sign on it and the Midland Bank will then discount it.

There are a number of other documents used in export.

Bill of Lading
This is the document of title of the goods, i.e. it is the document which the importer has to produce to lay claim to the goods. There are three copies:

1. One goes to the sender of the goods, i.e. Fortrex.
2. The second goes to the captain of the ship transporting the goods.
3. The third is sent, attached to the bill of exchange, to a bank – in our example a bank in Dortmund. The bill of lading is given to the importer only when he accepts the bill of exchange.

Airway Bill
If goods are sent by air the bill of lading is replaced by a document known as the airway bill, which is similar to the bill of lading.

Certificate of Insurance
This provides proof that the goods have been insured against loss or damage during transit and it is sent to the importer so that he can claim if there is damage.

Certificate of Origin
Some countries impose tariffs (import duty) on goods coming from certain countries. However, countries in the EEC (European Economic Community) have free trade arrangements between them. Goods from the UK to West Germany do not pay tariffs but, in order for the

West German authorities to be sure that the goods have not been made elsewhere and sent to the UK for further export, it requires a certificate of origin signed by an offical of the British government certifying that the goods sent by Fortrex are really British made.

The system of documentation is set out in Figure 12.4.

Figure 12.4 *Documents used in exporting*

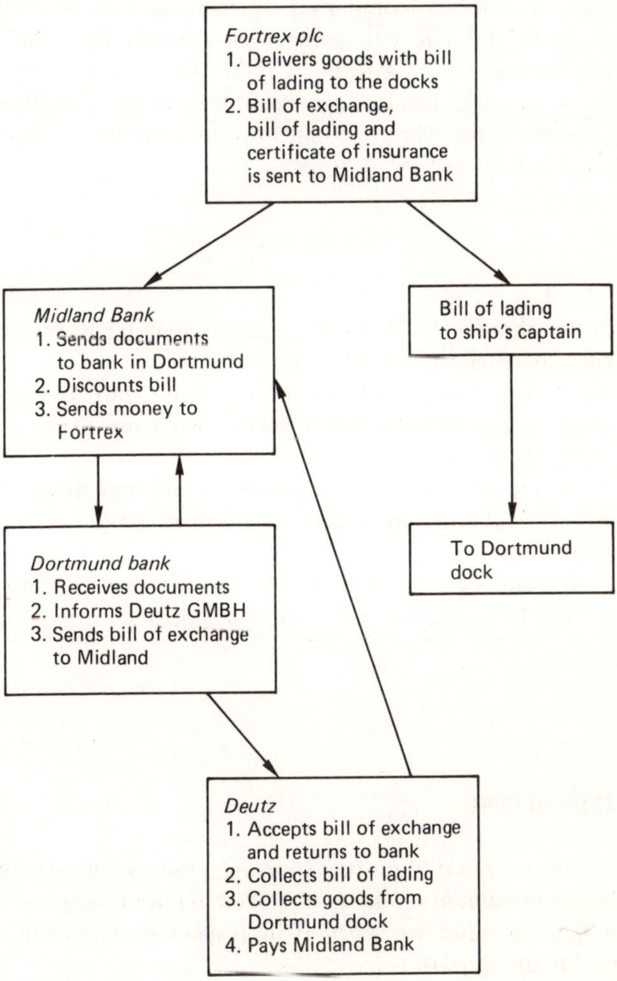

Insurance

When a company engages in overseas trade it is taking a greater risk than trading at home. If Fortrex for example exports goods it faces such problems as:

1. political troubles in the importing country, which may affect payment;
2. the company importing failing to pay;
3. civil war, which may interrupt payment;
4. new currency and import regulations which may be introduced.

In order to protect companies against such eventualities the government in the UK will provide insurance. The insurance is arranged through the Export Credit Guarantee Department (ECGD), which will insure exports under certain conditions. The ECGD operates just like a normal insurance company, though the premiums are kept as low as possible.

Exercise 2

1. Name three ways in which a country may try to protect its own industries against foreign imports.
2. Name five ways a company may obtain export orders.
3. Name the document which gives ownership in an export transaction.
4. If an importer is not well known, a bank may discount the bill of exchange only after a certain guarantee – what is this?
5. Name the organisation run by the government which is willing to insure the risks run by exporters.

12.4 IMPORTING

We have concentrated so far on exporting goods. However, there is a good deal of documentation, etc. involved in importing goods. In fact a good deal of what we learned in respect of exporting will be reversed for the importer.

Customs

Some goods, as we have learned, pay import duty and when goods arrive in the UK the importer must file an entry giving details of the goods. As pointed out earlier, importers provide a certificate of origin.

1. If the goods are duty free an 'entry for free goods' form is used. If the Customs officials are satisfied that the goods detailed on the form coincide with the goods to be imported they will be released.
2. If the goods carry duty an 'entry for home use ex ship' form is used; the amount of duty is determined and when it has been paid the goods are released.
3. In the case of goods paying large amounts of duty, e.g. spirits and tobacco, the Customs authorities will allow the goods to be stored in bonded warehouses and goods will be released to the importer gradually as the duty is paid. This service prevents the importer having to pay a large amount of duty on goods at once.

12.5 **TRADING BLOCS**

In order to encourage trade between countries and in order to promote more uniformity in economic affairs countries will often form themselves into groups. One example is the European Economic Community (EEC). The EEC comprises at present twelve countries in Europe, including the UK and the Irish Republic. Import duties between the countries in the EEC are gradually being abolished and duties paid on goods from other countries are uniform, i.e. goods imported from India will carry the same duty whether they are coming into West Germany or France or the UK. There are other examples of trading groups, e.g. ECOWAS – The Economic Community of West African States. There are sixteen member countries including Nigeria, Ivory Coast and Ghana.

Recently there has been quite a considerable amount of criticism of the EEC by people in the UK especially of what is called CAP (the Common Agricultural Policy). This has resulted, in the view of some people, in higher prices for foodstuffs and has given too much protection to farmers. The much criticised butter and grain mountains and the so-called wine lake have been compared with the terrible shortages of food existing in parts of eastern and central Africa.

Activity

Try to find out more about the working of the EEC and try to list the advantages and disadvantages to Britain of membership. Find out who the European Member of Parliament is for your area.

Activity

In 1992 the countries of the EEC will work as one market, i.e. a single European market. The Department for Enterprise (DTI) has produced an information folder '*Europe Open for Business*'. Try to obtain a copy by writing to DTI,1–19 Victoria Street, London SW1H OET, or ringing 01–200–1992, DTI's special 1992 hotline.

Exercise 2

The following review questions are based upon the whole of this chapter. Try to do them without reference to the chapter. If you find on checking the answers that you do not understand any particular part read the section over again.

1. Give four examples of invisible exports from Britain.
2. Give two examples of how a country might be able to finance an unfavourable current balance of payments.
3. Explain why manufacturers of cigarettes might store imported tobacco in bonded warehouses.
4. Explain the term 'discounting of a bill of exchange'.
5. What is the purpose of a certificate of origin?
6. Name the document used instead of a bill of lading if goods are transported by air.
7. When one manufacturer allows another manufacturer in another country to produce its goods this is known as . . . .
8. What does CAP stand for?

CHAPTER 13

TRADING DOCUMENTS

As we learned in Chapter 11, Fortrex plc is a company producing lifting gear and its reputation is growing in this field. It receives many enquiries in relation to its products and following a visit by one of Fortrex's sales staff a company in Carlisle, Redbridge Storage plc, make an enquiry. We will use this to trace the various documents which are involved in trading.

Now turn the page.

13.1 THE LETTER OF ENQUIRY

REDBRIDGE STORAGE PLC

Our Ref. FB/BWJ

40 Great Castle Street
Carlisle
CA4 8DJ
Tel Carlisle 463261
16.5.88

Dear Sir

Following a visit of your sales representative, Mr Sampson, we should be pleased to receive up-to-date details of your prices in respect of:

Fork lift trucks
Hand generated lifting equipment

Could you advise also on current delivery dates, carriage terms and discounts available.
Yours faithfully

G Brown

G Brown
Managing Director

This is a general letter of enquiry and as you can see the buyer Redbridge plc is asking for any discounts.

13.2 THE QUOTATION

Fortrex plc
Telephone: Swindon 23264
Telex: 43264

89 Railway Lane
Swindon
Wilts
SW4 6BT
20 May 1988

Dear Sir

I reply to your letter of the 16 May 1988 and have pleasure in enclosing our catalogue which contains details of the equipment you require. All prices include carriage to anywhere in the UK and terms are net. Delivery is within 6 weeks of an order.

I look forward to hearing from you.

Yours faithfully

S Lambert

S Lambert
Sales Director

As you can see the seller, Fortrex, has sent a catalogue and explained delivery dates. You will also have noticed that no discount is given, the terms are net which means that the prices are those in the catalogue.

13.3 THE ORDER

Order Form

Redbridge Storage plc
40 Great Castle Street
Carlisle
CA4 8DJ
Tel: 463261

Order No 88/1348

To: Fortrex plc
Swindon

26.5.88

Please supply

Quantity		Description	Price
1	Forklift Truck Cat. No. 43.26.321	Lifteasy	£3260
1	Hand operated lift Cat. No. 47.28.421		£1400
		Total	£4660

Deliver to above address within 6 weeks of the receipt of this order.

Signed G Brown

G Brown. Managing Director

This official order form tells the seller:

1. the goods and quantity required;
2. the place of delivery;
3. the expected date of delivery;
4. the price the buyer expects to pay.

Sometimes orders are placed by telephone. If this is so the telephone order will be followed up by a written order known as a confirming order. It will usually have the word 'confirmation' typed across it.

Orders will always bear a number, e.g. 88/1348, so that it can be identified and will be quoted on all correspondence in respect of the order.

13.4 THE ACKNOWLEDGEMENT

It is likely that Fortrex will send a note acknowledging they have received the order and advising Redbridge when they might expect delivery.

Fortrex plc
Telephone: Swindon 23264
Telex: 43264

89 Railway Lane
Swindon
Wilts
SW4 6BT
28.5.88

We hereby acknowledge receipt of your order no 88/1348 and confirm that we will deliver the specified goods within 6 weeks of the date indicated above.

Fortrex plc

You will note that Fortrex has quoted the order number.

Exercise 1

1. What does net terms mean?
2. What is a confirmation order?
3. Give the three stages from the letter of enquiry?

13.5 THE ADVICE NOTE

Fortrex will now send an advice note which is usually sent just before delivery advising Redbridge that they can expect delivery within the next few days.

Fortrex plc
Telephone: Swindon 23264
Telex: 43264

89 Railway Lane
Swindon
Wilts
SW4 6BT
23.6.88

Advice Note No. 4048

Dispatch by road	Order No. 88/1348	Terms Net
1 Forklift Truck Cat. No. 43.26.321		£3260
1 Hand operated lift Cat. No. 47.28.421		£1400

Delivery to Redbridge plc, Carlisle

13.6 THE DELIVERY NOTE

When the goods are delivered they will be accompanied by a Delivery Note which will look exactly like the Advice Note except that in place of Advice Note number it will have Delivery Note number 4048. Another difference is that no prices are shown.

Fortrex uses for this delivery West Wilts Haulage Service Ltd and the delivery note known also as a consignment note allows Redbridge plc to check the actual delivery against the details on the note.

Fortrex plc
Telephone: Swindon 23264
Telex: 43264

89 Railway Lane
Swindon
Wilts
SW4 6BT
23.6.88

Delivery Note No. 4048

Dispatch by road | Order No. 881348 | Terms Net

1 Forklift Truck Cat. No. 43.26.321	£3260
1 Hand operated lift Cat. No. 47.28.421	£1400

Delivery to Redbridge plc, Carlisle

13.7 INVOICE

Following delivery Redbridge will receive an Invoice which shows the amount of money owed by Redbridge for this delivery. It will also contain details of the Value Added Tax (VAT). VAT at present 15 per cent is charged only on the net price but in our example no discounts are allowed therefore the actual price quoted is the net price.

£3260 + 15 per cent VAT = £3749
(£489)
£1400 + 15 per cent VAT = £1610
(£210)

The invoice would look something like the invoice overleaf.

Fortrex plc				89 Railway Lane
Telephone: Swindon 23264				Swindon
Telex: 43264				Wilts
				SW4 6BT
				4.7.88

Invoice No. 84048

To: Redbridge Carlisle Order No. 87/1348 Terms net

Quantity	*Description*	*Price*		*Amount*
1	Forklift truck	Lifteasy	3260	
	Cat. No. 43.26.321			
		VAT	489	
				3749
1	Hand operated lift		1400	
	Cat. No. 47.28.421			
		VAT	210	1610
	Amount outstanding			5359

E & OE

Note that the order number is always quoted so the buyer can relate the invoice to a delivery. The Invoice always has a number. It always contains the letters E & OE which means 'Errors and Omissions Excepted'. This protects the seller should there be an error in the Invoice if the total had been typed out wrongly to read £53.50 then the seller has the right to change it and charge the buyer the correct amount £5350.

13.8 VALUE ADDED TAX

This is tax imposed by the government on goods and is presently 15 per cent of the value. You will remember that it is charged on the net price after any allowed discount.

Exercise 2
Grocery Suppliers plc supplies goods to the Corner Shop value £2500 with a discount of 25 per cent. Calculate the VAT and total price to be paid by the corner shop to Grocery Supplies plc.

Some goods pay no VAT and are known as zero rated VAT = 0 per cent. See if you can find examples of goods which are zero rated. Some goods are exempt which means that the buyer can reclaim the VAT back. If a school bought £2500 worth of goods from Grocery Supplies plc they would only pay £1875 because the VAT would be reclaimable.

13.9 CREDIT NOTES AND DEBIT NOTES

From time to time it is necessary for a supplier (e.g. Fortrex) to make adjustments to the purchaser (Redbridge). If Redbridge has overpaid or been charged too much they will receive a Credit Note, if they have under paid or been charged too little they will receive a Debit Note. To distinguish them the notes are usually printed on different coloured paper.

13.10 STATEMENT OF ACCOUNT

This is a summary of all the transactions over the last month and will show the amount outstanding which the customer has to pay. An example of a statement sent out to Redbridge appears below.

Fortex plc
Telephone: Swindon 23264
Telex: 43264

89 Railway Lane
Swindon
Wilts
SW4 6BT
1.8.87

To: Redbridge plc
40 Great Castle Street
Carlisle
CA4 8DJ

Date	*Details*	*Debits*	*Credits*	*Amount*
1.7.88	To account rendered June			£3250
4.7.88	Invoice No. 84048	£53.59		£8609
8.7.88	Credit Note 46326		£150	£8459
12.7.88	Debit Note 46328	£50		£8509
22.7.88	Cash Received		£3250	£5259
		Amount outstanding		£5250

E & OE

The Statement of Account shows:

1. Details of an account which has appeared in the July Statement 1.7.88.
2. Details of all invoices, credits and debits.
3. Details of cash paid by the customer – on 22 July 1988. Redbridge had settled the bill for £3250.
4. The amount outstanding is also shown.

You will note that the Statement of Account contains the letters E & OE.

Exercise 3
Try to answer the following review questions without reference to the chapter. If on checking your answers you find you have not understood some part then reread this.

1. If a supplier offers 15 per cent discount if the account is settled within ten days, what is the level of discount in £1000?
2. What does the term 'net' mean?
3. Explain the purpose of an Advice Note.
4. Give main differences between an Advice Note and a Delivery Note.
5. Calculate the amount payable on a £225 account + 15 per cent VAT.
6. What is the difference between zero rated and exempt?
7. What does E & OE mean?
8. What is another name for a delivery note when a supplier uses another firm to carry the goods?

CHAPTER 14

CONSUMER PROTECTION

Governments attach considerable importance nowadays to protection of consumers (buyers) against unfair business practices. Acts of Parliament have been passed to safeguard customers against such dangers as dishonest advertising, purchase of faulty goods and imposition of harsh credit repayment terms.

14.1 RIGHTS UNDER THE SALE OF GOODS ACT 1979

Bob Bleasdale is employed by an oil company and has to spend time working abroad. He earns very good money and, following a trip overseas, decides to purchase various items for his home, his wife and himself. Bob buys the following goods: a video recorder for £350, two continental quilts described as 'real eider', a secondhand pinewood dresser for £185, a camera for £250, purchased from a photographic shop.

Bob must be particularly unlucky. The video recorder fails to function, the continental quilts are not made of real eider, he learns that the pinewood dresser was stolen, and he has to return it and, finally, he discovers the camera is quite unsuitable for his purpose.

Bob is given some protection by the Sale of Goods Act 1979, which lays down that consumer sales, i.e. sales by a business to an individual, are governed by its terms. All Bob's purchases fall into the consumer sales category.

1. Goods bought in a consumer sale must be of merchantable quality. This means that they must work properly. If a video recorder costs £350, it is reasonable to expect that it will work. If it fails to function, it is not of merchantable quality and Bob can receive back his money. Obviously, goods bought very cheaply are not expected to last as long as expensive goods.

2. Goods which are bought by description must be as described. If the quilts packages say 'pure eider', but the filling is not of this material, the buyer can seek compensation by getting his money back.
3. Buyers are justified in assuming that the shopkeeper has, as the law puts it, 'good title' to the goods. This means the shopkeeper either owns the goods or, if he does not, has the right to sell them. If the goods are stolen, the shopkeeper does not have this right in reality, and Bob has the right to a full money refund for the pinewood dresser.
4. Where a specialist retailer is consulted, as in the case of Bob and his camera, the buyer is entitled to assume that the goods are 'fit for the purpose' advertised. Note that this provision applies only where a specialist retailer is consulted. It does not apply to advice received, say, from a supermarket sales assistant about the quality of a brand of washing powered.

Shopkeepers cannot deprive purchasers of their rights under the Sale of Goods Act, and manufacturers' guarantees or warranties, as they are usually called, often contain a statement to this effect, e.g. 'This warranty does not affect your statutory rights under the Sale of Goods Act.' 'Statutory' means by Act of Parliament.

Rights under the Sale of Goods Act do not apply to private sales, however. The term *caveat emptor*, 'let the buyer beware', applies to private sales. If, for example, you decide to buy a motor-car privately and this car fails to work properly, you will not be able to claim any rights under the Sale of Goods Act.

14.2 TRADE DESCRIPTIONS ACT 1968 AND 1972

It is illegal under this Act to describe goods wrongly. A trader who breaks the law faces criminal proceedings which could lead to a fine or imprisonment. In some circumstances the trader will be liable to pay the buyer compensation as ordered by the court. Fines of up to £2000 are possible and magistrates can order compensation up to this amount.

False Description of Goods

Philip wants to strip paint from his front door, and he sees in a shop a product called Remova, described as being able to remove all paint with just one application. Philip pays £14.20 for two boxes of the product. He follows the directions exactly but finds that little paint is removed. The shop stocking this falsely described produce has broken the Trade Descriptions Act 1968.

The *Trade Description Act* also applies to services and a holiday-maker, for example, may receive compensation if his holiday does not match the description.

Stanley Davey has booked a holiday in one of the Greek resorts and his hotel is described as being within walking distance of the sea and with breathtaking views of the surrounding coastline. Stanley pays £315 for a ten day stay with full en-suite facilities, but the hotel is seven miles from the sea and the view is across a housing estate. He has to walk along two corridors to the nearest bathroom.

If a case is brought under the Trade Descriptions Act then Stanley could be granted compensation from the travel agent who booked the holiday or the actual tour operator.

The Trade Descriptions Act makes it an offence to falsely describe the origin of goods. If goods are made in South Africa then this must be stated.

False Description of the Price of Goods

Rachel buys a dress in a sale for '£18.50, reduced from £25'. She later discovers that the shop at which the sale took place has never sold the dress for more than £18.50. The shop is liable to prosecution, therefore, under the Trade Descriptions Act 1968. The Act stipulates that cut-price goods must have been offered for sale at the higher price advertised for at least twenty-eight days in the previous six months.

The *Consumer Protection Act 1987* – extends the period for reductions to 28 days within one year rather than six months but it does allow shops to disclaim liability by indicating 'not all goods displayed in this shop have been on display at the old price for 28 days'.

Philip, Stanley and Rachel could refer their cases to their local branches of the Citizen's Advice Bureau, for that organisation to investigate and take up the complaints under the Trade Descriptions Act.

Exercise 1

1. What is a consumer sale?
2. A manufacturer's warranty given with a new product can reduce your rights under the Sale of Goods Act 1979. True/false?

3. State two offences created by the Trade Descriptions Act 1968.
4. What changes have been introduced by the Consumer Protection Act 1987.

14.3 OTHER ACTS OF PARLIAMENT WHICH PROTECT THE CUSTOMER

Prices Act 1974

Where goods sold by weight are prepacked, the weight must be shown and the price per pound indicated.

Weights and Measures Act 1963

Requires many items to have the quantity stated on the package.

Food and Drugs Act 1955

Makes it an offence to sell food which is unfit for human consumption. It also requires that the composition of food products be stated clearly on packaging. The percentage of artificial colouring, for example, must be clearly indicated.

Activity
Examine your next food purchases and look out for the statements on weight and composition of the products.

Unsolicited Goods and Services Act 1971

Goods sent by a supplier to someone who has not requested them are described as being 'unsolicited'. It is illegal, under the 1971 Act, to demand money from recipients of unsolicited goods. If the recipient requests that unsolicited goods be taken away, and this is not done within thirty days, the goods become the property of the recipient. Where no request is made by the recipient, the goods automatically become his property if the supplier does not reclaim them within six months.

Consumer Protection Act 1961

The government has powers, under this Act, to introduce regulations to safeguard consumers from risks caused by faulty goods.

14.4 OTHER PROTECTION

1. Traders often join together to form associations devoted to maintaining high standards of working practice in their industry. For example, most travel agents belong to the Association of British Travel Agents (ABTA).
2. Nationalised industries are scrutinised by consumer consultative councils which have powers to investigate complaints of malpractice.
3. The Consumers' Association is strongly established as a watchdog for customers' complaints. Its magazine *Which?* is read widely for its thorough reports on product quality and standard of service.
4. Standards labels: a number of institutions allow manufacturers to display a sign indicating the goods have come up to specification. The British Standards Institute safety mark is an example.

> **Activity**
> See if you can find other examples of standards labels on goods you have bought recently.

14.5 CONSUMER CREDIT

Shops carry many invitations to customers to buy goods on credit, and several credit arrangements are available to customers. It is possible to buy goods on hire purchase, credit sale or through a budget account with a shop.

> **Activity**
> Look out for the various types of credit arrangement which are available in your local shops.

The following example illustrates the difference between hire purchase and credit sales and also the way in which credit consumers are given protection under the Consumer Credit Act 1974. Mrs Amanda Harris is anxious to buy a bedroom suite priced at £450 from a departmental store known as Bargain Sales plc. She does not have enough money to buy the goods outright but is offered the chance of paying a deposit of £100 and paying the balance of £350, plus 10 per cent interest per year (£35 × 2), over two years. This would amount to a total payment of £350 plus two years' interest, i.e. £70, making £420 in all, which, divided by twenty-four months, requires instalments of £17.50 per month from Mrs Harris.

This agreement could be either a hire purchase agreement or a credit sale agreement. There is an important difference. In a hire purchase agreement the goods do not become the property of the buyer until the final payment is made. As the name suggests the goods are on hire and remain the property of the shop. If the hirer, i.e. Amanda Harris, defaults in payment the goods may be reclaimed by the store. Amanda could under no circumstances sell the goods under a hire purchase agreement because they do not belong to her. However, if Amanda had bought the goods under a credit sale agreement, the furniture would belong to her as soon as she signed the agreement. If Amanda defaulted in payment in a credit sale agreement she could not be forced to hand back the goods, though she could be taken to court by the store for recovery of the money.

Consumer Credit Act 1974

Agreements covered by this act are consumer credit agreements, i.e. where the borrower is an individual and not a business and the amount borrowed is £5000 or less. Such purchases are called 'regulated agreements' and Mrs Harris's agreement comes into this category. The Act requires:

1. The agreement must be in writing and must indicate the total interest charge payable (in our case £70), the rate of interest, i.e. 10 per cent, and the rights of termination available to the parties. Credit agreements must show the APR (average percentage rate – see page 141).
2. A copy of the agreement must be given to the borrower within seven days of signature.
3. If the agreement is signed away from the trade premises, the purchaser must be given the chance to change his or her mind.

This is known as a 'cooling-off period'. The law states that such a purchaser must receive a copy of the agreement by post. He or she has five days from receipt of the postal copy to change his/her mind and if he/she does so, the agreement is deemed never to have existed and he/she will receive back the deposit of £100.

4. In a hire purchase agreement, after one third of the total cost has been paid, the owner of the goods may recover them only by obtaining a court order.

Exercise 2

1. Which Act requires manufacturers of food products to indicate on the package or container details of the composition of contents?

2. If you receive 'unsolicited goods' you must pay for them. True/false?

3. Name the bodies which protect consumers in nationalised industries.

4. In a hire purchase agreement the buyer owns the goods as soon as he pays the deposit. True/false?

5. What do you understand by the term 'regulated agreements'? What sort of agreements fall into this category?

6. What protection is afforded to a buyer who signs a hire purchase agreement in his own home?

7. What does APR mean?

14.6 OTHER TYPES OF CREDIT

Credit Cards

We have already explained, on page 135, the way in which Access and Visa operate.

Budget Cards/Charge Cards

Many stores operate their own budget accounts, whereby customers can pay a monthly amount and receive credit of twenty-four times that amount; i.e. if a customer pays £5 per month, then he will be permitted to spend £120 (24 × £5). Interest at so much per month is charged on these accounts.

Increasingly shops are offering a system whereby the customer is given a credit limit and each month he/she either pays off what is outstanding or at least a minimum of 5 per cent of the outstanding amount. For example, if Lynne Pullin had an account with Marks & Spencer and had spent £200 she would need to pay at least £10, i.e. 5 per cent. This system operates just like the Access or Visa and, of course, interest is payable. At present 2 per cent per month i.e. on £200 £4 will be added.

Most of the large stores operate a system like those described above. Marks & Spencer, British Home Stores, Burtons and Debenhams are just a few examples of stores having budget or charge cards.

You have already seen an example of a Debenhams card. Below is an example of a Marks & Spencer card and a storecard which can be used at British Home Stores, Habitat and Mothercare.

Monthly Accounts

Some shops enable customers to hold accounts which they are asked to settle at the end of each month. Usually no interest is charged on such accounts.

Advantages of Credit

1. Customers can 'enjoy now and pay later'.
2. If goods are rising in price, there is an advantage in buying immediately.
3. Credit, by which purchasers may stretch out repayments, enables them to buy more expensive items than would be possible if they had to pay outright.

Disadvantages of Credit

1. Interest charges have to be paid.
2. Cards may be lost or stolen.
3. Credit can tempt people to live beyond their means.
4. If a person who buys on credit falls ill or becomes unemployed, he may encounter difficulty in meeting his repayment.
5. Often cardholders will take out insurance to protect themselves against loss or illness/unemployment.

Exercise 3
The following review questions are based upon the whole of this chapter. Try to answer them without reference to the chapter. If when you check your answers you find you have made mistakes read the relevant section again.

1. What sort of buyers are protected by the Sale of Goods Act 1979?
2. Explain the meaning of the term 'good title to the goods'.
3. Muriel sees dresses advertised as pure cotton. She buys a dress and finds that it is made of synthetic fibre. Is there anything she can do?
4. What is the purpose of the Consumer Protection Act 1961?
5. Explain the difference between a hire purchase agreement and a credit sale agreement.

6. State three advantages of credit.
7. State three disadvantages of credit.
8. Firebrand plc buys a lorry from Commercial Vehicles plc on a credit sale but decides to use its 'cooling-off' rights and cancel the agreement. Is this permissible?
9. What would be the APR for a 10 per cent flat rate on a loan of £100?
10. What is a charge card?

CHAPTER 15

BUSINESS AND THE GOVERNMENT

We have already learned that the government has an important influence on business. Nationalised industries produce a wide range of services and the government, either nationally or at local leve, is responsible directly for many other services. In Chapter 16 we will see that the government has a great deal of influence through the taxation system. There are other areas, however, where the effect of government is felt, and any business is constantly aware of its presence.

Fresh Foods plc started as a small company producing a range of dairy products – cheese, butter, cream and yoghurts. The company grew and, by mergers with other companies, widened its range considerably, producing a very large number of products for the grocery industry. It also formed its own retailing organisation and purchased a number of shops, which operate under the name Fresh Foods (Retailing) plc. Most of the company's production units are in the East Midlands, in the Leicestershire area, though its shops are found countrywide. So successful is the company that over 40 per cent of all dairy products sold in the UK are manufactured by Fresh Foods.

Fresh Foods is anxious to expand and decides to take advantage of the government's various incentive schemes to start a small factory in Devon and a large factory in Liverpool. It wishes to open new shops and plans to open a branch in Bakewell. This new shop is to be built on the site of a church hall which is no longer used.

A new managing director has been appointed and, wishing to maintain good profits, he sends a letter to all the shops which he supplies, i.e. the company shops and others, and lays down stated prices for Fresh Foods plc products. The letter goes on to say that any shop found reducing the price will have its supplies cut. The managing director decides he wants a more efficient secretary and sacks his present one. The sacked secretary decides to appeal to a tribunal. The managing director has also received complaints from his employees that the butter-making machinery is unsafe. The complaints are ignored but a recent visit from the Health and Safety Inspector leads to an *improvement order* to install safer machines.

Fresh Foods plc will find that the government has power to intervene in many of the situation set out above.

15.1 MONOPOLIES AND RESTRICTIVE PRACTICES

The Fair Trading Act 1973 set up the post of Director-General of Fair Trading and he can order the Monopolies and Mergers Commission to investigate the affairs of any company or organisation which has 25 per cent or more of the production of a particular product or service under its control. You will remember that Fresh Foods plc is responsible for 40 per cent of the total UK production dairy foods. The commission may carry out a thorough investigation of the company to see if its activities are in any way against the public interest. If the commission found that Fresh Foods plc prices were too high, or that it was restricting (reducing) its supply of foods to keep prices up, the director-general could either report the matter to the Department of Trade or more usually would himself negotiate with Fresh Foods, pointing out the difficulties and trying to obtain from the company an undertaking that its prices will be reduced and that it will give up the policy of reducing supply. Most companies will respond to the Director-General's recommendation because they know that failure to respond could lead to action from the Department of Trade.

The Director-General of Fair Trading also has the power to refer *restrictive practices* to a special court known as the Restrictive Practices Court. A restrictive practice is something which restricts trade. If, for example, Fresh Foods plc made an agreement with another large food manufacturer to restrict production to keep up prices at a high level, this would be a restrictive practice. If the court felt the practice was 'against the public interest', it would order it to be discontinued. It is likely that agreements designed to keep prices at too high a level would be regarded as against the public interest. In our example you will remember that the new managing director wrote to all the shops which Fresh Foods supplied and indicated that commodities had to be sold at a certain price. This practice, known as 'resale price maintenance', is illegal except in certain special cases and manufacturers can only recommend prices. Products often carry a price label stating 'manufacturer's recommended price'.

15.2 GOVERNMENT AID TO INDUSTRY

You will remember that Fresh Foods plc is anxious to expand its operations and two sites are planned for new factories:

1. on Merseyside
2. in East Devon

Both of these areas are higher than average unemployment areas and because of the difficulties of attracting industry to them certain financial incentives are available.

The Secretary of State for Industry can designate areas for special aid and both the areas in question at present qualify for aid. Areas may be designated:

1. special development areas
2. development areas
3. intermediate areas

A range of aid is available varying according to the status of the area, for example:

1. tax allowances
2. depreciation allowances
3. special employment grants
4. grants towards training
5. use of government built factories at a discount

In addition, areas such as Merseyside can receive aid through various inner-city schemes and the creation of Enterprise Zones.

The local authorities such as Liverpool City Council, Devon County Council/East Devon District Council are able to give grants for industrial development.

Activity
See if you can find from your newspapers examples of local authorities advertising a range of benefits to attract industry to the area.

Activity
Many local authorities advertise to manufacturers the attractions of coming to their area. The advertisements often contain details of what the local authority will offer. Some counties have set up development boards for the purpose. See if you can find examples of advertisements of this sort.

Exercise 1

1. In terms of the Fair Trading Act 1973, what constitutes monopoly?
2. Explain the term 'resale price maintenance'.
3. If two companies agree to fix prices at a high level, (a) what is this known as? (b) What would be the consequences?
4. Indicate four possible aids which could be given to a firm intending to start up business on Merseyside.

15.3 PLANNING PERMISSION

You will remember that Fresh Foods plc wanted to open new shops, one of them in Bakewell in Derbyshire. This particular shop is on the site of a church hall and the company would need to obtain planning permission because the company is intending a change of use from a church hall to a shop.

1. Application is made on the appropriate form to the local planning authority, which would be West Derbyshire District Council.
2. Detailed plans plus a drawing, together with a completed application form, must be deposited at the planning office.
3. Various applications with their plans and drawings are kept in a planning register, and any member of the public may inspect the register.
4. If the proposed building is more than twenty metres high, the planning application must be advertised in a local newspaper and a notice must be displayed on the site itself. Fresh Foods could not develop the land without obtaining planning permission.
5. West Derbyshire would consider the application at a meeting of its planning committee. If the committee decided to turn down the application, Fresh Foods could appeal to the secretary of

state, who could uphold (accept) West Derbyshire's decision or reverse (change) it.

If the land was developed without permission the local planning authority could serve on Fresh Foods plc, an enforcement notice requiring that the land be restored to its former use or that the present use be discontinued.

15.4 EMPLOYMENT AND THE GOVERNMENT

Various protection is provided by law to employees:

1. You will remember that the new managing director dismissed his secretary after she had worked with Fresh Foods plc for ten years. The secretary decided to appeal to an industrial tribunal, claiming she had been unfairly dismissed. The Employment Protection (Consolidation) Act 1978 lays down that employees who feel they have been unfairly dismissed can bring their case before an industrial tribunal. An employee can appeal only if he or she is employed full-time and has been with his or her company for two years or more. If the industrial tribunal finds that the secretary has been unfairly dismissed, it can order Fresh Foods to pay compensation to the secretary, order the company to reinstate the secretary or order it to re-engage the secretary in another job within the firm.
2. It is illegal for a company to discriminate, when employing people, on grounds of sex. With certain exceptions, therefore, it is illegal to advertise jobs as being for 'men only'. It is also illegal to discriminate on grounds of race, colour or nationality.
3. A business may terminate (end) a person's employment provided it does not act unfairly, but a proper period of notice must be given to the employee affected. The law lays down a legal minimum – a person who has been employed for up to two years must be given at least one week's notice. Thereafter an employee is entitled to one week for every year's service, e.g. two years = two weeks; three years = three weeks, up to twelve years, when an employee is entitled to twelve weeks' notice (the maximum period required by law).

   The period of notice which must be given is the minimum required by the law. In contracts of employment employers can require larger periods, for example in many jobs a month's notice is required right from the start. As long as an employer does not go below the minimum then he is within the law. An employer can pay an employee wages in lieu of notice, for example a person entitled to two weeks' notice could receive two weeks' pay instead.

4. Employees are given further protection through their entitlement to redundancy pay. Sometimes comanies are forced to lay off workers because of lack of business. Workers laid off are entitled to payment, provided they are over eighteen and have worked for the company for two years or more. There is a complicated system of calculation, which an example will explain.

   Barrie Marshall (age thirty) has been employed by Trenchard Engines Co. Ltd for six years at £150 per week. The company makes him redundant and Barrie is entitled to a lump sum payment of 6 × 150 = £900.

After a person's forty-first birthday the redundancy pay increases to 1.5 weeks for each year's completed service, for example if Molly Watkins, aged 50, who had worked for Leeds Cleaners Ltd for 15 years at £100 per week, was made redundant she would receive

9 years at 1.5 weeks =	1350
6 years at 1 week =	600
Total redundancy payment	£1950

Again remember that the examples quoted above are minimum payments required by the law. Companies can pay what they wish and we often hear of employees, particularly management, receiving quite lucrative 'golden handshakes'.

Exercise 2

1. Explain what might happen if a business failed to obtain proper planning permission to redevelop a piece of land.
2. It is quite legal to advertise a post with the words 'white men only should apply'. True/false?
3. Michael (twenty-eight) has been employed for three years with Olive Holdings plc. He is earning £100 per week. Calculate the period of notice he is entitled to and the redundancy pay he would receive.

15.5 HEALTH AND SAFETY

You will remember that Fresh Foods plc had received a visit from a health and safety inspector who had carried out an inspection of machinery in one of its factories. The Health and Safety at Work Act 1974 has made a big contribution to safety improvement in work places. Employers have a duty to provide safe places of work and to provide adequate welfare facilities for employees. Companies with more than four hundred employees must have a proper first-aid room and employ a full-time officer with responsibility for first aid.

Inspectors can make visits to factories and, following the visits, they may issue recommendations. However, if they think a particular process is too unsafe they may issue, as in our case, an *improvement order*, which is an order requiring the company to alter this unsafe system within a specified period of time. In our example, Fresh Foods was being asked to change its unsafe butter-making machinery. If a practice is considered extremely unsafe the inspectors may order that it be discontinued at once, i.e. *a closure order* or *prohibition order* will be issued.

Recently new regulations have been issued relating to health and safety notices in places of work. Different types of notices must be in different colours and, for example, first-aid boxes must be coloured green and this colour must be used for notices drawing attention to the location of the boxes. Blue is the colour used to draw attention to particular hazards.

Activity
See if you can find examples of notices required under the Health and Safety at Work Act. If you are at college you will see various notices posted around the building.

Special regulations have also been issued in respect of first-aid boxes and their minimum contents have been laid down by law.

Exercise 3
The following review questions are based upon the whole chapter. Try to answer them without reference to the chapter. If when you have checked your answers you find you have not understood any part of the chapter read that part again.

1. Name the body which has the power to investigate businesses which have 25 per cent or more share of the market.
2. The Restrictive Practices Court will investigate to see if a practice is . . . .
3. If a business is refused planning permission what can it do?
4. If an employee feels he has been unfairly dismissed, (a) what can he do? (b) If it is felt that he has been unfairly dismissed what might happen?
5. A health and safety inspector, following a visit to a factory, can take three possible courses of action. Name them.
6. Mark Stuart is 44, he has been with Glenbrook Glass plc for ten years at a wage of £150 per week. His company gives him notice and decides to pay him rather than ask him to serve his notice. Calculate the redundancy money and notice money to which he is entitled.

CHAPTER 16

TAXATION

The government of a country such as Britain is responsible for the provision of a range of services which sometimes people take for granted. Health services, education, the police, defence, the upkeep and maintenance of roads, the provision of housing – to name but a few. Some of the services are the responsibility of central government and some of the local authorities. Even those that are controlled by local authorities are subsidised by grants from the government. These services do not, however, come free and we pay for them through taxes and rates. These charges are levied on individuals and businesses.

16.1 DIRECT TAX

Direct tax is the tax paid directly by a person to the government, and some of the taxes coming under this category can be explained by reference to the following example.

John Drew is an engineer earning £20 400 per annum, or £1700 per month. In 1988 John used some of his savings to buy 7000 £1 shares. The company whose shares John had bought did particularly well and John was able to sell the shares in 1989 for £2 each and thereby gained £7000. John's father, who had been living alone, has just died and he has left John a house. John already has a house and sells his father's house for £130 000. Unfortunately John will have to pay taxes on these various sources of income.

Income Tax

John will have income tax deducted from his pay of £1700 per month. His employer will use the PAYE (pay as you earn) system of tax. John will be issued with a code number by the tax authorities (the

Inland Revenue). The tax code will be related to John's circumstances and will be used by his employer to determine the amount of tax to be deducted from his pay. Everyone receives a personal allowance. At present this is £2605 for a single person, while a married man receives an allowance of £4095. An allowance means that a sum of money can be earned before any tax is paid.

Let us return to our example of John. He is married and earns £1700 per month (£20 400 per annum). If we deduct from his annual income his married man's allowance we are left with £16 305; it is on this amount that he will pay tax. Joh's tax code, which his employer will use to work out his tax, will be 409H – this means that £4095 is allowed against his income and 'H' denotes he is married. If he were single the letter L would follow his code.

John will pay tax at the basic rate on £16 305, his taxable income. The basic rate is at present 25 per cent, so John will pay £4076.25 per annum, taken from his salary monthly at the rate of £339.69.

The rate of tax varies with the level of taxable income. The table below gives the details of the rates in 1988:

Taxable income	*Rate of tax (%)*
19 300	25
Over 19 300	40

Exercise 1

1. Explain the term 'taxable income'.
2. What would be the tax code of Bill Green, who is single with no other allowances?
3. Charles Harman is married and earns £40 000 per annum. What will his taxable income be and how much tax will he pay?

Activity

Find out from your local tax office full details of the rates of income tax and the level of allowances that are in force at present. The government has published a very informative leaflet, *IR34 Income Tax PAYE*, which is available from any tax office. You will also discover that besides a single person's and married man's allowance there are other allowances available.

Tax Relief on Mortgages

Until April 1983, people who were buying houses with the aid of a mortgage could claim tax relief on the interest payable, and their tax codes would be adjusted accordingly. This relief is still available but, instead of being given through income, the building societies now deduct the tax relief from the interest payments at source. This new system, known as mortgage interest relief at source (MIRAS), means that payments will be reduced by the basic rate of 25 per cent.

For example, Marc Holburn has bought a house with the aid of a £25 000 mortgage from the Halifax Building Society at an interest rate of 9.8 per cent. The interest payments, therefore, will be £2450 per annum (£25 000 × 9.81 per cent); but because 25 per cent is (the tax relief) the payments will be reduced by £612.50 to £1837.50. (This was explained more fully in Chapter 10.)

Capital Gains Tax

You will remember that John has sold his £7000 worth of shares for £14 000 and has thus made a gain of £7000. This is known as a capital gain and is taxed by means of capital gains tax. At present capital gains tax is payable on capital gains which exceed £5000. John has gained £7000 and he will pay tax on £2000. The rate for capital gains tax is the same as the rate for PAYE income tax. In John's case the rate is 25 per cent, so he will pay £400 (25 per cent of £2000).

Capital gains tax is also payable when a house is sold at a profit. However, a person who owns only one house is exempt. If Bill Smith sold his house for £100 000, having purchased it for £30 000, the £70 000 gain would be exempt from tax provided that the house was Bill's sole residence.

Exercise 2
Michael Allcock owns four houses. He sells one for £110 000, having purchased it for £70 000. Calculate the capital gains tax payable. Assume Michael is liable at 40 per cent.

Inheritance Tax

From 17 March 1986 the capital transfer tax was replaced by a tax known as inheritance tax. You will remember that John was left a house by his father worth £130 000 which John sold. Unfortunately for John he has to pay tax on this. The first £110 000 is exempt from tax so therefore John will only pay tax on £20 000. Since April 1988 there is just one flat rate on inheritance and that is 40 per cent.

John would therefore pay £20 000 at 40 per cent = £8000

The tax just described is payable on death but tax may also be payable on a gift. If John's father gave his son the house a year before he died then John would still have to pay £8000. However, if Mr Robert Maxworth gave his son £200 000 and dies 10 years later no tax would be payable. A table shown below shows what percentage of the inheritance tax is paid on gifts and you will see it depends on how long before death the gift was made.

Interval in years	*Percentage in tax paid*
0–3	100
3–4	80
4–5	60
5–6	40
6–7	20
7+	0

Exercise 3

Lady Mary Roberts gives £310 000 to her only daughter and dies $4\frac{1}{2}$ years later. Calculate the tax to be paid by the daughter. daughter.

Corporation Tax

John works for a large company known as United Engineering plc and like many companies United Engineering makes a profit. Profits are, like other income, subject to a tax known as Corporation Tax. You may remember from Chapter 2 that companies could either plough back profit or distribute it. In some circumstances the government will reduce the level of taxation on profit ploughed back in order to encourage investment. This tax relief, as it is called, applies especially to spending on buildings, machinery and plant. A company has to pay corporation tax before it distributes to its shareholders.

The present rate of corporation tax is 35 per cent but small companies pay a special lower rate of corporation tax currently 25 per cent. Companies which have charitable status are exempt from corporation tax. A good example of this is a company providing an education or training service as their sole business.

Tax on Business other than Companies (i.e. Sole Traders, Partnerships) Schedule D

Corporation tax is a tax on company profit. Other sorts of businesses pay their tax through a system known as Schedule D.

Alf Roberts runs a small grocery shop. He must submit to the Inland Revenue a set of accounts for each year. These accounts set out his income and expenditure. The present system allows someone like Alf to set some of his expenses against a tax allowance. Expenses such as rent, rates, electricity charges, vehicle expenses including depreciation are rightly regarded as costs and are exempt from tax.

A leaflet entitled 'Starting Your Own Business' which explains the Schedule D system is available from your local tax office.

All the taxes we have considered so far are known as *direct* taxes because they are paid directly to the government.

16.2 INDIRECT TAXES

There are taxes which are not paid directly to the government but are taxes on spending. The best-known example of such a tax is the value added tax or VAT.

Value Added Tax (VAT)

This is a tax on sales and it is paid at each stage of a product's progress from raw material to the final consumer. The 1988 rate of tax is 15 per cent.

For example, a retailer sells a suit for £100. The suit was bought from a wholesaler for £80; the wholesaler bought the suit from a manufacturer for £60. The manufacturer bought the cloth, etc. for £40. These are four stages in the chain leading to the purchase by the customer. If the value added tax is 15 per cent, each stage would add 15 per cent.

1. The cloth would be sold for £40 + 15 per cent = £46. The tax is £6, which is paid to the government.
2. The manufacturer sells the suit for £60 + 15 per cent = £69. The tax is £9 but only £3 is paid to the government. £9 – £6 = £3.

3. The wholesaler sells the suit for £80 + 15 per cent = £92. The tax is £12 but only £3 is paid to the government £12 − £3 = £9.
4. The retailer sells the suit for £100 + 15 per cent, i.e. £115. The tax is £15 but the retailer pays only £3 to the government. £15 − £12 = £3.

The government receives the full tax in four amounts: £6 + £3 + £3 + £3 = £15. The tax is known as value added tax because it is levied at each stage, as value is added.

Zero Rated Goods and Exemptions

Zero Rated Goods
Certain goods are zero rated, that is VAT is not payed on them. The list of zero rated goods is quite large. Below is an example of some categories of goods that are zero rated:

1. certain foods and drinks
2. books, newspapers and periodicals
3. coal, coke, gas and electricity when used as fuel
4. passenger transport charges

Exemptions
Certain organisations and persons are exempt. This means they pay VAT, but then reclaim it. Examples are:

1. educational establishments such as schools, colleges and universities.
2. hospitals, chemists, opticians, dentists and general practitioners.

For example, a college buys ten Amstrad PCWs 9512 at £499 + VAT each. The total bill payable to supplier will be (10 at £499 + £74.85) £5738.50. The college will then reclaim the VAT, a saving of £748.50 (see p.217).

Other Indirect Taxes

We have already pointed out that certain products coming into the country pay tax known as *excise duty*, payable on petroleum products and alcoholic drinks. Other goods pay *import tax*, sometimes known as *tariffs*. An indirect tax is also levied on *betting and gaming*.

Exercise 4
1. Name four types of direct tax.
2. Name four types of indirect tax.

There is also a special tax payable on the purchase of cars currently 8.31 per cent. VAT is then added at 15 per cent. This is the reason why cars are more expensive in the UK than they are in Europe.

16.3 OTHER FORMS OF GOVERNMENT REVENUE

National Insurance

All employees pay a sum to the government which is deducted from their wages or salaries. National insurance is used to help finance the national health service and to contribute to the funds needed to meet unemployment and sickness benefits. The rate of deduction of national insurance varies with the size of income of the employee – the higher the income, the bigger the deduction.

The employer also pays a national insurance contribution for everyone employed by him.

An example of the system of payments is given below but remember changes do take place. Make sure you keep up to date. The figures given relate to April 1988.

Weekly earnings	*Employer contribution (%)*	*Employee contribution (%)*
Below £41	Nil	Nil
£41–69.99	5	5
£70–104.99	7	7
£105–154.99	9	9
£155–305.00	9	10.45
Over £305	9% of £305	10.45% of all earnings

The employer is responsible for the payment of both contributions but is entitled to deduct from the employee's wages the employee's contribution.

Local Authority Rates

Many key services are provided by local authorities, e.g. by counties such as Kent or Derbyshire, and by districts into which counties are divided. It is the districts which charge the rates, but a proportion is paid to the counties. Counties and districts provide such services as education, roads, road lighting, refuse collection, museums, parks, public conveniences, police and fire. Some money for these services is provided by the government through a direct grant called 'rate support grant'. The rest is provided by the rates. The following example will show how rates are calculated.

J. and J. Jones, husband and wife, own a small grocery shop. A grocery shop, just like any other property, will be given a rateable value by its local authority. The rateable value will depend upon the size, location, etc. of the property. A large shop in a main street will have a much larger rateable value than a small corner shop. Let us assume that the grocery shop owned by J. and J. Jones has a rateable value of £300. The local authority (i.e. Canterbury City District) will then fix a rate poundage or in other words will state how much rate to the £ must be paid.

Local authorities charge different rates for domestic property (ordinary homes) and commercial property (businesses). In 1988–9 the rates in Canterbury were 201.80p for domestic property and 220.30p for commercial property. J. and J. Jones would pay £300 × 220.30, i.e. £660.90p per annum. For each £ raised in 1988–9, Canterbury City District took 28.30p and the remainder, 192.00, went to Kent County Council.

Exercise 5

Calculate the annual rates payable by F. Lees & Co. Ltd on property with a rateable value of £500 where the rate poundage is 250p in the £ for commercial property and 229p in the £ for domestic property.

Activity

Leaflets on capital gains tax and capital transfer tax, and on starting your own business, are obtainable from tax offices. Your local council will provide you with details of rates, how they are collected and how they are spent. Try to obtain these leaflets, which will tell you more about the various means which the government uses to collect revenue. Local authorities will usually send explanatory leaflets with the rates (see p.215).

Exercise 6
Calculate the national insurance contribution paid by both the employer and employee in respect of:
Michael Jennings who earns £450 a week working for United Foods PLC.

Poll Tax

This system of local rates will be phased out in 1990 in England and Wales. The starting date in Scotland is 1989. Under the new Poll Tax arrangements every adult will be liable to pay the tax. Instead of local taxes being levied on houses it will be on adults. There will also be one rate for businesses set by the government.

Some adults will be exempt, for example.

1. severely mentally handicapped
2. people in gaol
3. patients in hospital
4. old people in residential homes.

People on low incomes will get up to 80 per cent rebates and students will pay 20 per cent in the area in which they are studying.

In England the system will be fully in place by 1994 and calculations show that some of the likely charges will be: Reading, £168; Bristol, £237; Bradford, £238; Coventry, £219; Manchester, £272; Canterbury, £152.

Exercise 7
John Hartley lives with his wife and two sons aged 25 and 27 in Canterbury. His house has a rateable value of £202.

1. On the basis of a rate of 201.80p calculate the rate he would pay.
2. Now calculate the amount of poll tax his family would pay.
3. How much more/less will they pay under the new system?

Activity
Try to find out the effect of the Poll Tax in your area. What will be the effect on your own family.

RATES 1988–89

AN EXPLANATION

Rates are a tax on the occupation of properties throughout the country whether domestic, industrial or commercial.

The Rateable Value of all properties is decided by a Central Government department, not by the City Council. The factors affecting the Rateable Value of individual properties are very wide-ranging including size, standards, services, facilities and location.

The total Rateable Value of all properties in Canterbury is some £16.2 million.

The total rate you have to pay is made up as follows:-

Canterbury City Council Rate	28.30
Kent County Council Rate	192.00
FULL RATE	220.30p*
for every £1 of Rateable Value payable by Industrial and Commercial Ratepayers	
Less Domestic Rate Relief from Central Government	18.50
DOMESTIC RATE	201.80p*
for every £1 of Rateable Value payable by Domestic Ratepayers	

*Plus the PARISH RATE (where appropriate)

The average household (with a Rateable Value of £186) will pay (after Domestic Rate Relief), about £48 for the City Council's Rate Fund services in the coming year. This is equivalent to about 93 pence per week per property.

CANTERBURY CITY COUNCIL

This leaflet contains both information for the benefit of ratepayers, and data required to be shown by Central Government (i.e. the section called 'Summary—Kent and Canterbury').

The government not only provides many services either directly or through nationalised bodies, but it also has an enormous influence on commerce and industry through monopoly control, health and safety legislation, and aid to industry. It is important, however, to remember always that it has a very big influence through its power to raise revenue through taxation. If the government wishes to reduce or increase spending, it can operate through the tax system. If the government wishes to stimulate (give a boost to) the economy it may do so by reducing levels of taxation so that people and firms have more money to spend.

This chapter has explained the various ways the government raises revenue, based upon the system existing in 1988. However, changes do take place – by obtaining the various leaflets mentioned you can keep up to date.

Exercise 8

These review questions are based upon the whole of this chapter. Try to do the questions without reference to it. If on checking your answers you find that you have not understood any particular part read over that section again.

1. Explain what you understand by the term 'tax code' and explain how one is determined.
2. At what level of capital gains is tax deducted?
3. Profits on sale of houses are exempt from capital gains tax. True/false?
4. What is inheritance tax?
5. How can a company gain relief from corporation tax?
6. Explain the term 'value added tax'.
7. Which type of local authority levies rates?
8. Local services are paid for partly by rates and partly by the government in the form of . . . .
9. What is VAT zero rated?
10. What is VAT exempt?

16.4 SUMMARY

This book has covered the main branches of business and supplied the background to the business environment. Try to build on the information contained here by reading as widely as possible from interesting and readily available sources. The business pages of newspapers especially *The Times*, The *Guardian*, *Independent* and *Financial Times* carry excellent coverage of share price changes, company performances, bankruptcies and government policy towards industry and commerce.

To keep up to date try to read one of these newspapers at least once a week.

The exemptions from VAT mentioned on page 211 are likely to change following a decision in a recent legal case: '*Commission of European Communities* v. *United Kingdom* [1988]. In this case it was argued that certain exemptions were illegal given the UK's membership of the EEC.

Schools and hospitals in the private sector will no longer get exemption from VAT and this is likely to lead to higher fees being charged by these schools and hospitals.

This provides a good example of the constant change taking place in business and emphasises the need to keep up to date.

ANSWERS TO EXERCISES

CHAPTER 1

Exercise 1

Your pie chart should have looked something like this:

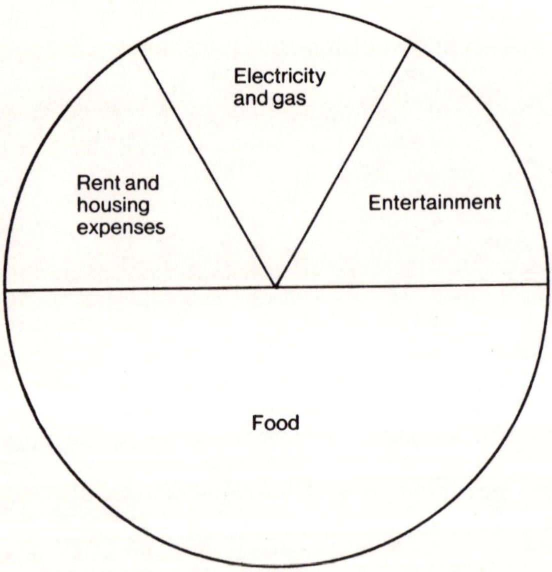

Exercise 2

1, 4, 5 and **7** are clearly 'consumable goods; **2, 3, 6** and **8** are 'durable' goods.

Exercise 3

1, 3 and **4** are services; **2, 5** and **6** are goods.

Exercise 4

1. Bus services are provided both publicly and privately. Public sector: coal, gas, law and order, postal services, Russian-produced Lada cars.
2. Private sector: milk, beer, televisions, washing machines, snack bars, furniture.

Exercise 5

If, for example, the exchange rate of the £ falls from £1 = 3.3 DM (Deutschmarks to £1 = 3 DM, it will cost £1100 to buy German goods which would have cost £1000 previously.

Exercise 6

1. 15 per cent.
2. Increase in oil prices; high labour costs; low exchange rate for £ sterling.
3. False. This has fallen from 20p in the £ to 15p in the £.
4. Often, both husband and wife go out to work which has resulted in an increase in demand for such products.

Exercise 7

2, 7 and **8** are primary; **1, 3, 5** and **10** are secondary; 4, 6 and 9 are tertiary.

Exercise 8

1. Possible reasons are (a) technological changes resulting in labour-saving machinery; (b) low demand for goods and services; (c) high wage rates; (d) competition from abroad.
2. Your bar chart should have looked something like Figure 1.4. on page 15.

Exercise 9

1. Furniture and the television video recorder are regarded as

durables because they are items which are likely to last for some time, whereas the biscuits, the shoe polish and the shampoo are likely to be used (consumed) immediately and they are known as consumables.

2(a) *Not* true – electricity is mainly produced by a public corporation, i.e. the Central Electricity Generating Board, and distributed by regional boards, e.g. Norweb (North West Electricity Board), SEEboard (South East Electricity Board).

(b) Not true – this is an example of a service.

(c) Not true – British Rail is publicly owned.

(d) True – the National Coal Board (NCB) now British Coal is publicly owned.

(e) Is not true – an accountant is an example of a tertiary occupation.

3(a) True – less money per £ was spent on food 1970–80.

(b) False – more money was spent in the £ on services between 1970 and 1980.

(c) False – the average rate of inflation was 15 per cent.

(d) True – more money in the £ was spent on housing, therefore there was a relative increase (in relation to other goods and services) and, of course, more money in total was spent on housing because of inflation.

4. There are many examples you could have chosen: *primary* – iron ore miners; *secondary* – mechanics and factory workers; *tertiary* accountants, clerks.

5. (a) tertiary, (b) secondary (c) primary.

6. *Advantages:* more goods produced, workers can concentrate on what they are best at; *disadvantages:* monotony in some instances, workers who are too specialised are vulnerable to demand change.

7. Your pie chart should look something like this one.

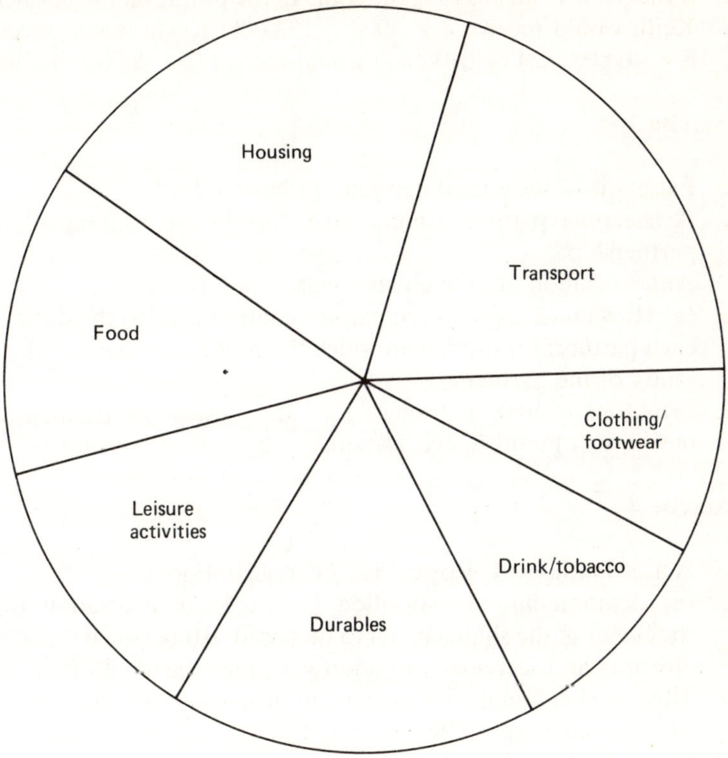

CHAPTER 2

Exercise 1

1. (a) Sole ownership, (b) sole responsibility for decisions, (c) sole responsibility for profits and losses.
2. False – there has been a steady decline in the number of sole trader type organisations.
3. False – this requirement was abolished in 1981.
4. False – a sole trader does not need to give information.
5. Michael could lose more than the £50 000 because as a sole trader he has 'unlimited liability'.

Exercise 2

1. 'Plough back' means to spend some of the profits on the business.
2. Keith would receive 8 × 4000 = £32 000; Kevin would receive 6 × 4000 = £24 000; Wendy would receive 2 × 4000 = £8000.

Exercise 3

1. False – it is not a legal necessity to have a deed.
2. A 'sleeping partner' cannot take part in the running of the partnership.
3. An association of individuals engaged in business.
4. (a) How much capital each partner contributes; (b) the duties of each partner; (c) the way in which the profits are shared; (d) the salary of the partners.
5. (a) More capital; (b) sharing of the burden of running the business; (c) more specialisation.

Exercise 4

1. Act of Parliament, Royal Charter, registration.
2. (a) Memorandum of association, (b) articles of association, (c) a statement of the share capital to be raised, (d) personal details of directors and secretary, (e) address of the registered office.
3. This is a clause in the memorandum of association which sets out what the company is being set up to do.
4. False – because Surefit (Shoes) Ltd is a legal entity; the company itself will be prosecuted.
5. False – if Keith wishes to leave he must first get rid of his shares, so the company does not end; it gets different shareholders.
6. A private company cannot sell its shares to the public.

Exercise 5

1. True – the words 'public limited company' or 'plc' must appear in its title.
2. By using a prospectus or an offer to sale issued by a merchant bank.
3. The public need to be sure that they can resell the shares, and the investigation by the Stock Exchange ensures that they are dealing with a reputable company.
4. It needs a certificate of trading.

Exercise 6

1. (a) CEGB (Central Electricity Generating Board) provides electricity; (b) a number of boards are responsible for distribution, e.g. Norweb, EMEB, SWEB, SEEboard.
2. The Treasury.
3. A minister is responsible; (b) the government appoints the board and the chairman; (c) accounts have to be presented annually to Parliament.
4. It is the only provider of rail services.
5. False – the BBC is a public corporation, not a public company.

Exercise 7

1. The owner is liable for debts over and above his investment in the business.
2. A sleeping partner is a partner who has no say in the running of the partnership.
3. John £6000, Frank £4000, Joanne £2000, William £4000, total £16 000.
4. (a) The company name, (b) the situation of its registered office, (c) objects clause, (d) a statement that liability is limited, (c) a statement of its share capital.
5. False – it must also have received a certificate of trading.
6. A public company can advertise and sell its shares to the public.
7. 'Public limited company'.
8. (a) Shareholders, (b) shareholders.
9. The investors and borrowers.
10. Because the building society keeps the deeds of the house.
11. 63%
12. Shareholders.

CHAPTER 3

Exercise 1

The Managing Director and Sales Director, as their titles suggest, but also the Chief Accountant and the Production Manager indicated by the letter 'D'.

Exercise 2

12.5p in the £, or 12.5 per cent.

Exercise 3

1. (a) To send out the agenda and minutes for the board meetings.
   (b) To submit accounts to Company House.
   (c) To ensure that the company complies with the company law.
2. (a) To promote the company's products.
   (b) To organise the company's advertising.
   (c) To ensure the correct product range is available.
3. (a) To obtain a highly trained workforce.
   (b) To ensure a contented workforce.
4. A director who does not work in the company.

Exercise 4

1. 30 per cent.
2. (a) full discussions with employees;
   (b) guarantees on redundancy;
   (c) better salaries;
   (d) good training.

Exercise 5

1. The shareholders.
2. The board of directors.
3. One who works in the company.
4. Managing Director
5. Production Manager
   Chief Analyst
   Health & Safety Officer
   Works Manager
6. It improves communications and helps the implementation of decisions.

CHAPTER 4

Exercise 1

1. That the product or service is what customers want and it can be provided bringing an adequate return to the business.
2. The 'matching process' is the process whereby the resources of a company or business are matched to market needs so that a

product or service is provided which is mutually beneficial, i.e. useful to the customer and giving a return to the business.

3. To find out the potential market, to find out the size of the market, to find out what sort of product or service the customer wants.
4. Desk research is research which is conducted using any statistical or written information to provide some of the answers in relation to the market. It does not involve going out but can be conducted in the office or at home.

Exercise 2

1. A representative sample is a proportion of a group chosen in such a way that is exactly like the group.
2. Whether the price is likely to attract customers and whether it will bring an adequate return to the company.
3. Product, price, place, promotion.

Exercise 3

1. You should have mentioned such functions as information giving, persuasion and reminding.
2. The brand might be advertised merely to keep its share of the market and it is likely that the cost would be passed on to the consumer in the form of higher prices.
3. 'Advertising media' means those places where advertising can be placed, e.g. newspapers, magazines, TV, radio.
4. To make sure that standards are kept high. The Advertising Standards Authority will investigate complaints and will try to ensure that advertisements are within the code of practice.
5. It is likely to result in existing customers staying and it is likely that a good reputation for after-sales service will result in increased sales.

Exercise 4

1. Because the research is carried out on information available without going out to the public. Often the research takes place in the office and, therefore, is called desk research.
2. This means taking a representative group of particular population; e.g. it may be a sample of working wives in the age group 20 to 35.

3. This means developing a product in line with the needs of customers which have been identified through market research.
4. What group of people the media might reach. The cost.
5. Possible answers are: (a) it provides information about product and service; (b) it promotes competition and keeps prices down; (c) it promotes increased sales which may result in lower prices.
6. (a) Newspapers lay down conditions to their advertisements; (b) the Advertising Standards Authority. Some of you may have mentioned the Trade Descriptions Act. This is certainly a good example of protection, which we will be considering in Chapter 14.
7. Market research, product planning, pricing, policy marketing through advertising, selling the product, after-sales service.
8. Product design and promotion would seem to be the important aspects in launching a product with a high fashion content.
9. This means the way in which a firm tries to mix the various marketing ingredients to achieve good sales.

CHAPTER 5

Exercise 1

1. Small shops cannot buy in bulk and therefore cannot sell the goods at low prices. People will sometimes pay higher prices when they are buying for convenience.
2. (a) Convenience of location, (b) convenience of time, (c) personal service, (d) shopkeepers are happy to keep going on small returnS, (e) credit facilities.

Exercise 2

1. As the name suggests, a multiple specialist store is concerned with a small range of goods, e.g. shoes, clothes, motor accessories, books, whereas a multiple variety chain store sells a very wide range of goods. There are many examples you could have chosen: multiple specialist stores Chelsea Girl, Peter Lord, Halfords, W. H. Smith; multiple variety chainstores Woolworths, British Home Stores, Littlewoods, Boots.
2. A departmental store is really a number of different shops under one roof.

3. Retail co-ops have attempted to halt their decline by: (a) amalgamation of societies, (b) employing skilled managers.
4. (a) (i) A supermarket has 186 square metres of floor space or more; (ii) a hypermarket has over 2500 square metres of floor space.
   (b) Bulk buying, quick turnover, stocking a wide range of goods, low labour costs are some of the reasons for the supermarkets' success.
5. Some independent retailers have joined groups such as Mace and Spar so that they can reduce the costs of buying goods.

Exercise 3

1. (a) The offer of credit, (b) shopping can be done at home.
2. Postage, commission, and producing an expensive catalogue.
3. They do not need to provide large numbers of staff.
4. The supplier can assist with: (a) training, (b) advertising, (c) shop fitting.
5. (a) Breaking of bulk, (b) preparation of goods in a saleable condition, (c) providing goods where they are required, (d) measuring consumer preferences.

Exercise 4

1. (a) Bulk buying, (b) own branding, (c) good stock control, (d) specialist buying, (e) advantage of self-service, (f) new aids to efficiency, (g) large turnover.
2. (a) Lack of personal service, (b) inflexibility of hours and location, (c) no provision for specialist goods, (d) losses due to pilfering.

Exercise 5

1. Because the wholesaler occupies a place between retailer and manufacturer.
2. Because as retailing comes increasingly into the hands of the large-scale retailer some of the advantages of the wholesaler are not so important.
3. These are wholesalers who sell goods for cash to be taken away immediately by retailers.
4. There are many examples of these types of goods: Christmas ware and summer clothes are seasonally demanded. Fruit and vegetables are seasonally produced but regularly demanded.

5. Manufacturers need not pay transport costs to take goods to large numbers of retailers. Since each order needs separate paperwork the manufacturer by selling directly to the wholesaler will save the administrative costs involved.
6. The wholesaler can pay the manufacturer immediately so that the manufacturer has more money to buy raw materials but he can offer the retailer credit.

Exercise 6

1. The Baltic Exchange in London.
2. Where goods are ordered at a present price to be delivered and paid for in the future but at the agreed price.
3. Where buyers and sellers are brought together.
4. He can buy seasonally demanded goods throughout the year and can buy seasonally produced goods for sale throughout the year.
5. They are paying for convenience and flexibility.
6. Mace; Spar.
7. (a) The turnover is £40 000. (b) The mark-up is 33.3 per cent.
8. (a) Where goods are produced specifically for a retailer. (b) Where goods are packaged specially for a retailer.

CHAPTER 6

Exercise 1

1. Liabilities include opening capital and profit. Assets include debtors, equipment, cash in bank.
2. The loss in value is known as depreciation.
3. Because the profit is owed to the owner of the business.
4.

Liabilities		*Assets*	
Capital	£15000	Equipment	£7500
		Furniture	£2500
		Cash in bank	£5000
	£15 000		£15 000

Exercise 2

£50 000–£30 000 = £20 000
£20 000 is the gross profit.

Exercise 3

Gross profit £20 000; net profit £12 000.

Exercise 4

1. Gross profit is the difference between revenue and the costs of goods or services.
2. Net profit is the difference between gross profit and all other costs.
3. The accountant's view of profit is net profit while the economist's takes into account what the owner of the business might have earned by being employed together with his interest on investing his capital elsewhere.

Exercise 5

Annual interest on the lathes would be £2500 while interest on the factory would be £6250, i.e. a total of £8750.

Exercise 6

A private company can only sell its shares privately but a public company can advertise its shares and sell them to the general public.

Exercise 7

1. Because the preference shareholder comes before ('takes preference over') the ordinary shareholders when profits are shared.
2. Dividend.
3. False – the debenture holder is a creditor.
4. Plough back.
5. The ordinary shareholders would receive £1600, i.e. 32p in the £, or 32 per cent.

Exercise 8

1. You could have included insurance companies, investment trusts, pension funds, trade unions.
2. Underwriting.
3. False – this would be known as 'above par'.
4. Offer for sale.
5. True – shareholders are given the right to buy additional shares.

Exercise 9

1. A balance sheet is a statement which shows how a business stands financially.
2. Because the business owes the owner the £20 000 and any money owed is a liability.
3. False – money is owed by the business to the creditor; therefore it is a liability.
4. Her true profit is £10 900; her previous earnings + her interest when £6000 was invested (£600).
5. This is where money is lent against the security of property.
6. When a business pays tax on its profits it can deduct from the profit the interest payments.
7. It means 'public limited company' and signifies that shares can be offered to the public.
8. If a preference shareholder does not get his interest one year then it is held over to be paid if possible the next year.
9. (a) He may obtain a dividend from the company; (b) he may sell his shares for more than he paid.
10. It means the shares have been listed on the Stock Exchange which idicates that the Stock Exchange has approved the company and the issue.

CHAPTER 7

Exercise 1

1. End of October 1986.
2. Tokyo and New York.
3. 500 × 50p = £250.
4. You may have mentioned abolition of scales of minimum charges, scrapping of the division between Brokers and Jobbers, the introduction of an electronic market.

CHAPTER 8

Exercise 1

1. The premium:

$$\frac{\text{the total value of claims £5000}}{\text{the number of insured 100}}$$ plus the administrative cost of

£10=£50 + £10 = £60.
The value of claims is 5 per cent of the total insured, i.e.

$$\frac{5000}{100\ 00} \times \frac{100}{1} = 5 \text{ per cent.}$$

2. The premium is the charge made for the insurance which enables the company to pay out compensation.
3. Pooling of risks.

Exercise 2

1. False – this risk is not insurable.
2. Because this event will occur; i.e. a person with life insurance will die at some time.
3. Utmost good faith.
4. False – it is not possible because there is no insurable interest.
5. Indemnity means being compensated in full but no more if you suffer a loss.
6. You would not get £5000 but only the secondhand value of it. this is because of the principle of indemnity.
7. Each insurance company would pay 50 per cent of the claim under the principle of contribution.
8. Anything of value after a full claim for loss has been made belongs to the insurer. The insurer takes the place of the insured.
9. Consequential loss.
10. Under the average clause the insurance company would pay out half, i.e. £250, because only half the value of the antique is insured.
11. Because the risk of the insurance company having to pay out earlier is greater.

Exercise 3

1. Fidelity guarantee insurance.
2. Cargo insurance insures the cargo of a ship while freight insurance insures the owner's freight charges if they should have to be refunded.
3. Whole life insurance relates only to life and payments are made only on death. Endowment insurance relates to a period of years after which a lump sum payment is made.
4. Underwriters.

Exercise 4

£3760 @ 50p in the £ is £1800.

Exercise 5

1. A premium.
2. Because under the principle of indemnity the insured can get only the value of his loss, no more; therefore the additional premium is a waste.
3. Average clause.
4. Consequential loss.
5. If someone wishes to end his endowment insurance before the date of payment then it is said to be surrendered and usually a money payment is made.
6. Underwriters.
7. A receiving order.
8. The *London Gazette* and a local newspaper.
9. Liquidation.
10. False – it may be voluntarily wound up if the company wishes to discontinue business or amalgamate.
11. Fully paid up.

CHAPTER 9

Exercise 1

1. True – interest is paid by the bank on a deposit account.
2. A cash dispenser.
3. Money is transferred directly from one account to another.
4. £50 per month: £600 ÷ 12.

5. Statement.
6. (a) The amount of money in the account, (b) the number of transactions.

Exercise 2

1. Insufficient funds, death of drawer, the cheque is stopped, the figures and words to not coincide, the cheque is out of date.
2. Michael is the drawer; Janette is the payee; Barclays is the drawee.
3. It means that the payee should refer to the drawer and usually it is because there are insufficient funds in the drawer's account.
4. Three days.

Exercise 3

1. (a) Standing order, (b) direct debit.
2. Bank giro.
3. The cheque may be paid only into the payee's account.
4. True – this is the purpose of a crossing.
5. False – a banker's draft can be paid out on immediately.
6. By asking the customers to support the cheque by a cheque card.

Exercise 4

1. Because business A will pay 15 per cent for the whole year and business B will pay on the daily amounts outstanding.
2. Midland, Lloyds, National Westminster.

Exercise 5

1. Firms do this by direct transfer system. Their accounts are debited and the employees' accounts are credited.
2. False – bank charges are never paid on deposit accounts, in fact interest is earned on this type of account.
3. False – the purpose of a budget account is to pay regular bills and this might involve overdrawing.
4. This is the person receiving the cheque, i.e. his name appears after 'Pay . . . . '
5. He can ask someone with an account to cash the cheque but the cheque must be endorsed.
6. The shop or business concerned will require to see a £50 cheque card and the number on the cheque card will be written on the reverse of the cheque.

7. A standing order is an order to pay a specific amount at regular intervals. Direct debit means that the account is directly debited (money taken from it). Unlike the standing order the amount can vary.
8. False – overdrafts are allowed for day-to-day trading but not usually for equipment.
9. 33 per cent (16 per cent × 2 + 1 per cent = 33 per cent).

CHAPTER 10

Exercise 1

£137.50 – Annual interest rate £22 000 × 10 per cent = £2200 less 25 per cent = £1650.40 per year.
This represents a monthly repayment of £1650 ÷ 12 = £137.50.

Exercise 2

£120.83.

Exercise 3

The three differences are:

	Credit sale	*Hire purchase*
1.	The goods (the car) passes to the buyer immediately.	The goods remain the property of the finance company.
2.	The company are not able to recover the goods.	The company can seize back the goods.
3.	The borrower does *not* hire the goods.	The buyer does hire the goods.

Exercise 4

1. £12.50, i.e. 5 per cent of £250.
2. (a) With American Express the whole of the outstanding amount is payable this is not the case with Access and Visa.
   (b) With American Express a subscription is payable but this is not the case with Access or Visa.
3. Visa – TSB, Barclays, Bank of Scotland.
4. Access – Midland, National Westminster and Lloyds.

Exercise 5

£675 at 6.75 per cent interest.

Exercise 6

£35 576, a gain of £25 576.

Exercise 7

£25 000, £15 000 gain + £10 000 originally invested.

Exercise 8

1. £6500; 2. £250 + £57.50 = £307.50.

Exercise 9

1. £208.33 monthly.
2. (a) £68.75 monthly.
   (b) Tax relief £22.92 per month or £275 annually.
3. 30 per cent.
4. The credit firm would be acting illegally if they tried to recover the goods. Remember it is not a hire purchase agreement.
5. With Visa customers can pay 5 per cent of the outstanding debt with American Express the whole amount must be paid.
6. The gains and losses are as follows:
   (a) £1 875 gain.
   (b) £168.75 gain.
   (c) £312.50 loss.
   (d) £125 gain.
   An overall gain of £1856.25.
7. Securities and Investment Board.

CHAPTER 11

Exercise 1

1. Economy, speed, convenience, regularity.
2. Because trains travel to and from the centre of large cities.
3. High maintenance and staff costs.
4. Containerisation, special wagons and the Red Star parcel service.

Exercise 2

1. False – there has been a decline in the number of miles of railway track.
2. Social costs are the environmental costs of traffic, i.e. pollution, noise and the need for police to control road transport.
3. False – inter-city rail and internal air transport are far speedier than road transport between major cities.

Exercise 3

1. Coal, because it is bulky and expensive to transport, would probably be taken by sea or, depending on the siting of the electricity power station, maybe by rail.
2. It is likely that air transport would be used because the item is expensive and the size small.
3. A consortium known as Trans Manche Link (TML).

Exercise 4

1. False – the service was withdrawn in October 1982.
2. Word processors.

Exercise 5

1. Armfield plc would consider speed, cost, reliability, regularity and convenience in choosing its means of transport to destinations in the South of England.
2. Ordinary postal services, registered letters, recorded delivery, express delivery, freepost, airmail.
3. You may have included secretarial work, accounting, stock control, payroll, management information.

CHAPTER 12

Exercise 1

1. Visible balance
2. **a** Import, **b** import, **c** export, **d** export.
3. Current balance.

Exercise 2

1. Tariffs, quotas, subsidies.
2. Buying agents, export houses, overseas exporting agents, licensing, direct dealing.
3. Bill of lading.
4. By getting the bill of exchange signed by an acceptance house.
5. Export Credit Guarantee Department (ECGD).

Exercise 3

1. You might have included banking services, insurance services, holidays in Britain, payment of foreign troops in Britain, shipping services.
2. (i) To use its reserves, (ii) to borrow from the IMF.
3. To avoid paying all the duty on one payment. The duty is paid as the tobacco is used.

CHAPTER 13

Exercise 1

1. Net means as stated there will be no discount on the price.
2. It is a written order which follows the telephone order.
3. Enquiry, quotation, order, acknowledgement.

Exercise 2

£2500 less 25 per cent = £1875
VAT = £281.25
Total price = £2156.25

Exercise 3

1. £150.
2. The amount after discount if any has been deducted.
3. To advise the customer that the goods are about to be delivered.
4. The delivery note will not show the prices.
5. £258.78.
6. 'Zero rated' means some goods do not carry any VAT whereas exempt means certain types of organisation do not need to pay

VAT on any purchases.

7. 'Errors and omissions excepted' if the supplier makes a mistake he can rectify it.
8. Consignment note.

CHAPTER 14

Exercise 1

1. A purchase by an individual from a business is a consumer sale.
2. False – no warranty can reduce your statutory rights.
3. (a) She can complain to her Citizen's Advice Bureau and the seller could be prosecuted under the Trade Descriptions Act 1968.
   (b) She could sue under the Sale of Goods Act.
4. (a) Sale goods must have been on display for 28 days in its last year.
   (b) Shops can no longer disclaim liability by a notice.

Exercise 2

1. Food and Drugs Act 1955.
2. False – you need not pay for them and the goods become your property if not collected within a six-month period.
3. Consumer consultative councils.
4. False – he does not become the owner until the last payment is made.
5. Agreements which come under the Consumer Credit Act 1974, i.e. agreements between individuals and firms where the amount borrowed does not exceed £5 000.
6. He can cancel the agreement within five days of receiving his postal agreement.
7. The annual percentage rate.

Exercise 3

1. Individual buyers who buy from sellers who are running businesses.
2. This means that the seller owns the goods or has the right to sell them, i.e. is selling them for someone else.
3. (a) She can complain to her Citizen's Advice Bureau and the seller could be prosecuted under the Trade Descriptions Act 1968. (b) She could sue under the Sale of Goods Act.

4. It allows the government to issue regulations to protect consumers against unsafe goods.
5. The main difference is in ownership. The goods do not become the property of the buyer until the last payment is made in a hire purchase agreement; but in a credit sale agreement the goods immediately become the property of the buyer.
6. (a) The buyer can 'enjoy now – pay later'; (b) it may protect the buyer against inflation; (c) the buyer can buy more expensive goods than would be possible otherwise.
7. (a) Interest has to be paid; (b) credit may tempt a buyer to live beyond his means; (c) if unemployment or sickness occurs, too heavy a credit obligation may cause problems.
8. It is not permissible because this agreement between two companies is not protected by the Consumer Credit Act 1974.
9. The APR would be around 21 per cent.
10. There are certain cards available from certain stores which give customers credit, i.e. they can make purchases on presentation of their cards without parting with any cash.

CHAPTER 15

Exercise 1

1. Where one business has control of 25 per cent or more of the production of a good or service.
2. This is where a manufacturer lays down the price at which his goods will be sold in shops.
3. (a) This is known as a restrictive practice. (b) It could be referred by the Director-General of Fair Trading to the Restrictive Practices Court.
4. Tax allowances, grants towards training, depreciation allowances, employment grants.

Exercise 2

1. The local authority could order that the land be restored to its former state and that the present use be discontinued.
2. False – it is illegal to discriminate on grounds of sex or colour. This advertisement discriminates against women and non-whites.
3. Michael is entitled to three weeks' notice and 3 × 100 = £300 redundancy pay.

Exercise 3

1. Monopolies and Mergers Commission.
2. Against the public interest.
3. It can appeal to the secretary of state.
4. (a) He can appeal to an industrial tribunal. (b) He might be compensated, reinstated or re-engaged.
5. He can (a) make recommendation, (b) issue an improvement order, (c) issue a closure or prohibition order.

CHAPTER 16

Exercise 1

1. Taxable income is the income when all the allowances have been deducted.
2. Bill Green's tax code will be 260L.
3. Charles Harman's taxable pay is £35 905 and he will pay £11 467, i.e. £19,300 at 25%; £16605 at 40%.

Exercise 2

Michael's gain is £40 000, but he will pay only £35 000 (£40 000 – £5000), which will be £14 000 (£35 000 at 40 per cent).
A leaflet explaining capital gains tax is available free of charge from any local Inland Revenue (tax) office.

Exercise 3

The tax on inheritance of £310 000 is £200 000 × 40 per cent = £80 000 but the interval of 4.5 years reduces this to 60 per cent £48 000.

Exercise 4

1. Income tax, corporation tax, capital transfer tax, capital gains tax.
2. VAT, excise duty, import tax, betting and gaming tax.

Exercise 5

£500 × 250 in the £ = £1250.

Exercise 6

Employer (United Foods plc) 10.45 per cent of £450 = £47
Employee (Michael Jennings) 9 per cent of £305 = £27.45.

Exercise 7

1. Rates £407.64; 2. Poll Tax £608 (4 × £152); 3. £200.36 more.

Exercise 8

1. A tax code is used by an employer to deduct tax. It is determined by reference to a person's circumstances, e.g. marriage.
2. At £5000.
3. False – only profit on a house which is the seller's only home is exempt.
4. This is a tax paid on property which is transferred on death or by a gift.
5. By ploughing back its profit.
6. This is tax which is levied at every stage from raw material to final purchase. A tax is levied as value is added.
7. Districts levy rates.
8. Rate support grant.
9. Goods or services that do not pay VAT.
10. Organisations which can claim VAT payment back.

INDEX

A

acceptance house 172
accounts 88–91, 166
acknowledgement 181
advertising
  cost of 57
  functions of 57
  media 56, 57
  protection of consumers 58
advice note 182
after-sales service 60
agents for export 170
air transport 156
airway bill 172
articles of association 28
assets 89, 90
assurance 110
average clause 113

B

balance of payments 166–9
balance sheet 88
banking
  accounts, types of 125–6
  direct debit 133
  cheque cards 132
  cheque clearing 128–9
  cheques 127–32
  credit cards 136
  credit transfer 133
  functions 124–5
  loans 134–5
  overdrafts 134
  standing order 133
  statements 126
bankruptcy 119–20
bill of exchange 171–2
bill of lading 172
big bang 105
board of directors 31, 41–4
bonded warehouse 175
branding 78
British Standards Institute 192
brokers
  insurance 117
  stock 102–3
budget accounts 126
building societies 37
buyer, rights of 188–9

C

capital
  capital gains tax 208
  capital transfer tax (inheritance tax) 209
cash and carry stores (discount stores) 74, 80
certificate of
  incorporation 28
  insurance 172
  origin 172
  trading 30
chain of distribution 64, 81
channel tunnel 157
chief accountant 42
cheque
  clearing 128–9
  crossing 130
  dishonouring 129–30
communications
  postal 160–1
  telecommunications 159
  transport 153–7
  word processors 162
companies
  articles of association 28
  dividends 96, 122
  formation 26–31
  incorporation 28
  memorandum of association 26–7
  private 26–9
  public 29–31
  registration 26
company secretary 42
company takeovers 31–2
computers 162
Connect card 135–6

consumer credit 192–4
Consumer Credit Act 193–4
containerisation 155
cooperative societies 71
corporation tax 209
credit
  bank 134–5
  cards 71, 136, 195
consumer protection 188–95
current account 125–6
customs 175

D

debentures 97
delivery note 182
departmental stores 69–70
deposit accounts 126
depreciation 90
desk research 49
direct tax 206–10
Director-General of Fair Trading 199
discount stores 74
distribution, chain of 64, 81
distribution of labour 13
dividends 96, 122
documents in exporting 171–3

E

Ecowas 175
EEC 175
endowment assurance 110
European single market (1992) 176
expenditure, consumer 7
export
  documentation 171
  Export Credit Guarantee Department 174
  visible and invisible 166–7
express delivery 161

F

Fair Trading Act 199
fax 160
fidelity guarantee insurance 115
Food and Drugs Act 1955 191
franchise, retailing 74
freepost 161
free trade 175, 176
freight market 85
futures 85

G

government
  aid to industry 200
  employment protection 202
  health and safety 204
  monopolies and restrictive practices 199
  planning 201

H

hedging 85
hire purchase 141–2
HOBS (Home and Office Banking System) 135, 136
hypermarkets 72

I

import
  customs 169–70, 175
  visible and invisible 166–7
indemnity 112
independent retailer 66–7
inheritance tax 209
internal communications 44
institutional investors 99
insurable and non-insurable risks 110
insurable interest 111
insurance
  accident 114–15
  assurance 110
  average clause 113
  brokers 117–18
  cargo 117
  certificate of 172
  comprehensive 115, 116
  consequential loss 114
  contribution 112
  fidelity guarantee 115
  freight 117
  hull 117
  indemnity 112
  insurable interest 111

insurance (*cont.*)
  liability 114
  life assurance 115, 116
  Lloyds 118
  marine 116, 117
  market 117, 86
  national insurance 212
  pooling of risks 108, 109
  premiums 108
  principles of 111, 113
  proposal form 108
  proximate cause 113
  subrogation 112
  types of 114, 117
  underwriters 118
  utmost good Faith 111
interest 92, 97, 98, 138–46, 147
International Monetary Fund 169
investors
  institutional 99
  trust 149, 150
investment management 150–1
invisible trade 167

J

jobbers 105

L

large-scale retailing 76–7
letter of enquiry 178
leasing 94
liabilities 88, 89
liability
  limited 26–8
  unlimited 22
liquidation 121–2
limited companies 26–31
Lloyds 118
local authorities 212–13

M

mail order 73–4
managing director 41–2
market research 48–51
market surveys 50–51
markets
  freight 85
  futures 85
  insurance 85, 117–18
  stock 84
marketing 47–48
memorandum of association 26–8
middlemen 80
mobile shops 66
monopolies 35, 199
multiple shops 68

N

national insurance 212
nationalised industries 5, 32–6
non-executive board members 41

O

occupations, specialisation of 14–17
offer for sale 30, 99
overdrafts 134–5
order (cheques) 128
order (Health and Safety Act) 204

P

patterns of retailing 76–7
patterns of expenditure 8–9
partnerships
  deed 23–4
  formation 23
Pay As You Earn (PAYE) 206
personnel officer 43
ploughing back 93
poll tax 214
Post Office 160–2
privatisation 33–4
private company 26–31
production
  primary 10
  secondary 11
  tertiary 11
profit and loss account 91–2
profit-sharing 45
promotion of product 53–6
prospectus 30, 99
protection and free trade 169–70
proximate cause 113
public company 29–30
public corporations 32–6
public goods and services 5–6

Q

quotas 170

R

rail transport 154–5
rates 212–15
recorded delivery 161
registration, of business names 21
retailers
  cooperative 71
  departmental 69
  functions 75
  hypermarket 72
  independent 66–7
  large-scale 77–80
  multiple 68
  nature of 76
  supermarket 72
road transport 155–6

S

Sale of Goods Act 1979 188–9
sales marketing director 43
services 4–15
shares
  certificate 97
  ordinary 96
  preference 96
sole trader 19–22
standing order 133
statement
  Account 185–6
  Bank 126
Stock Exchange 102–6
subrogation 112
supermarket 72
Switch 135–6

T

tariffs 169
tax
  capital gains 208
  capital transfer (inheritance tax) 208–9
  corporation 209
tax (*cont.*)
  direct 206–10
  income tax (PAYE) 206–8
  indirect 210–12
  value added tax 210–11
teletex 160
telephone 158–9
teleprinters 159
trade
  free 175, 176
  visible and invisible 166–7
Trade Descriptions Acts 1968 and 1972 189–90
trading blocs 175
transport
  air 157
  rail 154–5
  road 155–7
  sea 157–8
turnover 77, 79

U

underwriters
  insurance 118
  shares 99
unit trusts 149–50
Unsolicited Goods and Services Act 1971 191
utmost good faith 111

V

value added tax (VAT) 210–11
variety chain stores 68
vending machines 74
visible trade 166
voluntary retail chains 72–3

W

warehouses, bonded 175
Weights and Measures Act 1963 191
whole life assurance 115
wholesalers, services of 81–3
word processors 162–3